Better Homes and Gardens®
Vegetable & Fruit
Gardening Made Easy

Meredith Consumer Marketing
Des Moines, Iowa

Better Homes and Gardens
Vegetable & Fruit
Gardening Made Easy

MEREDITH CONSUMER MARKETING
Vice President, Consumer Marketing: Janet Donnelly
Consumer Product Marketing Director: Heather Sorensen
Business Director: Ron Clingman
Consumer Marketing Product Manager: Wendy Merical
Senior Production Manager: Al Rodruck

WATERBURY PUBLICATIONS, INC.
Contributing Editor: Karen Weir-Jimerson, Studio G, Inc.
Associate Design Director: Todd Hanson
Contributing Copy Editor: Amy Kuebelbeck
Contributing Proofreader: Carrie Schmitz
Contributing Indexer: Donald Glassman

Editorial Director: Lisa Kingsley
Creative Director: Ken Carlson
Associate Editors: Tricia Bergman, Mary Williams
Associate Design Director: Doug Samuelson
Production Assistant: Mindy Samuelson

BETTER HOMES AND GARDENS® MAGAZINE
Editor in Chief: Gayle Goodson Butler
Managing Editor: Lamont Olson
Creative Director: Michael D. Belknap
Deputy Editor, Gardening: Eric Liskey

MEREDITH NATIONAL MEDIA GROUP
President: Tom Harty

MEREDITH CORPORATION
Chairman and Chief Executive Officer: Stephen M. Lacy

In Memoriam: E.T. Meredith III (1933–2003)

Pictured on the front cover:
Carrots, apples, and tomatoes are just a few of the crops you can grow in your home garden.

Photographers credited may retain copyright to the listed photographs. Howard F. Schwartz, Colorado State University, *bugworld.org:* *108, top center, 109, top center* Gerald Holmes, Valent USA Corporation, *bugworld.org: 108, bottom right*

All of us at Meredith® Consumer Marketing are dedicated to providing you with information and ideas to enhance your home. We welcome your comments and suggestions. Write to us at: Meredith Consumer Marketing, 1716 Locust St., Des Moines, IA 50309-3023.

Grow your favorite fruits, vegetables, and herbs right outside your door. The inspiring images and easy-to-follow planting, growing, and harvesting advice on the following pages will yield a bountiful harvest and months of scrumptious, garden-fresh meals.

Contents

Chapter 9

ALL ABOUT PRUNING

Spur fruiting trees and shrubs to produce abundantly with a few basic pruning practices.

Chapter 10

GARDEN PLANS

Use these easy-to-follow planting plans to create your homegrown feast.

Chapter 11

VEGETABLE ENCYCLOPEDIA

Each entry describes when and how to plant, as well as harvest tips. Favorite vegetables, such as tomatoes and peppers, are highlighted as well as lesser-known plants.

Chapter 12

FRUIT ENCYCLOPEDIA

Hardy tree fruits, citrus, and fruiting shrubs are covered in this in-depth guide to growing fruit.

Chapter 13

FOOD PROCESSING

After you've grown the garden of your dreams, gather up the produce and enjoy.

CHAPTER ONE

From Garden to Table

Grow your own flavor-filled, nutrient-packed vegetables and fruits. Your home garden can become your own personal farmer's market.

Raise your own food

A simple backyard garden can yield the freshest food you'll ever eat for three seasons—from early spring through late autumn.

With a backyard garden, you know all kinds of things about the vegetables and fruits you harvest to create meals for your family. To begin, count on intense flavor. Produce tastes best when it is fresh—plucked from the vine when it is perfectly ripe and eaten soon after. Your homegrown tomatoes will be sweeter than those from the supermarket, and just-picked lettuce will be deliciously tender and flavorful. If you're not careful, the best of your harvest will not make it to the table as you delight in a gardenside snack.

When the field-to-table distance is mere feet instead of hundreds of miles, putting together a spur-of-the-moment meal is as easy as stepping out the door, harvesting what is ripe, and combining the produce with some kitchen staples. A mesclun salad topped with slivers of baby radishes and a handful of sweet peas is the perfect starter for a springtime supper. Or you can harvest a handful of cherry tomatoes and combine them with fresh goat cheese, grilled chicken, and basil leaves to make a meal right off the menu of a trendy restaurant.

A backyard garden can infuse your breakfast, lunch, and supper with fresh flavor from midspring through fall. And what you don't eat fresh, you can put away for the rest of the year. Freeze, dry, and can your produce and you will be able to feast from the garden 12 months a year.

Delicious, nutritious, and safer food

More often than not, backyard garden produce boasts more nutrients than supermarket counterparts. Research shows that the shorter the time between when a fruit or vegetable is harvested and when it is consumed or preserved, the more nutrients it contains. So a pepper that is harvested in South America and arrives on your grocery store shelf four or more days later has notably fewer valuable nutrients than the glossy green fruit you plucked from your garden 20 minutes before supper was served. Fresh-picked also affects flavor. You can actually taste freshness.

Along with harboring more nutrients, homegrown produce can come in contact with fewer chemicals. In fact, a chemical-free, totally organic produce patch is easy to accomplish with a few pest-free strategies. And if you use compost, you won't need to purchase chemical fertilizers. In this way, gardening organically can also save you money.

Food safety is an issue with many families, and when you raise your own fruits and vegetables, you know you are eating exactly what you planted and nothing more. A backyard orchard and vegetable patch can give you the peace of mind that you are providing your family produce without traces of chemicals that are commonly used on large-scale farms.

Colorful means good for you

Garden produce is more than just delicious. If you eat enough fresh fruits and vegetables, they will have powerful effects on your health. Researchers are continuously studying the benefits of a diet rich in fruits and vegetables, and their findings have led to a new way of thinking. As it turns out, your mother's advice to eat your vegetables has been scientifically validated.

Aim to eat produce in a rainbow of colors, instead of focusing on eating a particular number of fruit and vegetable servings each day. Researchers have found nutrients and powerful antioxidants vary by color, and eating many different colors of produce allows you to harness maximum benefits. Use the chart, opposite, to plant a rainbow in your garden this year.

EAT A RAINBOW

RED

Beet
Red cabbage
Cherry
Red grape
Red pepper
Red potato
Radish
Raspberry
Rhubarb
Strawberry
Tomato
Watermelon

ORANGE AND YELLOW

Yellow apple
Apricot
Butternut squash
Cantaloupe
Carrot
Corn
Lemon
Mango
Nectarine
Orange
Peach
Pear
Yellow pepper
Pumpkin
Rutabaga
Sweet potato

GREEN

Green apple
Artichoke
Asparagus
Avocado
Green bean
Broccoli
Brussels sprout
Cucumber
Green grape
Honeydew melon
Kiwifruit
Lettuce
Lime
Green onion
Pea
Green pepper
Spinach
Zucchini

BLUE AND PURPLE

Blackberry
Blueberry
Eggplant
Fig
Purple grape
Plum
Prune

WHITE

Cauliflower
Garlic
Onion
Parsnip
Potato
Turnip

above left A neat and tidy way to grow fruits, vegetables, and herbs, raised beds not only look good, but they are good for plants, too. These quick-draining garden plots promote healthy, vigorous plants.

above right Midsummer is ripe with colorful produce. Easy-to-grow tomatoes, peppers, and cucumbers are especially productive. Share your nutrient-rich harvest with friends.

Plant what you eat

Enjoy your produce as it ripens, and you will truly be in sync with your garden and the seasons.

Think of your edible garden as your sweetly convenient personal produce section. Your garden will not have pineapple and fresh green beans year-round like your supermarket, but it can offer fresh produce at different times throughout the year.

Deciding what to grow in your edible garden is as simple as making a grocery list. Recall recent trips to your local grocery. What was in your cart as you were leaving the produce section? Make a list of the vegetables, fruits, and herbs you commonly buy. Perhaps carrots, tomatoes, apples, lettuce, garlic, and potatoes top your list. Good news—you can grow all of these foods in a home garden. If bananas, oranges, and kiwifruits are popular with your family, you can grow these fruits, too, if you live in a warm climate.

In addition to growing the fruits, vegetables, and herbs that you commonly eat, a backyard garden is a low-cost opportunity to try new foods. For just a dollar or two you can introduce your friends and family to edamame, leeks, or garden-fresh cauliflower. Don't worry if you're unsure about the particulars of growing something; the encyclopedia section at the back of this book is stocked with all the information you need to grow produce.

Another way to approach the subject of what to grow in your edible garden is to think about what kinds of cuisine your family enjoys. Are Italian dishes a popular menu item? Do you frequent a favorite Mexican restaurant? Or is your refrigerator full of take-home boxes from a local Asian establishment? Specific fruits, vegetables, and herbs combine to lend these cuisines their telltale flavors. Plant an Italian-theme garden and make your own fresh spaghetti sauce with homegrown herbs and vegetables.

PLANT AN EXTRA ROW
In addition to filling your table with fresh produce, your garden can also supply valuable nutrients to people in need. Consider adding an extra row of potatoes, peppers, tomatoes, or other favorite vegetables and donating the produce to your local food bank. Fresh fruit is often in short supply. Plant an extra row of raspberries or another apple tree and share the bounty. Contact your local homeless shelter or soup kitchen to learn about its specific food needs and how your garden can meet those needs.

Freeze, dry, and can
When deciding what to grow, also think about how you will consume your produce. Most likely you'll eat most of it fresh, but if you take a few extra hours throughout the growing season, you can turn a summertime harvest into a year-round smorgasbord.

Freezing, drying, and canning are popular food preservation methods that capture the flavor of fresh produce. Turn a bushel of apples into many pints of applesauce, or freeze a few cups of blueberries for use in a midwinter blueberry crumble. Make dried fruits and vegetables for lost-cost snacks.

opposite A small garden plot can yield a wide array of produce. Carrots, cucumbers, onions, and radishes are among the vegetables that are the easiest to grow.

Get planting

You don't need to have a green thumb or a degree in horticulture to raise delicious homegrown produce.

In a few short weeks, your empty balcony or forlorn patch of turf can be the site of a fruitful garden. Use this book as a resource for need-to-know answers throughout the growing season. From site selection to when to harvest the first red tomato of the season, the following pages are packed with everything you need to know to plant and care for vegetables, fruits, and herbs.

Site selection and preparation

One of the most important tasks in creating any garden is to choose the appropriate site. All plants have particular soil and sun requirements, and the following pages will help you match your site conditions with vegetables, fruits, and herbs that will thrive in those conditions. Once you determine the site, it's time to create the best growing conditions possible. Removing sod for a garden bed and choosing soil for a container garden are just two of the site-preparation tasks covered.

Picking what to plant

The most popular vegetables and fruits are covered in detail in the encyclopedias. Each entry has specific planting advice, care tips, harvest information, and cultivar recommendations, along with colorful photos.

Seeds vs. transplants

Whether you start plants from seeds or transplants purchased at your local nursery, you'll find tips and techniques to ensure that young plants put down roots. Get a jump on the gardening season by starting seeds indoors with the help of the indoor seed-starting section.

Care tips

Timely weeding, watering, and pest control will promote a bountiful harvest. Look for time-saving tips for accomplishing these garden chores, as well as environmentally friendly pest-control techniques.

Harvesting

Picking vegetables, fruits, and herbs at optimum ripeness allows you to capture the fruits' maximum sugars and valuable nutrients. You'll find harvest tips throughout the book.

opposite Direct-seed beans in a raised-bed garden after all danger of frost has passed. Get a jump-start on the season with pepper transplants. And dress up the bed with flowering annuals such as marigolds and alyssum. **above** Vegetables require a steady supply of moisture to be productive. Apply water to the base of the plant and avoid wetting the foliage to prevent disease problems.

BHG TEST GARDEN TIP | PACE YOURSELF

If you are planting a vegetable garden for the first time, don't be overzealous about your selections. Plant no more than you can use or take care of. It's easy to get caught up in the fun of planting without thinking about the time you'll need to weed, water, and harvest.

CHAPTER TWO

Edibles in the Landscape

Plant fruits and veggies anywhere: in a traditional kitchen garden, tucked into front-yard landscaping, or in containers on a balcony or patio.

Pick a good garden site

Food crops aren't demanding. But they need sun, good soil, and water to thrive.

Choosing a site for growing edibles is a little like choosing a home. If your dwelling satisfies your basic need for shelter, you're more likely to be happy and productive. Apply the same principle to growing edibles, and they'll reward you with armloads of produce.

Sweet sun

Choose a site that receives 8 to 10 hours of sun a day. While some leafy vegetables will thrive in less light, most edible plants need eight or more hours of sunlight a day. Opt for direct light. Sunlight filtering through a tree canopy does not provide plants with the same light qualities as direct sunlight. Choose a spot where plants do not have to compete with trees and shrubs for sunlight.

Rich soil

Choose a site with nutrient-rich soil; color is often a good indicator of soil nutrient content. Dark brown or black soil often has the most available nutrients. And look for a quick-draining site. Waterlogged soil will quickly suffocate plant roots. Choose a site that drains quickly after a rain. Avoid depressions and swales where water collects. A relatively level spot promotes good drainage and is also easier to plant and care for than an undulating site.

Even healthy garden soils benefit from a rejuvenating layer of compost. Whether you garden in a pot or a backyard plot, plan to give your soil a boost by incorporating amendments every year.

Water wonders

Locate your garden near a water source. In general, vegetables require frequent irrigation. Fruit trees need minimal watering after establishing a deep root system.

Pay attention to soil texture. A soil's texture often determines how well it will hold water and then share that water with a plant. The best soil for an edible garden crumbles easily in your hand when you gently squeeze it.

BEWARE OF BLACK WALNUT TREES

Some vegetables can't grow beneath these trees, so steer clear when planting garden beds.

AVOID TREE SECRETIONS Black walnut trees secrete a substance called juglone through their roots into nearby soil. Juglone is also present in the plants' leaves, twigs, and hulls and can leach into the soil as the plant parts decompose.

SUSCEPTIBLE VEGGIES Some plants are very sensitive to juglone and quickly wilt and die in its presence. Tomato, pepper, cabbage, eggplant, and potato are the most sensitive edibles. Melon, squash, bean, carrot, and corn all show good resistance to juglone, as do peach, cherry, nectarine, and plum trees.

PLANT ELSEWHERE The best defense is to steer clear of planting near black walnut trees. The greatest amount of juglone is found under the tree canopy. A mature tree's toxic zone extends about 50 feet from the trunk of the tree.

opposite Lettuces and herbs thrive in this patio-side raised-bed garden. The garden's close proximity to the house simplifies watering and harvest.

Plant a traditional vegetable garden

Planted in rows, a traditional garden is easy to weed by running a small tiller down the length of the rows every two weeks.

A traditionally designed edible garden is usually rectangular or square. But don't let shape stop you from adding creative flair to your produce patch. Not only aren't you constricted by shape, but you can grow vertically as well as horizontally. For example, grow pole beans up a collection of twig towers, or edge the garden with a border of knee-high zinnias. Traditional vegetable gardens are as unique as the people who tend them.

A good choice for a large sunny yard, a traditional garden is firmly rooted in function. A row-style planting scheme makes it easy to water and weed young plants and harvest produce. End-of-the-season garden chores are as simple as removing all the leaves, stems, and plant debris. Then it's a cinch to spread compost over the swath of open ground and till it in.

The size of a traditional edible garden depends on the types and amounts of vegetables and fruits you wish to grow and how much time you have for garden chores. The best-size garden is large enough to be enjoyable and offer space to plant a variety of vegetables but small enough not to be a burden. If you are just starting out, begin with a simple 10×10-foot plot. Both manageable and productive, a 100-square-foot garden offers many opportunities.

Design know-how
Combine a geometric plot and a few rows of plants and you're well on your way to designing a traditional edible garden. Increase your garden's production while simplifying plant care with these traditional garden design tips.

Honor spacing suggestions. In your exuberance to pack as many tantalizing vegetables into a defined space, it's easy to downsize plant-spacing recommendations to squeeze in just one more row of heirloom carrots. Resist, resist. An exceptionally dense planting scheme may look great on paper and even appear possible at planting time, but plant growth will prove

otherwise. Densely planted gardens are difficult to weed and water effectively, more susceptible to pest problems than well-spaced counterparts, and frustrating to harvest. In short, you will harvest more if you plant more judiciously.

Plan for paths. An easy access route through the garden is essential for quick maintenance and hassle-free harvest. Aim to create paths that are at least 2 feet wide, and blanket them with a weed-inhibiting layer of organic mulch or shredded bark. To make your garden as hospitable as it is productive, think about adding a bench for seating as well as a spot to keep tools you'll use on a daily basis, such as pruners or a trowel.

Cluster annuals. For easy cleanup and soil preparation at the beginning and end of the season, plant annuals together in one contiguous area while grouping perennials and woody plants in another space. This arrangement allows you to pull up end-of-season annual vegetables (such as bolted lettuce) and replant an empty bed. Perennial crops such as blueberries, sage, and other long-lived plants can grow undisturbed when you prepare soil for the annual vegetable crops.

Think about making maintenance as easy as possible. Plan a weeding strategy. If you want to run a small tiller between rows to eliminate weeds, allocate ample space—at least 3 feet between rows. Add stepping-stones into beds so you have a place to stand while weeding or harvesting. And make watering chores easy by grouping water-loving plants, such as raspberries and blueberries, together near a convenient water source. You'll spend less time hauling water or grappling with hoses.

PRODUCTIVE AND PRETTY

Dress up an edible garden with pretty and productive elements to make it a backyard focal point.

1 ARBOR
Frame the garden entry with an arbor cloaked with pole beans or kiwifruits. Or add color with the blooms of climbing roses, clematis, or morning glories.

2 FENCE
Surround the garden with a low decorative fence. A simple picket, rustic twig, or stately stone fence will define the garden border and maybe even keep pests away.

3 FLOWERS
Wake up a sleepy green vegetable garden with edible flowers such as nasturtiums, calendula, and lavender.

4 OBELISK
Add height with an obelisk. Made of wood or stone, an obelisk is an ideal focal point. Train sweet peas or climbing edibles up the sturdy structure.

5 TREES
Use dwarf fruit trees to unite the edible garden with the surrounding landscape. Plant trees along the garden edges or one on each corner.

Grow edibles in your landscape

Invite edibles into beds and borders to add color and taste.

If a traditional vegetable garden isn't your style or your lot is short on space, consider an edible landscape. Plant fennel near your foundation and border your patio with peppers. Not only does an edible landscape make it possible to grab a snack as you mow your front lawn or harvest a handful of beans as you grill a steak, but it also maximizes growing space.

Get started designing your edible landscape by taking stock of your current yard. Look for lackluster nonedible plants that can be replaced with edibles. For example, instead of enclosing your backyard with a traditional hedge, consider a row of blueberries. Springtime flowers, summer fruit, and colorful fall foliage make blueberries an excellent landscape plant.

When adding trees to your lot, go with edibles. Apple, peach, and pear trees provide food for your family, friends, neighbors, and wildlife. Avoid planting fruit trees near patios, driveways, and walkways because they are bound to drop fruit, creating a mess on paved surfaces.

Annual excitement

Carrots, radishes, squash, and other annual edibles make excellent landscape plants, too. For year-round good looks, pair these short-lived plants with shrubs or perennials. Perennial edibles such as raspberries, sage, thyme, and many other herbs are good choices. The key to success is matching plants with their preferred growing conditions. Don't plant vegetables in the dry environment under your home's eaves, and beware of too much shade.

Some edibles lose their beauty at the end of the season. For example, the foliage of potato plants dies down as the tubers mature, and foliar diseases occasionally plague tomatoes. Plant these productive (but not-so-pretty) plants in a backyard planting bed while reserving prominent planting space for eye-catching vegetables such as lettuce, peppers, eggplant, and herbs.

FRONT-YARD WORTHY

Neat and tidy growing habits, minimal pest problems, and bountiful production make these edibles perfect for garden beds. Don't hesitate to plant them in a prominent place. Their consistent good looks will add edible decoration to your landscape.

VEGETABLES	FRUITS	HERBS
Artichoke	Apple	Basil
Beet	Apricot	Chives
Broccoli	Blueberry	Lavender
Carrot	Cherry	Lemon verbena
Chard	Grape	Oregano
Kale	Kiwifruit	Parsley
Kohlrabi	Mango	Rosemary
Leek	Peach	Sage
Lettuce	Pear	Thyme
Onion	Plum	
Pepper	Strawberry	
Radish		
Rhubarb		
Tomatillo		

opposite Lettuce, cabbage, and kale are neatly contained in a tidy planting bed bordered by a boxwood hedge.

Plant an orchard

A few fruit trees can pump out the sweetest harvests.

Integrate fruit trees into an existing shrub bed, and they instantly become landscape plants. Whether you choose to grow two or three fruit trees or a half-acre orchard, here are some tips.

Site for sun

Selecting a site for a fruit tree involves taking stock of the planting site's current conditions and predicting the site's future conditions. Fruit trees, like most vegetables, require full sun for good growth and fruit production. When selecting a planting site, pay close attention to nearby trees, which may cast shade on the young fruit tree in 5 or 10 years as the plants grow and mature. And fertile, well-drained soil is essential. Like most edibles, fruit trees will grow poorly, if at all, in heavy clay soil.

Plan for pollination

Several types of fruit require more than one variety for pollination and subsequent fruit production. These plants set fruit only when they receive pollen from a nearby plant of a different variety. These types of plants are called self-sterile and include some peaches, apricots, and crabapples and most apples, pears, plums, and sweet cherries. 'Royal Ann' sweet cherry, for example, must be within 100 feet of another cherry tree with compatible pollen that blooms at the same time as 'Royal Ann' or it will not produce cherries.

Water wisely

Deep watering is essential during the first year after planting. To encourage strong root growth, soak the tree's root zone every week or two during the first year after planting. Drought conditions will require more frequent watering. Prevent competition for moisture by removing weeds and grass from underneath the tree's canopy.

right top Most sweet cherries require pollination from another cultivar. *right middle* Plant care and pollination are often simplified when several different fruit trees are planted together in a small backyard orchard. *opposite* There is an apple cultivar for nearly every climate and even the smallest urban landscapes.

 BHG ASK THE GARDEN DOCTOR

I have a small yard. Can I grow fruit trees?

ANSWER: Even the smallest yard usually has space for a fruit tree. For years, scientists have been working to select and produce small, productive fruit trees for the home landscape. A standard-size apple tree can grow 20 to 40 feet high and spread 25 to 40 feet. Dwarf apple varieties, by contrast, can be held to a height of about 10 feet with a 10-foot spread. Expect similar results from dwarf apricots, cherries, nectarines, oranges, peaches, and plums.

Check the fruit encyclopedia for a list of dwarf cultivars for most fruit trees. When shopping at the nursery, check the plant tag for information about the tree's height and spread.

Take advantage of small spaces

Even the smallest growing spots can host a vibrant edible garden.

Edibles will thrive on a 5-foot-square balcony, in a sunny front entryway, or in a minuscule backyard plot. Vegetables and fruits prefer spacious plots but can be just as productive in tight quarters, especially if you provide ample water and nutrients. Make the most of your limited planting space with these ideas.

Embrace containers

Filled with quick-draining soil and bathed with ample sun, a container will play host to nearly any edible plant. Station a pot of small tomatoes and peppers outside your kitchen door for quick picks. You can even grow small fruit trees in containers. Choose a hardy dwarf cultivar and a large pot, and you'll be harvesting fruit on your patio in a few short years.

Add height

Maximize space by growing plants up instead of out. A vining cucumber takes much less space when trained on a trellis rather than allowed to sprawl on the ground. Instead of growing a row of green beans, send plants skyward by planting a pole bean cultivar.

Choose petite cultivars

In recent years researchers have worked hard to select small or dwarf cultivars of many edibles—from fruit trees to tomatoes—that thrive in ever-shrinking landscapes. These petite cultivars are often nearly as productive as their full-size relatives.

Practice succession planting

Succession planting is all about maximizing planting space. It is a planning and planting process that allows the garden space to be continuously in production from spring to fall. For example, follow a fast-growing spring crop of arugula, radishes, spinach, or peas with a summer crop of bush beans, cucumbers, or eggplant in the same planting space. Then tuck cool-season plants such as broccoli and lettuce into open areas among the summer vegetables for a late-fall or winter harvest.

Take advantage of intercropping

This technique pairs fast-maturing crops with those that are slower to grow so valuable garden space won't lie empty. Intercrop by sowing lettuce or cilantro seeds in the spaces between tomato plants. By the time tomatoes take up their full space and are fruiting, the lettuce or cilantro will have happily been harvested.

Plant a community garden plot

Community garden plots offer urban residents an expanse of open soil perfect for growing prized edibles. Along with providing coveted growing space, a community plot will connect you with local gardeners.

Reserve prime, full-sun space near your home for frequently harvested edibles such as herbs, cherry tomatoes, and lettuce. Plant other favorite crops in the more expansive community plot.

opposite left Garden anywhere with containers, even on a gravel patio. Here, tomatoes, peppers, and herbs are planted in galvanized buckets dressed up with a colorful coat of paint.
opposite, top right Delineated by flagstones set on edge, this tiny raised-bed garden is carved out of a busy courtyard.
opposite, middle right A good example of intercropping, rows of lettuce flank tiny kale plants. After the lettuce is harvested, there will be plenty of space for the kale to mature.
opposite, bottom right Petite tomatoes and peppers thrive in surprisingly small spaces.

CHAPTER THREE

Growing Produce in Pots

Whether you garden on a half acre or 4 square feet on a patio, growing edibles in containers makes it possible to harvest favorite foods outside your door.

29 30 36 39

Tomato
Red Cherry

Grow edibles anywhere

Containers make it possible to grow juicy tomatoes, spicy peppers, and sweet strawberries almost anywhere.

Turn a barren front walkway into an edible symphony of texture and color by lining it with pots of leafy lettuce. Add taste to a desolate courtyard with containers brimming with juicy red tomatoes and fragrant herbs. It's surprising where you can tuck in a few edible plants.

Not only do edible container gardens offer tasty fruits, vegetables, and herbs, but they are also valuable landscape elements. Lend privacy to a patio by grouping three to five large container gardens to form a living screen. Frame an entry by flanking it with containers of neatly trimmed dwarf apple trees. Use an edible container garden to dress up a lackluster section of a perennial border or shrub garden. When planted in bold containers, a portable garden is an instant focal point that can be moved around the landscape as needed.

Container gardens are especially useful where in-ground gardening is not possible. Balconies, decks, and housing association covenants often limit gardening, but containers make it possible to harvest a sprig of rosemary or a handful of parsley at a moment's notice.

Don't be confined to ground level when planning your edible container garden. Go vertical. Hanging baskets and window boxes will help you make the most of every square inch of growing space.

Seek sun

Just like an in-ground edible garden, container gardens generally need 8 to 10 hours of direct sun for good growth. Rooftop gardens and south- and west-facing locations usually offer ample sunlight. Gardening on the north or east side of a building or in the shade of a tree limits the number of edibles you can grow but doesn't eliminate edible gardening. Instead of growing sun-loving tomatoes and peppers, grow spinach, lettuce, and herbs that tolerate partial shade. The encyclopedia section details the sunlight requirements for edibles.

Water is another necessary ingredient in a container garden location. Water should be easily accessible as container gardens require watering at least daily, if not twice a day, on the hottest days of summer. A nearby spigot makes filling a watering can or delivering water with a hose a quick and easy task.

BHG TEST GARDEN TIP

STURDY SUPPORT

Hanging baskets and window boxes make great container gardens, but these sky-high gardens can become very heavy as the fruit ripens. Use sturdy supports or brackets, attached to wall studs where possible, to anchor baskets and boxes.

opposite Containers filled with tomatoes, peppers, lettuce, alpine strawberries, and herbs turn a deck into a productive edible garden. **above** Herbs are especially easy to grow in containers. Grillside seasoning is easy with an enamelware container filled with rosemary and two types of thyme.

Design a container garden

Think of a container garden as a petite version of an in-ground garden.

Combine rich, well-drained soil with ample sunlight and healthy plants, and you'll be rewarded with luscious produce. In a container garden, just as in an in-ground garden, grow the edibles you commonly use in the kitchen, and introduce your taste buds to new flavors by setting aside space for new plants.

Pot-friendly plants

Many vegetables and fruits grow as well in containers as they do in the ground. They are typically short, stocky, and exceptionally good at withstanding strong winds and rigors of growing in a confined area. Researchers are constantly working to develop cultivars for container gardens.

Container-friendly tomato plants often produce slightly smaller fruit than their in-ground counterparts, but they are just as prolific and are gems at standing tall when laden with many pounds of fruit. Bush forms of the traditional vining cucumber make it possible to grow these summer staples on your patio without a trellis.

Some plants, though, are not well-suited to containers. Corn, melons, and several varieties of squash require vast amounts of space or extensive trellising to grow in containers. Purchase these crops at your local farmer's market, and use the container space to grow other pot-friendly plants instead.

Fruit trees require more effort than easy-to-grow vegetables and herbs, but the results are well worth it. In a container, it's possible to grow 'Improved Meyer' lemons in Michigan and peaches in North Dakota because their mobility makes it easy to move them to shelter when cold weather comes.

Container considerations

Choose the largest container possible for your edible garden. The larger the container, the more soil moisture it will retain and the

TAKE FIVE

Tomatoes, peppers, and herbs are popular edibles for container gardens. Here are five great tomato and pepper cultivars and five herbs that are easy to grow in pots. Count on these plants to be deliciously prolific and well-behaved.

TOMATOES	PEPPERS	HERBS
'Bush Big Boy'	'Bell Boy'	Basil, 'Minimum'
'Patio'	'Gypsy'	Parsley, curly
'Pixie'	'Jalapeño'	and flat-leaf
'Saladette'	'Red Cherry'	Thyme
'Small Fry'	'Sweet Banana'	Oregano
		Sage

less frequently you'll need to water. With that concept in mind, it is possible to choose a container that is too large if you intend to move it during the growing season. Pots at least 10 inches across can hold herbs, green onions, lettuces, and other small crops. For tomatoes, peppers, and other large plants, choose a pot that holds 5 to 15 or more gallons of soil.

Almost any vessel can be converted into a container garden. Tubs, buckets, and half barrels work well, as do a variety of items from flea markets and salvage yards. Garden and home centers offer hundreds of colorful ceramic, plastic, and concrete options. The key to a perfect pot is drainage holes in the bottom. Otherwise water collects in the soil, displacing necessary oxygen and eventually suffocating plant roots.

opposite A collection of herbs, Swiss chard, and bush-type cucumbers spill out of stone containers. The obelisk provides support for cucumbers.

above Densely planted containers rely on nutrient-rich potting mixes, such as those that contain slow-release fertilizers to sustain fast growth.
left The best soil for edible container gardens is a quality potting soil. A soil-base potting mix provides nutrients and drainage necessary for healthy plants.

Start with soil

Soil is a plant's lifeline. It helps make water, nutrients, and air available to plant roots.

Great soil is essential to plant growth and fruit production. It pays to invest in good-quality potting soil that will sustain plants from planting time until the first frost, or for years in the case of fruit trees. Before planting your edible containers, use these tips to search out the best soil for a rich harvest.

The ideal soil will not come from your yard—garden soil is too heavy, compacts too easily, and drains poorly in pots. Instead, the best soil is formulated to drain well but still hold moisture; it is light enough to use in a portable container but heavy enough to keep the pot from toppling in a strong wind.

For convenience, use an all-purpose potting mix that includes a blend of ingredients, such as peat, vermiculite, perlite, sand, and bark, suited to most potted plants.

Look for a soil-base mix that is made with sterilized loam. It is a dense soil that will hold moisture and nutrients well. The package will tell you if it is a soil-base or soilless mix (made primarily with peat, coir/coconut husk, bark, wood chips, or sawdust), which will be lightweight and dry out too quickly for most edibles.

Compost is a valuable addition to a soil mix. Many packaged soil mixes contain compost, and the package label will list percentage of compost by volume in the mix. Compost contains nutrients plants need for growth, but because it releases those nutrients slowly over time, additional fertilizing is often needed for a continuous harvest of edibles.

Customize a potting mix by incorporating compost made in your own backyard, slow-release fertilizer, and water-holding polymer crystals, which will lessen feeding and watering but not eliminate the chores. Be sure all purchased soil additives are labeled for use with edible plants.

Go organic with an organic soil-base mix. There are many on the market. Look for one that is specially formulated for edibles; it will likely contain more valuable nutrients than general mixes.

THE DRAIN GAME

Every container needs drainage, giving excess water an escape route. Placing pot shards in the bottom of a container is no longer recommended—this technique hinders drainage instead of improving it. Try one of these methods instead.

SCREEN If a container's drainage hole is large, cover it with screening, newspaper, or a coffee filter to prevent soil from leaking out.

GRAVEL If a container has no drainage hole and you prefer not to drill one in it, create a drainage area using a 2-inch layer of gravel.

LINER When lining a container with landscape fabric or plastic, cut several drainage holes in the liner for water to escape.

Plant your container garden

Do you have 10 minutes? You have time to plant an edible garden!

Containerized edible gardens are quick to plant and quick to care for, thanks to their petite size. Even though you can plant a container faster than you can make a trip to the grocery store, it's important to pay attention to details at this stage to ensure strong, healthy plants. Plant with care now, and you'll be shopping for fruits and vegetables on your patio instead of at the supermarket.

Use the last frost date for your area as an indicator of when to plant. Plant cool-season vegetables such as lettuce, spinach, and radishes as well as hardy herbs two to three weeks before the last average frost in your region. Wait until after the chance of frost has passed to plant warm-season crops such as tomatoes and peppers. Don't know when your last spring frost date is? Contact your local extension service.

Plant in place if the container will be too heavy to move after it is planted.

Before planting in terra-cotta, soak the container in water. A dry clay pot absorbs moisture from soil.

Fill a container half to three-fourths full with potting mix. Blend in slow-release fertilizer and water-retentive crystals, if desired. Top with plain potting mix.

Place the largest plant in the center of the container for a symmetrical design, or off to one side for asymmetrical balance. Leave adequate space for stakes, particularly around tomatoes, if necessary. Rearrange plants until you're pleased with the display.

Remove one plant at a time from its nursery pot, starting with the largest. To dislodge a large plant from a nursery pot, gently lay the pot on its side and press firmly on it with your foot. Roll the pot to the opposite side and repeat the process. Then slide the plant out of the pot.

JUST THE RIGHT SIZE

Size matters when it comes to the perfect container for edibles—if the pot is too small, your tomato plant might topple. If a fruit tree is planted in a massive container, you'll have a tough time lugging it inside at the end of the season. Use these sizes as a guide.

POT SIZE:	POT SIZE:	POT SIZE:
1 gallon (10-inch diameter and at least 6 inches deep)	4 to 5 gallon	5 to 7 gallon
	Beet	Dwarf fruit trees
	Carrot	
Herbs	Cucumber	
Lettuce	Eggplant	
Onion	Green bean	
Spinach	Pepper	
	Potato	
	Tomato	

To plant, set the plant in the container and add potting mix around the root ball. Set smaller plants in place. Fill in between plants with soil mix without packing it.

If you wish to plant seeds, sow them directly in a container filled with potting mix. Use a water wand or sprinkler can to gently moisten the seedbed before planting. Follow planting instructions on the seed packet.

Leave 2 inches between the top of the soil mix and the container rim for water and mulch.

After planting, moisten the potting mix thoroughly (until water runs out of the pot's drainage hole). Elevate the pot with pot feet or bricks so water can escape freely.

opposite Plant thyme near the edge of a container. As it grows, its vigorous, trailing stems will spill over the side of the pot.

Watering tips

Regular watering is essential to a bountiful container garden harvest.

Unlike their in-ground counterparts, container-grown edibles can't send out roots to mine for additional moisture because they are confined. So they rely on you to provide ample water, especially on hot, dry summer days when they are funneling all their resources into producing juicy fruit or foliage. Diligent watering, sometimes as often as twice a day, will yield weeks of fresh produce.

Containers usually require watering daily during summer or every two or three days during cooler periods, unless nature handles it for you. Hot, dry weather and small pots can necessitate twice-daily watering.

Plants suffer from too much water as much as from too little. Determine if a container garden needs water by poking your finger into the soil up to the second knuckle. If the soil feels dry, it's time to water. Check pots daily.

Saturate the potting mix thoroughly. You know you have saturated the soil when excess water drains out the drainage hole. Quick, efficient drainage is key. Soil sours, roots rot, and mineral salts build up in a container that drains poorly.

If a soilless mix dries out completely, re-wet it by standing the pot in a large vessel of water overnight.

Watering early in the day is best. It allows plants to soak up what they need before afternoon heat causes excessive evaporation.

Use a watering can to water only a few containers. Group pots and water them all at once. For faster watering by hand, use a hose and watering wand to deliver water to many containers.

Using drip irrigation set on a timer takes the work out of watering. A drip system also saves water by delivering it near plants' root zones with as little evaporation and runoff as possible. Check the system seasonally to make sure the timer works and lines are not clogged or punctured.

Self-watering pots feature built-in reservoirs that deliver moisture to the soil. They require less-frequent watering.

Water-holding mats fit into the bottom of hanging baskets and other containers, wicking moisture into the soil.

EARLY RISER

The best time to water plants is in the early morning. Daytime sun and wind will quickly dry leaves, thwarting the development of fungal diseases. Take 10 minutes before you leave for work to thoroughly soak your container gardens.

opposite Watering wands are a fast, gentle way to water container gardens. A sturdy, long-handle wand makes easy work of watering tough-to-reach hanging baskets, too. **above** When set on a timer, a simple irrigation system can take care of your watering chores. It is especially useful for watering edibles, like this lemon verbena, when you are away from home for days at a time.

Grow healthy container gardens

As long as they are watered regularly, container gardens are undemanding.

An investment of 10 minutes a week to mulch, stake, feed, and tidy a trio of edible container gardens will reap produce all summer long.

Fertilize

Choose organic fertilizers when possible. Not only do they enrich the soil, but most also improve soil structure. Organic fertilizers include compost, well-rotted manure, fish emulsion, and kelp products.

Gradual-release fertilizer blended into a potting mix before planting offers an easy way to fertilize container plants continuously. The coated granules release nutrients slowly, usually over three to nine months. Many packaged potting soils include a gradual-release fertilizer in the mix. If your mix does not, blend one in according to package directions.

Water-soluble plant food is an alternative. Make a solution of plant food and water, sprinkle it on the soil, and reapply it regularly throughout the growing season.

Plants show signs of nutrient deficiency particularly in their foliage. Clues include pale or discolored leaves, weak or slow growth, and small leaves and flowers.

Mulch

Mulch prevents soil from washing out of pots and splashing on foliage when you water plants. It also insulates soil and plant roots, helping them stay cooler during the hot days of summer.

Organic mulches, such as cocoa shells and chipped or shredded bark, decompose gradually and add nutrients to the soil mix.

Spread a 1- to 2-inch layer of mulch on top of the soil after planting. Apply it loosely and evenly; avoid compacting mulch or piling it up around the plant stems.

STAND TALL

Staking top-heavy fruits and vegetables in containers is not necessary, but it will promote a larger harvest and create a more attractive pot garden. Many tomatoes and some peppers and eggplants benefit from staking. Help wayward plants stand tall with these tips.

START YOUNG Put stakes or trellises in place at planting time to avoid disturbing roots later in the season. Staking at planting also ensures that the supports are in place as soon as plants begin to grow.

STRENGTH IS ESSENTIAL Wood dowels, thick twigs, commercial tomato cages, and a variety of found objects all make good plant supports as long as they are sturdy. Choose strong stakes to support tomatoes, which often have several pounds of fruit hanging from their vines.

SECURE STEMS Use small pieces of nylon or cloth to tie plant stems to stakes. Or thread branches through sturdy tomato cages or trellises.

opposite Vigorously growing plants, especially flowering ones such as these edible yellow calendula, require regular nutrients. For no-hassle fertilizing, use a soil mix that includes slow-release fertilizer.
above Prevent excessive soil-moisture evaporation by topping containers with a layer of mulch. Shredded bark is easy to find at garden centers.

CHAPTER FOUR

All About Climate and Seasons

Take cues from climate and seasons when choosing which fruits, vegetables, and herbs to plant and when to plant them.

43

44

49

Know your Zone

Growing plants depends on where you live in the country.

In an effort to help gardeners select plants that will survive the winter in their region, the U.S. Department of Agriculture developed a map that divides North America into Zones based on lowest recorded temperatures. Zone 1 is the coldest and includes portions of Alaska and Canada. Zone 11 is the warmest and is primarily in southern Mexico.

Zone and plants

Plants are classified by the coldest temperature they can endure. For example, plants hardy to Zone 6 survive where winter temperatures drop to –10°F, while those hardy to Zone 8 die long before it's that cold. These plants may grow in colder regions but must be brought indoors over the winter or replaced each year. Keep in mind that soil conditions, sun and shade, and wind also influence a plant's ability to overwinter.

Plants rated for a range of hardiness Zones can usually survive winter in the coldest region as well as tolerate the summer heat of the warmest one.

Plant for your Zone

A plant tag or seed packet lists a plant's Zone unless the plant is typically grown as an annual, meaning it grows from seed, bears fruit, and dies in one year. Tomatoes are annual plants. They complete their life cycle in one year. Peppers, eggplant, beans, potatoes, and the majority of other vegetables are annual plants.

Fruit trees and shrubs are grown as perennial plants. Hardiness Zone is particularly important when selecting trees and shrubs. Cold temperatures can injure buds and prevent fruiting while leaving the plant unscathed. The opposite is also true. Some plants, like apples, require a specific amount of cold temperatures to spur fruit development.

opposite Gardening zones are based on low winter temperatures.
right Rhubarb is a tough, hardy perennial that overwinters in Zones 2–9.

WHAT IS A MICROCLIMATE?

A microclimate is the climate in a small area that is different from the climate around it. The small area might be warmer or colder than a nearby area.

YOUR HOUSE and other buildings create microclimates by absorbing heat during the day and radiating it into the landscape at night. The south side of a building is typically the warmest. The west side is also warm.

BALCONIES AND ROOFTOPS are unique microclimates because they are above ground level. The elevation sometimes helps them escape frosts that kill tender plants at ground level. Keep in mind that cold, dry winds may mitigate any heat gain.

FENCES, WALLS, AND LARGE ROCKS can protect plants from wind and can radiate heat, creating sheltered spots.

PAVED SURFACES such as patios, driveways, and sidewalks can absorb heat during the day and radiate it into the landscape at night, moderating nighttime temperatures.

Fruit crops and climate

Fruit crops are particular when it comes to climate, but when you satisfy their requirements, they'll produce with abandon.

Learn what fruit crops your climate will support, and enjoy your unique backyard fruit salad.

Too cold

Cold is the most common factor limiting the growth of fruit trees and shrubs. Cold temperatures thwart the growth of the plants' roots, stems, and leaves and also bring about a late-spring frost that will nip tender buds. The frost may not damage the plant, but it will kill the buds, preventing fruit from forming.

Abiding by Zone requirements is key to successful growth and fruit harvest. Only grow fruit crops that are hardy in your Zone. For extra protection, choose plants that are hardy to one Zone lower than yours. For example, if your garden is Zone 5, plant varieties that have a hardiness rating to Zone 4.

Too warm

Most fruit trees also need a specific amount of heat to produce fruit while having a low tolerance of high temperatures. Peaches and nectarines generally require long, hot summers to produce high-quality fruit. Apricots, on the other hand, prefer cooler summers and do not reach peak flavor in regions where the heat is ideal for a flavorful peach crop.

Some fruit crops react poorly to warm winter weather, too. These crops require chilling, meaning the temperature must be below 45°F for a specified number of hours. Apples, cherries, pears, and peaches all require winter chilling.

Just right

Most fruiting plants have a wide adaptation to temperature and produce fruit in all but extremely hot- or cold-summer areas. For reliable crops, stick with plants that are hardy in your Zone. If you see a new offering, check its hardiness rating.

EXCEPTIONAL HARDINESS

Hardiness varies greatly within a species. A species may be generally classified as hardy to Zone 6, but plant breeders may have developed hardier cultivars that can tolerate the rigors of Zone 4, for example. This exceptional hardiness is becoming common as researchers breed plants for cold tolerance.

Contact your local extension office or garden center to learn about notably hardy cultivars of your favorite fruits. Or do research on the Internet by visiting the University of Minnesota, Cornell University, and Texas A&M University websites and searching the term "hardy fruit."

BHG ASK THE GARDEN DOCTOR

How do I protect a tender fruit tree from cold temperatures?

ANSWER: Increase the hardiness of marginally hardy fruit trees with these easy-care practices. First, make all fertilizer applications before mid-June. The tree will absorb the nutrients in a timely manner and not produce tender, new growth at the end of the season when it can be injured by freezing temperatures. Water regularly. A drought-stressed tree is more susceptible to winter injury than a tree growing in moist soil.

opposite The grapes scrambling up this arbor are hardy to Zone 4, but the pomegranate tree behind the stone wall is hardy to only Zone 8. Planted in a container, it is moved inside for winter.

Vegetables and climate

Relative to climate, vegetables are divided into two groups: cool-season and warm-season crops. Each has its own growing considerations.

Working with the idiosyncrasies of their climate, gardeners in most regions can successfully grow cool- and warm-season crops. A solid understanding of the crops' climate needs will help you know when to plant your favorite vegetables.

Cool-season vegetables

Cool-season vegetables grow best when temperatures range between 40°F and 75°F. In most areas, they can be planted two to four weeks before the last spring frost. These crops are most often those that develop edible roots, stems, leaves, or buds.

Most cool-season crops don't mind frost. After frost blankets their leaves, they will show little or no signs of damage and continue to grow, unfurling new leaves. Some cool-season crops are frost-hardy, meaning they tolerate prolonged freezing temperatures.

Cool-season crops are also unique in that their seeds germinate best in cool soil. The root systems of these plants are shallower and the plants themselves are smaller. Cool-season crops stop producing in early summer when temperatures range above 80°F.

Cool-season crops are typically planted as soon as the soil can be worked in spring. In regions where nights remain cool, you can sow them every two weeks or so for a continuous harvest that extends into fall. This planting method is called succession planting and ensures a bountiful harvest from spring to fall.

In warmer regions, plant cool-season vegetables as early as possible in late winter or spring, and plant seeds or transplants again in late fall for harvest in winter.

There are also cold-hardy vegetables that can survive throughout winter in some regions, especially under an insulating blanket of snow. These include carrots, parsnips, and garlic.

Warm-season vegetables

Warm-season vegetables, such as tomatoes, peppers, corn, and okra, originated in tropical climates. These are the crops that develop edible fruits as opposed to cool-season crops, which usually develop edible roots, stems, leaves, or buds. Warm-season crops are killed by frost and won't perform well if temperatures fall below 50°F. Planting before the soil and air temperatures have adequately warmed in spring has poor results. Wait until about two weeks after the average last frost date in your area to plant warm-season crops.

You can encourage many warm-season crops to continue growing, albeit slowly, into fall by protecting them from frost with row covers, cold frames, and other season-extending devices. But warm-season crops perform best during the height of summer.

left Kale and loose-leaf lettuce thrive in cool weather. Plant this combination as soon as the soil can be worked in early spring.
opposite top Corn, tomatoes, and beans are warm-season crops, requiring long, hot days to produce fruit. Cauliflower, on the other hand, thrives in the cool temperatures of spring and early summer.

COOL-SEASON CROPS

These vegetables love cool soil and cool temperatures. Plant them in early spring.

Asparagus	Kohlrabi
Beet	Leek
Broccoli	Lettuce
Brussels sprout	Onion
Cabbage	Parsnip
Carrot	Pea
Cauliflower	Potato
Celery	Radish
Chard	Rhubarb
Collards	Rutabaga
Garlic	Spinach
Kale	

WARM-SEASON CROPS

Heat makes these vegetables produce fruit. Plant them in the garden after the last chance of frost passes.

Artichoke	Peanut
Bean	Pepper
Corn	Squash
Cucumber	Sweet potato
Eggplant	Tomatillo
Melon	Tomato
Okra	

Get an early start in spring

With a little planning, you can harvest garden-fresh vegetables for six months, nine months, or even year-round if you live in a tropical climate.

The majority of gardeners in Zones 3–8 can easily increase their garden harvest season by at least one month when they plant early-spring vegetables. The same goes for fall—cool-season crops thrive at the end of the season, too.

Spring ahead: when to plant

Soil temperature is the best indicator of when to plant crops, no matter what climate you live in. Some cool-season crops readily germinate in soil as low as 40°F; others do best when the soil is 50°F. Use a simple soil thermometer to check soil temperature in early spring.

The workability of garden soil is another factor when planting an early-spring garden. Avoid planting in soggy soil that is still full of moisture from snow or spring rains. Wait until the soil dries and can be cultivated.

What to plant

Cool-season species, such as greens, broccoli, and peas, thrive in the cool air and soil temperatures in early spring, or in winter in Florida, the Gulf states, and Southern California.

For extended cold hardiness, choose varieties with notable frost tolerance. For example, 'Coronado Crown' broccoli tolerates frost better than many other broccoli varieties.

Warm-season crops can be planted indoors. An early start indoors gives warm-season crops a jump on the growing season.

Where to plant

Choose a protected planting location if possible. A warm microclimate, such as a south-facing slope, the south side of a building, or a spot protected from cold northwestern winds, will be a few degrees warmer than other planting locations.

Soil covered with dark organic mulch, such as compost or shredded leaves, will warm faster in early spring than bare soil.

TEMPERATURE MATTERS

Purchase a soil thermometer next time you're at the garden center. These cool-season vegetables germinate from seed at the prescribed soil temperatures.

40°F	50°F	60°F
Arugula	Chinese cabbage	Beet
Fava bean	Leek	Broccoli
Kale	Onion	Brussels sprout
Lettuce	Swiss chard	Cabbage
Parsnip	Turnip	Carrot
Pea		Cauliflower
Radicchio		
Radish		
Spinach		

Raised beds offer many advantages in spring. Not only do they drain faster than an in-ground planting bed, but the soil in a raised bed also warms faster.

Layer of protection

Even though soil is warm enough to plant cool-season crops, a hard frost could still harm young plants. Cover plants with a sheet or cotton blanket in an occasional late-spring frost.

A cold frame, a miniature greenhouse made of glass or plastic, is placed over plants, increasing the air temperature by 3–6 degrees. This increase, combined with warm soil, can bump up the harvest of cool-season produce by two to six weeks.

opposite Spring bulbs are a cue that it is time to plant lettuce, peas, and other cool-season crops. Wait for bulb foliage to emerge, and then plant your vegetable seeds.

Harvest through fall

Ripe watermelons and brilliant-orange pumpkins signify the end of the gardening season for many, but the warm days and cool nights of fall are perfect for growing many vegetables.

A rich end-of-the-season harvest depends on careful planning and planting when you're in the middle of harvesting tomatoes, peppers, and eggplant. Use this simple late-season gardening calendar as a guide, and you'll enjoy an additional month or more of fresh produce.

Three months before fall frost

Note: If you don't know the first fall frost date for your area, contact your local extension service or inquire at your local garden center.

Make a list of fall crops you would like to grow. In most regions, cool-season crops such as lettuce, carrots, and radishes are popular fall crops. Gardeners in Zone 8 and above can grow a second crop of tomatoes, peppers, and other warm-season crops.

Select a planting site for your fall crops. The ideal planting site might be home to beans, tomatoes, or another warm-season crop three months before the first fall frost, but if you anticipate that crop to finish producing in about a month, it is a great site for fall vegetables.

Eliminate weeds. Summer weeds can wreak havoc on a fall garden. Their extensive root systems will quickly crowd out seedlings and transplants. Get rid of weeds in preparation for planting. Cover the weed-free area with a 2-inch-thick layer of mulch.

Buy seeds or transplants. Vegetable seeds and transplants can be hard to find in late summer.

If plants are not available in your area, the Internet is a valuable option. When choosing varieties, pay close attention to the "days to maturity" label found on most seed packets and plant tags. All vegetables planted in late summer should mature in 80 days or less to prevent the chance of frost damage.

Gardeners in Zones 8 and higher should opt for fast-maturing warm-season plants. 'Bingo', 'Celebrity', and 'Carnival' tomatoes produce fruit in about 75 days.

Two months or so before frost

Spread a layer of compost over the planting site to enrich the soil. After clearing existing plants on the site, spread a 2-inch layer of compost over the soil.

Plant seeds or transplants about 60 to 80 days before the first expected frost. Use the variety's "number of days to maturity" as a guide. Mesclun greens are ready for harvest in just 40 days, so they can be planted much later than beets, which require about 60 days of growth.

Water regularly after planting. Periods of dry weather are common in late summer and early fall. Aim to provide seedlings and transplants with about 1 inch of water per week.

One month before frost until harvest

Keep frost protection in the form of blankets or sheets on hand to cover plants if temperatures dip below freezing in early fall.

Continue to water regularly to promote healthy plants and fruit production.

Harvest frost-tender plants such as tomatoes, peppers, and sweet corn before frost hits. Most cool-season crops will weather a light frost with ease. In fact, the flavor and texture of carrots and parsnips are distinctly improved by a touch of frost.

opposite left Pumpkins and squashes signify the end of the summer growing season. Continue harvesting homegrown produce by planting cool-season crops in late summer. *opposite, top right* Leeks are some of the last crops to harvest in the fall garden. Requiring nearly four months to mature, they taste sweetest after they are nipped by a fall frost. *opposite, middle right* Harvest all tomatoes if a frost is predicted. Green tomatoes can be wrapped in newspaper and ripened indoors. *opposite, bottom right* Large storage onions require as many as five months to mature and are often harvested in early fall. They are ready to pull when about half of the bulbs' tops bend over.

CHAPTER FIVE

Good Earth

Every delicious tomato, peach, and carrot begins with properly prepared soil. Invest time and effort in preparing soil, and you'll reap edible dividends.

54 58 64

Build soil knowledge

Before adding amendments to your soil, take a couple of minutes to gather some soil sense.

Think of the following discussion as a soil primer. Once you know how soil is formed and its basic components, you'll be ready to get your hands dirty and assess and improve the good earth that is in your backyard.

What is soil?

Soil is simply weathered rocks and minerals combined with organic matter, water, and air. Rain, snow, ice, and varying temperatures pulverize rocks into tiny particles. Different kinds of rocks and the ways that weathering affects them result in the wide variety of soils.

Soils that develop in warm, wet environments weather quickly. In these soils, many of the minerals that act as plant nutrients are washed away by frequent rains. Soon the soil becomes acidic and contains a large percentage of iron. The soil takes on a red or yellow color and often needs fertilization in the form of compost or commercial fertilizer for plants to thrive.

Hot, dry environments often produce soil that is low in nutrients, too. Since weathering is slow in arid regions and water is scarce, salts that are detrimental to plant growth accumulate. Incorporating compost and watering deeply is one way to discourage salt buildup and to infuse nutrients into the soil.

Essential organic matter

Organic matter is the most dynamic component of soil. It may be living or dead, composed of plant or animal material, and easily visible or infinitesimally small. A teaspoon of healthy soil contains an entire universe of microorganisms. The organisms are working to decompose plant and animal parts. When the organic matter finally stabilizes and stops decomposing, the result is humus—a naturally rich, dark, crumbly material that increases soil fertility.

Most often called compost when it is added to the soil, organic matter improves the workability and structure of all soils. It helps break apart clay particles, allowing soil and air to move through the soil. And organic matter improves sandy soil, helping it to better retain water and nutrients.

Soil types

Sand Soils made of sand have the largest particles and the largest amount of pore space—or space for water and air to move through the soil. Sandy soil drains quickly and can be worked shortly after rain. In cold climates, sandy soil is appreciated because it warms faster in spring than clay soil, allowing gardeners to plant vegetables early.

Sometimes water passes through sandy soil so quickly that roots cannot supply plants with enough water. And as water passes through the soil, it takes nutrients with it, which is why sandy soil is usually low in fertility.

Silt Tiny rounded soil particles make up silt. Because the small size results in more surface area and smaller pore spaces than in sand, silty soil drains more slowly than sandy soil and retains more nutrients.

Clay Individual clay particles are microscopic. An ounce of soil contains millions of clay particles. The miniscule particles often pack together so tightly that roots have a hard time making their way through the soil. Clay is sticky when wet and can be brick-hard when dry. Even though clay is moisture-rich, the water may not be available to plant roots because the clay particles are holding it so tightly. The same goes for clay's holding power on nutrients. Soils with a high percentage of clay are difficult for gardening.

opposite Healthy soil produces healthy plants. The bright-color stems of Swiss chard indicate the soil is nutrient-rich and drains well. **opposite, top right** Raised-bed gardening offers the opportunity to customize your soil. Combine native soil with compost and peat moss for a nutrient-rich, well-drained soil mix. **opposite, middle right** Soil rich in organic matter is easy to sink a spade into because it has a crumbly texture. **opposite, bottom right** Whether you make your own compost or purchase a bagged product, an annual application of a 2-inch-thick layer will boost soil nutrients and improve soil structure.

Size up your soil

When talking about soil, gardeners throw around terms such as "well-drained," "loose," and "moderate pH."

What do these terms mean in relation to the garden? And most importantly, how does your garden rate? Use the following guide to take a close look at the texture and drainage abilities of your garden spot. If you're inclined to learn more about your soil's nutrient content, check out the soil-testing information.

Texture

Soils are almost always a mixture of sand, silt, and clay. The ideal is a loamy soil, which scientists classify as consisting of 40 percent sand, 40 percent silt, and 20 percent clay. Loam is ideal because it holds moisture and nutrients, yet it has plenty of pore space for air, water, and roots.

Nature, however, is seldom easily classified, and the percentages of sand, silt, and clay can vary widely. Your garden soil may be a sandy clay loam, a silty clay, a loamy sand, or myriad potential combinations. Testing your soil's texture is as easy as moistening ½ cup of soil with water. Roll it into a ball and try forming it into a ribbon between your hands.

Clay soil (opposite, top right) If the soil packs together and easily forms a ribbon, the soil is clay or has a high clay component. Soils with a high percentage of clay are sticky and will probably stain your skin. If the soil ribbon feels smooth instead of sticky, it is probably silty clay. If gritty, it is sandy clay.

Loam (opposite, middle right) If the soil ribbon holds together but is looser and tends to crumble, it contains a high amount of silt, sand, or organic matter, and likely a loam soil.

Sandy soil (opposite, bottom right) If the soil will not hold together, breaking apart regardless of how much water you apply, it is a sandy soil.

opposite left Good soil texture and drainage are key to growing carrots with a uniform shape. Loam or sandy soil is ideal. Grow carrots in a raised bed if your soil is sticky clay.

DRAINAGE

Good drainage. Gardeners everywhere talk about good drainage or creating the conditions for good drainage. What is good drainage? Basically, drainage is how much and how fast water moves through the soil. Soil with good drainage has a good supply of oxygen, which is vital to root and plant health. In short, clay soils drain slowly and sandy soils drain rapidly. To test your soil's drainage ability, grab a shovel and head for the garden.

1 DIG A HOLE
Use a spade to dig a hole about 12 inches deep and 8 to 12 inches in diameter in soil that is moist but not soggy.

2 ADD WATER
Fill the hole with water. Allow it to drain. Refill it 12 hours later, noting the time.

3 TIME IT
If the soil drains well, all the water will be gone in 2 to 3 hours. But if it takes 10 or more hours to empty, it is poorly drained, and most plants will struggle to survive in that area.

SOIL TESTING

A soil test can pinpoint nutrient deficiencies and excesses and pH values, as well as guide you toward materials that will help correct problems. Soil tests can be time- and money-saving and earth-friendly tools because they point out exactly which amendments are needed.

Test soil if plants show poor or stunted growth over the course of the growing season. Other reasons to test soil? If you're starting a garden in an urban area or near a building where lead paint chips may have contaminated the soil. Or if you're growing a crop that is pH sensitive, such as blueberries, which prefer acidic soil.

Find a soil-testing lab in your area for the most accurate results. Most county extension services will perform soil tests or provide referrals to commercial labs. Request a test kit from a lab. The kit will include a bag to gather a soil sample as well as instructions on how to take an accurate sample. The soil report will include recommendations for improving your soil.

Assess your soil's nutrients

All plants require several nutrient elements for growth. Your soil will perform its best with the right nutrients.

Plants source carbon, hydrogen, and oxygen from the atmosphere and water. They mine the soil for nitrogen, phosphorus, potassium, and other important elements. Plants use these elements to fuel their food-making process called photosynthesis.

It's a gardener's job to make sure the reservoir of soil nutrients does not become depleted. One of the quickest ways to deplete a nutrient reservoir in a vegetable garden plot is to remove all the foliage, stems, and shoots at the end of the growing season. Instead of removing dead plant material, consider leaving disease-free plant parts in the garden over winter. The plant parts will decompose and add nutrients to the soil. The natural nutrient reservoir depends on this annual recycling of elements to rebuild stockpiles after a long growing season.

How does your soil rate?

Often soil, especially soil enriched with compost, has all of the mineral nutrients a plant needs for strong growth and fruit development. Loam soils are particularly nutrient-rich. Clay soil usually has many nutrients, too, but the clay binds to the nutrients so tightly that plant roots cannot access them. Excessively sandy soil, on the other hand, is often lacking nutrients; these valuable minerals quickly wash out of sandy soil.

Stunted growth, poor fruit development, and discolored foliage are all signs of a potential nutrient deficiency. The only surefire way to determine the nutrient content of your soil is to submit a sample for testing. Contact your local extension service for soil-testing information. The test results will include suggested soil amendments if there are deficient nutrients.

There are many ways to boost the nutrient content of your soil. The following pages address several popular, earth-friendly choices including nutrient-rich compost, which you can make in your own backyard.

opposite Tomatoes are voracious nutrient consumers, but they are easy to satisfy when the soil is enriched with well-decomposed compost or a slow-release fertilizer.

PLANT TALK

Plants cannot speak, but they are expert communicators. They use their leaves, stems, and overall growth habit to communicate their general well-being. With a little experience you'll soon be able to spot an unhealthy plant. Sometimes poor growth, discolored leaves, or dead foliage indicates a low nutrient level in the soil.

If your plants exhibit deficiency symptoms, take a soil test. If the soil test identifies a deficient nutrient, apply a synthetic or organic fertilizer as recommended by the testing lab.

Nitrogen deficiency symptoms: Yellowing leaves beginning with the oldest leaves and then younger leaves. Slow, stunted plant growth.
Phosphorus deficiency symptoms: Unusually dark green or purple foliage. Few flowers or fruits. Slow growth.
Potassium deficiency symptoms: Scorching on the margins of the oldest leaves. Weak stems and shriveled fruit.

EARLY RISER

BHG TEST GARDEN TIP

Some edible plants balk at nutrient-rich soil. Lavender and rosemary are two examples. Originating in the Mediterranean where low-nutrient sandy soils are the norm, when planted in high-nutrient soil these plants tend to produce many floppy, vigorous stems with mild flavor. For intense flavor, plant them in well-drained, sandy loam. If your garden soil doesn't fill this bill, grow the plants in a container.

Add a layer of compost

Compost's many attributes might make you think it is too good to be true.

Compost improves drainage in poorly drained soils, making it possible to garden in clay soil. You can mix compost with clay soil to make it loose and workable over time. It can also help excessively sandy soil hold more water. And compost adds nutrient content. Well-made compost is packed with more nutrients and beneficial microorganisms than many other soil amendments. It's easy to see why compost is called black gold.

You can buy compost at many garden centers, but if you have a few feet of space, you can make compost. Here are a few common composting methods and bins; choose the best for you.

Holding units are a good choice for apartment dwellers and those with limited space. These units do not require turning. Layers of green and brown materials are simply piled in the unit, moistened, and left to decompose. Because holding units are not turned, the decomposing material is not infused with oxygen and the composting process takes as long as two years.

Turning units are designed to promote aeration. These units produce compost in a few months because oxygen is supplied to bacteria working inside the pile. These units may be a series of bins or a structure that rotates, such as a ball or barrel. Most often materials must be saved until a unit can be filled to the correct level. Once these units are filled and the turning process begins, new materials should not be added.

Heaps do not require a bin or structure. A compost heap is a layered pile of compostable material, preferably located in part shade and on top of soil or a pallet if poor drainage is a concern. Do not create a compost heap on cement or asphalt. Contact with soil will provide necessary bacteria for the pile. Turning a heap is optional, but the composting process will be faster if the pile is turned. Aim to turn a compost heap every two weeks.

opposite Each spring before planting, spread a 2-inch-thick layer of compost over your garden and mix it into the top few inches of soil. It will boost soil nutrients and improve soil structure over time.

MAKE YOUR OWN COMPOST

Make a compost heap by spreading a 3-inch-layer of brown material on the soil. Top the brown material with a 3-inch-layer of green material. Continue layering as materials become available, and water the pile until it is as moist as a wrung-out sponge. Turn the pile once every two weeks.

1 BROWN MATERIAL
Leaves, dried grass, small wood chips, twigs, soil, and shredded newspaper contribute valuable carbon and microrganisms to the pile.

2 GREEN MATERIAL
Fresh grass clippings, kitchen scraps from fruits and vegetables, and garden waste provide compost with valuable nitrogen.

3 WATER
Add water to the pile to encourage bacteria to grow and decomposition to take place. Turn the pile every two weeks, and you'll have nutrient-rich humus in a few short months.

How do I keep pests out of my compost pile?

ANSWER: When adding items to your compost pile, don't add meat, bones, and fatty foods such as cheese, salad dressing, and oils. These foods ferment, cause odors, and can attract rodents. Also avoid adding disease-infected plants to the pile. Although the heat generated from the compost process may kill some diseases, some organisms may survive and be returned to the garden.

Boost soil nutrients

As edible fruits, vegetables, and leaves are growing, the plants are harvesting nutrients from the soil.

It's a gardener's job to replenish the soil's nutrients so it can continue to provide all the elements necessary for plant growth.

The nutrients plants use in large qualities that might be deficient are nitrogen (chemical symbol N), phosphorus (P), and potassium (K). If you are starting a new vegetable garden plot or your edibles are showing symptoms of nutrient distress (see page 59), take a soil test and follow fertilizing recommendations. Established gardens with healthy plant growth usually have adequate supplies of phosphorus and potassium, and thus nitrogen is the primary focus of fertilization.

Label lingo

Fertilizers are labeled or described according to the percentage of N, P, and K they contain. Take a look at a fertilizer label, and you're likely to see three numbers separated by hyphens, such as 10-10-10, on the front of the package. The first number represents N; this product contains 10 percent nitrogen. The second number represents phosphorus, and the third number represents potassium.

More often than not, vegetable gardens benefit from a fertilizer that is high in N and lower in P and K, because nitrogen readily dissipates in the soil over time but P and K are more lasting. Herbs and fruit crops are often fertilized less often and benefit from a balanced fertilizer, or one that contains equal amounts of N, P, and K.

opposite Water-soluble fertilizer is a quick and efficient way to deliver nutrients to plants when it is applied using a hose-end applicator like this one.

AMENDING SOIL AT A GLANCE

Healthy soil promotes healthy plants. Build healthy soil with these soil-amendment tips:

When: Timing depends on the type of amendment and the crop. Synthetic slow-release fertilizers are mixed into the soil before planting. Compost is often mixed into the soil before planting and then again in midseason.

What: Use products specifically formulated for edible gardens. Do not use lawn fertilizers; they often contain herbicides that harm vegetable plants. Low-cost organic options such as compost are best choices because they supply valuable nutrients while improving the soil structure.

How: Purchased products have specific application instructions. Strictly follow directions, because overapplication or improper timing could damage plants and the environment. Spread a 2-inch-thick layer of homemade compost over the garden prior to planting. Till it into the top 6 to 8 inches of soil.

NUTRIENT SOURCES FOR EDIBLE GARDENS

1. **SYNTHETIC FERTILIZERS** are available as granular products or liquids. Liquid forms deliver nutrients to plants faster than granular products. There are many different N-P-K combinations and even crop-specific formulations. Synthetic fertilizers are convenient and simple to apply, but do so carefully; overapplication can burn plants.

2. **BLOOD MEAL** is dried, powdered blood collected from cattle slaughterhouses. It has a formulation of 12-0-0 and is a rich source of nitrogen. Apply it carefully; it can easily burn plants.

3. **COMPOST** is decomposed plant parts. Make it yourself or purchase it in bulk at your local garden center. Most commercial compost has a chemical formulation of 1.5-1-1. Compost not only contains nutrients, but it also has microbes, which improve soil structure.

4. **COTTONSEED MEAL** is a byproduct of cotton processing. This 6-3-2 product poses little danger of burn.

5. **COVER CROPS** are planted in fall or early spring and tilled into soil two to three weeks before planting. Annual ryegrass and oats are two popular cover crops. Formulation varies among crops, but all are high in nitrogen. Cover crops add valuable nitrogen to soil.

6. **FISH EMULSION** is a partially decomposed blend of finely pulverized fish. The odor can be offensive during application, but it dissipates in a day or two. It has a formulation of 4-2-2. Apply fish emulsion after plants have sprouted, to boast initial growth. The nutrients are quickly available to plants.

Improve soil structure

Just because your garden soil is excessively sandy or dense clay doesn't mean you have to tolerate poor plant growth.

There are many simple things you can do to improve soil structure and nutrient content. Time is your major investment. Incorporating amendments will take a few hours, depending on the size of your plot, and waiting for the soil to radically transform will take years. You'll enjoy some success immediately, but the soil will continue to improve as it weathers. Enjoy greater improvement by adding compost and amendments annually.

Plant a cover crop. Often called green manure crops, cover crops are grains, grasses, or legumes that grow during the fall and winter and are tilled under in the spring. Their roots penetrate and help loosen heavy-texture soils, allowing better air and water movement in the soil. Cover crops also add valuable nutrients to the soil when they are tilled in—a benefit to both sandy and clay soils. Plant winter rye or wheat, hairy vetch, or crimson clover in fall, and turn it under in spring. For a spring cover crop, plant buckwheat, alfalfa, or oats, and turn the crop under two to three weeks before planting edibles.

Add a layer of organic mulch. As mulch slowly decomposes, it adds organic matter to the soil. A slow addition of organic matter to clay and sandy soils improves the soil structure. Mulch also works to mediate the compaction of clay soil and to prevent an impenetrable crust from forming on top of the soil.

Incorporate compost. Any composted material that has been reduced to humus is a good soil amendment. Homemade or purchased compost is a good choice, as is rotted animal manure. The key is to add enough compost to make an impact. To make a significant change, the volume of compost must equal one-third of the volume of soil you are amending.

opposite A layer of straw mulch around plants has many benefits. It prevents weeds, slows soil moisture evaporation, and slowly decomposes, improving soil structure.

HOW MUCH COMPOST DO YOU NEED?

Significantly changing soil structure requires an addition of compost or well-rotted manure in a proportion of at least one-third of the volume of soil you are amending. For example, to amend a garden to a depth of 12 inches, you need to add 4 inches of amendments. How much material is this? Here's how to calculate using a 10×20-foot garden as an example.

1. MULTIPLY the width and length to get the area.
10 × 20 = 200 square feet

2. MULTIPLY the area by 0.33 (one-third of a foot) to get cubic feet. 200 square feet × 0.33 = 66 cubic feet

3. DIVIDE cubic feet by 27 to get cubic yards. (Large quantities of amendments are usually sold in cubic yards) 66 cubic feet / 27 = about 2.5 cubic yards

BHG ASK THE GARDEN DOCTOR

My tomato plants' leaves turned brown after I fertilized them. What happened?

ANSWER: Most likely you overfertilized your plants, and the excessive nitrogen scorched the leaves. This can happen to any type of plant, most frequently with liquid or granular fertilizer products. Avoid overfertilizing by carefully following application directions. Aid scorched plants by watering them deeply to wash the fertilizer away from the plants' root systems.

Build a raised bed

Raised-bed gardening is often the best way to rise above frustratingly sticky clay soil.

With a small monetary investment and a few hours of work, you can build a raised bed over poor soil. Sites with slow-draining, clay, or rocky soil are not the only benefactors of this smart garden practice—it's a great solution for small gardens, too.

Edibles can be planted more intensely in a raised bed—ideally spaced just far enough apart to avoid crowding but close enough to shade out weeds—because no space has to be set aside for paths. This intense planting scheme is a good fit for urban and rooftop gardens where planting space is at a premium. Raised beds elevated 2 feet or more also reduce bending and stooping.

Construction particulars

Size. To prevent walking in a raised bed, build it no wider than 4 feet. At this width, it's easy to access the bed from either side. Opt for short beds with 2-foot paths in between to eliminate unnecessary steps walking around an extremely long bed. The best beds are 12 to 24 inches tall, which allows adequate rooting space and easy construction.

Materials. Stone, brick, concrete block, and untreated wood make fine building materials for raised beds.

Soil. Before filling the raised bed with quality topsoil, loosen the ground-level soil by rototilling it or turning it over with a spade. Then mix the native soil with topsoil to fill the raised bed.

Maintenance

Water. Raised beds dry out faster than traditional gardens during the heat of summer. Be prepared to water frequently. Spread a 2-inch-thick layer of organic mulch, such as shredded leaves or finely shredded wood mulch, around plants.

opposite Remedy slow-draining soil with an easy-to-build raised bed. Looseleaf lettuce, cabbage, and peas thrive in this well-drained raised bed framed with wood planks.

STEP-BY-STEP: RAISED BED

What's not to love about raised-bed gardening? These tidy, efficient gardens rise above slow-draining, compacted soil and reduce the need to bend and stoop as you care for plants. Build a raised bed in an afternoon with these easy instructions.

1 SELECT A SITE AND REMOVE SOD
For ease of construction, choose a level site for the raised bed. Also pay attention to sunlight. Most edibles require at least eight hours of direct sunlight per day. Delineate the edges of the bed with white marking paint, and use a sharp spade to skim the sod off the site. If this is your first garden, start small—a 4×4-foot bed will provide plenty of planting space.

2 CONSTRUCT THE FRAME
Build the bed frame using a raised-bed kit, available at home improvement stores and on the Internet, or make your own using untreated lumber. A simple design involves using 4×4s for the corner posts and attaching 2x6s to form side rails.

3 LOOSEN THE SOIL
Set the course for a well-drained bed by loosening the native soil. Most likely compacted during the construction process, the native soil has the potential to thwart the good drainage of the raised bed by not allowing water to percolate into the ground below the bed. Use a sharp spade to turn soil to a depth of about 8 inches.

4 ADD SOIL
Fill the new bed with topsoil. Mix in a generous amount of compost and other amendments, if a soil test indicates they are necessary. Don't skimp on soil for your raised bed; fill it with high-quality, nutrient-rich soil. Garden centers stock many bagged products that contain ample nutrients and have excellent drainage for raised-bed gardening.

5 MIX IT TOGETHER
Using a small tiller or a spade, combine the topsoil, soil amendments, and a few inches of the native soil to form a uniform mixture.

6 PLANT YOUR GARDEN
Raised beds are perfect for growing plants from seeds or transplants. You can even grow perennial plants, such as blueberries or brambles, in raised beds, if you like.

CHAPTER SIX

Planting Time

Soil, seeds, water, and time produce delicious results in an edible garden. Start planting today with tips for growing plants indoors and out.

71 72 76 80

Getting started: seeds or transplants?

Gardening is full of choices—from what to plant, to where to plant, to when to harvest.

Starting plants is no different. Plants can be grown from seeds or transplants. If you choose to start vegetables and herbs from seeds, you have the choice of planting the seeds indoors or planting them directly in the garden.

Starting from seed

Although many vegetables can be bought as transplants at your local garden center or home improvement store or on the Internet, it's fascinating to watch plants develop from seeds.

Starting vegetables from seed has practical advantages as well. Seeds offer the greatest selection at negligible cost. They are a practical way to grow a large number of plants for you or to share with friends and family. Some seeds are best sown directly in the soil, while others need to be planted indoors for transplanting into the garden later on.

Fruit plants are rarely started from seed. Tree fruits, such as apples, and most berries usually are started from nursery-grown transplants.

Indoors or out?

Where to plant seeds is mostly a question of timing. Some plants benefit from a few extra weeks of growing time. By starting seeds indoors, you give them a jump on the growing season before the soil and air temperatures are warm enough for planting outside. Tomatoes, peppers, eggplant, and several more warm-season crops demand an early start in order to mature and set fruit in many climates. Lettuce, carrots, radishes, and beans thrive when seeded into the garden.

Large seeds that germinate quickly are easier to sow outdoors. Small seeds that germinate slowly or germinate best at a specific soil temperature are easier to manage indoors. Bottom line: Sow seeds indoors or in the garden, whichever better suits your

INDOORS OR OUTDOORS

Some plants are easiest to start from seeds planted directly in the garden. Others do best when planted indoors or started from purchased transplants. Here's a suggestion of what to plant where.

SOW IN THE GARDEN

Bean	Onion
Beet	Parsnip
Carrot	Pea
Chard	Peanut*
Corn	Pumpkin
Cucumber	Radish
Lettuce	Rutabaga
Melon	Spinach
Okra*	Squash

*start indoors in Zones 6 and below

SOW INDOORS OR START FROM TRANSPLANTS

Artichoke*	Eggplant
Broccoli	Kale
Brussels sprout	Leek
	Pepper
Cabbage	Tomatillo
Cauliflower	Tomato
Collards	

*difficult to grow from seeds; best grown from transplants

season and temperament. Just follow the planting directions on the seed packet for best results.

Transplants

Some seeds are tricky and time-consuming to start indoors or to sow directly in the garden. Buy these vegetables and herbs as transplants at your local garden center, or place an order with a plant company on the Internet and transplants will be shipped to your door at planting time. When shopping for transplants, look for sturdy, short plants that have a strong stem and disease-free, healthy foliage.

opposite Growing plants indoors does not require fancy equipment. Recycle clay pots or create a pot out of newspaper. Degradable peat pots can be planted right in the garden in spring.

Start seeds indoors

Technology has made seed-starting indoors a hobby rather than a necessity for most gardeners.

Hundreds of vegetable cultivars are available as small transplants from local garden centers and Internet sources. Even though ready-to-plant seedlings are just a click away, it is still a joy to plant a few seeds while snow and cold winds blow outdoors. With modern methods and products, starting seeds indoors is simple.

Containers

As long as a container has drainage holes or you can create drainage holes, it will make a fine seed-starting vessel. Recycle yogurt cartons, egg cartons, and waxed paper cups into containers. A popular option is peat pots, small containers made of pressed organic material, such as compost or peat moss. Seeds are planted directly in the pots, and you plant the entire pot without disturbing the roots. The pot slowly disintegrates into the soil. Peat pellets are similar. These little discs expand in water to form a 2-inch-tall cylinder. Plant a seed in the expanded disk, which you then treat like a peat pot.

Soil

The best soil for starting seeds indoors is a mix of peat moss, perlite, and starter fertilizer. Look for a commercial seed-starting mix at your local garden center. Don't use garden soil; it compacts easily, preventing tender roots from expanding.

Light

Most vegetable seeds don't need light to germinate, but once they begin to grow, they need adequate light so they don't produce long, floppy stems. An indoor lighting setup that includes fluorescent lights provides dependable, consistent light.

opposite Peat pellets provide the perfect conditions for starting broccoli and other plants from seeds. When the plants are ready to go into the garden, plant the entire pellet, reducing transplant shock.

BHG TEST GARDEN TIP

PLANTING HOLES

The eraser end of a pencil is the perfect size for making small planting holes for many seeds. Lightly press the eraser into the potting soil, drop in a seed or two, and sprinkle soil over the planting hole.

STEP-BY-STEP: STARTING SEEDS

Plant seeds indoors six to eight weeks before you plan to plant them outside. Tomatoes and peppers are some of the most popular edibles to start from seeds. These easy-to-grow plants germinate readily and grow rapidly.

1 CHOOSE A CONTAINER
Start seeds in any type of container that drains readily. Peat pots and peat pellets are especially easy to use because they can be planted directly in the garden. You can also recycle nursery containers; be sure to clean them well before seeding.

2 ADD POTTING SOIL
Unless you are using peat pellets, it is necessary to add potting soil to your container. A seed-starting potting mix is ideal, but you can also use an all-purpose potting soil. Quick drainage is essential, and a slow-release fertilizer is a good addition. Use a straight edge, such as a small ruler, to level the potting soil, being careful not to compact it.

3 PLANT SEEDS AND WATER
Using your fingers or a piece of cardstock folded into a trough, drop two or three seeds into each pot or pellet. Planting depth depends on the plant. Some seeds are planted ½ inch deep, while others grow best when they are planted just ⅛ inch deep. Check the encyclopedia section beginning on page 136 for planting-depth recommendations. Using a spray bottle, mist the soil daily until seedlings emerge.

4 PLACE SEEDLINGS UNDER LIGHT
After the seedlings germinate, move them to a bright location. Fluorescent lights are ideal. Use two bulbs—one cool white and one warm white—to provide ample light for 14 or so hours per day.

Grow healthy seedlings

Warm soil and adequate moisture trigger seedlings to germinate in short order.

Follow these tips and you'll have healthy seedlings for transplanting into the garden in a few weeks.

Germination

Seeds tend to need warmer temperatures to germinate than to grow. Most vegetables germinate fast in warm soil. The faster seeds germinate, the less likely they are to rot or be damaged by insects. Under ideal soil temperatures, most seeds will germinate within one week. However, some vegetables, such as leeks, may take longer.

Setting pots or seed trays in a warm spot will speed germination. The top of a refrigerator or any place that provides a little extra warmth is all you need. Commercial warming mats, similar to heating pads, are also available.

Spur germination by keeping the soil moist; water gently with a mister, or place pots in a watertight container and pour 1 or 2 inches of water in the bottom of the container. Water will naturally travel into the dry soil. Remove the container from the water tray as soon as the top of the soil is moist.

Light and transplanting

As soon as seeds germinate, move them to a place that has bright light or put them under a bank of seed-starting lights, available online and at home improvement stores.

Once seedlings form a second set of leaves, thin them to one per pot. Use scissors to snip off the weakest seedlings at the soil line. Large plants, such as tomatoes, peppers, and eggplant, might need to be transplanted into a larger pot before planting outside. Figure that once a seedling's height is three times the diameter of the pot, it's time to move it into a larger pot.

BEWARE OF DAMPING OFF

The biggest hazard in starting seeds indoors is damping-off disease. This fungus literally attacks overnight and can wipe out a whole tray of seedlings by morning. The telltale sign of damping-off disease is seedlings that have rotted at the soil line. The disease thrives under damp conditions with little air circulation.

To prevent damping-off fungus from attacking, don't overwater seedlings. Water until the soil is moist, allowing it to dry slightly between waterings. Also generously space seedlings and encourage good air circulation by placing a fan nearby so it gently moves air around the plants.

Acclimate to the outdoors

One week before you're ready to transplant seedlings into the garden, harden them by acclimating them to outdoor conditions. Find a location that's protected from wind and receives morning sun. Place the seedlings outside, ideally on a cloudy, windless day that's above 50°F, for a few hours, then bring them indoors. Gradually extend the amount of time they are outdoors over a one-week period. By the end of the week, you can leave them outdoors overnight.

opposite Acclimate seedlings to their new environment by placing them outside for a few hours every day for a week. A simple cold frame will moderate cold winds.

left A potato fork is handy for turning soil and working compost into the top 8 or so inches of soil. Soil that crumbles easily in your hand is dry enough to work. **above** Mix in a 2-inch-thick layer of compost to a depth of about 8 inches.

Prepare a seedbed

Planting seeds or transplants in the garden begins with preparing the soil.

Little preparation, other than adding compost, is needed when vegetables are planted in existing landscape beds to form an edible landscape. New landscape beds and vegetable plots require just a few hours of time, some muscle power, and compost to prep for planting. Here's a quick summary to guide you through the process.

Remove sod. Your soon-to-be vegetable garden is most likely blanketed with turf grass. Begin by skimming away the sod and as many roots as possible. There are several ways to accomplish this. A low-cost option that requires some strength and stamina is to use a sharp shovel to slice under the grass, cutting below the sod's 2- to 3-inch-deep root zone. Be sure to slice deep enough to remove all visible roots and prevent the grass from regrowing as a garden weed.

Sod can also be removed with a sod cutter. Rent this small machine at a home improvement store for the day and use gas power to make quick work of removing sod. Adjust the sod cutter's cutting depth to ensure it removes as much of the sod's root zone as possible.

Toss the sod into a compost pile. It will quickly decompose, turning into compost that can be spread on the garden next spring.

Check soil dryness. Before tilling or turning the soil, check the soil moisture. Tilling wet soil results in hard-to-break clods that will plague you and your plants all season long. To determine when the soil is dry enough to work, press a handful in your fist and squeeze. If the soil readily crumbles, you can till or turn the soil. If water oozes out when you squeeze, it's still too wet. Wait a few more days and check the soil again.

The soil in raised-bed gardens often dries more quickly than in-ground garden soil. If it takes your soil more than a week to dry in spring after a heavy rain, consider gardening in raised beds.

SMOTHER GRASS

If you have time—four to eight weeks or more—you can kill grass by covering it with sections of newspaper and topping the paper with wood mulch. Cover the grass with newsprint, overlapping sections to create a mat that is at least 10 sheets thick. Top the newsprint with a 4-inch-thick layer of shredded wood mulch. Water the mulch well to prevent the newsprint from blowing. Over time, the grass will die and the newspaper will decompose. Till or turn the soil, incorporate compost, and plant seeds or transplants.

Add compost. It is easier to amend the soil prior to planting. Before planting, you have no obstacles in your way, making spreading and mixing in compost a breeze. Spread a 2-inch-thick layer of well-decomposed compost over the garden. Add compost annually in fall or spring, and mix it in the soil prior to planting in spring.

Loosen soil. Topsoil in a vegetable garden should be finely textured and free of large clods so sprouts can punch through the soil surface and water can seep into the root zone. Use a tiller or long-handle spade to turn the soil and break up clods. After tilling, smooth the soil with a stiff garden rake, gathering up rocks and large clods as you go.

Time to plant

The first warm, sunny day after a long winter might spur you to begin planting, but hold off.

Plant seeds and transplants of cool-season crops before the last frost date in your area. They'll thrive once the soil reaches about 40°F and is fairly dry. Plant seeds and transplants of warm-season crops outdoors about two weeks after the last average frost date for your area.

Look to seed packets

Much of the information you need for planting, including the best planting time, is at your fingertips on the back of a seed packet. Seed packets detail plant spacing and planting depth as well as mature plant size. They also give an estimate of how many days from planting time that you can expect ripe produce, listed as "days to maturity" on the packet. Seed packets also detail special treatments seeds might require prior to planting, such as soaking in water to soften the seed's outer covering.

Planting

The most common way to plant seeds is in straight, narrow rows. Refer to the seed packet for planting depth, and use a hoe or tool handle to make a depression in the loose soil. To make a straight row, run a plumb line from a stake at either end of the planting bed. Place seeds in the furrow, spacing them as directed on the seed packet and covering them with loose soil, again as directed on the seed packet. Firm the covered row with your hand to ensure seed-to-soil contact, and water gently.

Another way to plant seeds is in wide rows, which offer efficiency in small spaces by eliminating pathways. Wide rows should be no wider than 4 feet across so you can comfortably reach the center of the bed.

Vining crops, such as melons and pumpkins, are traditionally grown on mounds of soil called hills. Create a 3-foot-diameter, flat-top mound on heavy soil or just a circle on the ground on sandy soil. Plant five or six evenly spaced seeds per hill, and space the hills based on the individual vegetable you're growing. Thin out all but the strongest two or three seedlings to the proper spacing. Hills give vining vegetables room to spread.

TOMATO PLANTING TIPS

Tomatoes are usually grown from transplants planted directly in the garden after the last average frost date. When shopping for tomato transplants, look for short, stocky plants. They will withstand strong spring winds more easily than tall, lanky plants.

STAKE PLANTS AFTER PLANTING. Whether you use a traditional wire tomato cage or a sturdy dowel sunk into the soil alongside the plant, stake your tomato at planting time to prevent damage to the root ball or foliage that can happen when staking a large plant.

PLANT THE STEM. Tomatoes produce roots along their stems. Bury the stem of an exceptionally tall and lanky transplant to encourage it to produce roots that will anchor the soon-to-be top-heavy plant. Plant the transplant in a 3-inch-deep trench, bending the tip of the plant up so that three or four sets of leaves are above the soil and the rest of the stem and root ball are below the soil. The stem will quickly sprout roots.

TEST GARDEN TIP — TASTY ROW MAKER

Carrots are notoriously slow to germinate. Remember where you planted them by sowing a crop of radishes in the same furrow as the carrots. Radishes spring out of the ground quickly, marking the row. The radishes will be ready for harvest shortly after the carrots germinate.

opposite Transplants are a quick and easy way to plant your garden. These lettuce and kale transplants will produce edible leaves in just three to four weeks.

Seedling care

Nature throws a bevy of diverse weather conditions at tender young seedlings in spring—from sudden snowstorms to scorching heat.

More often than not, seedlings will tolerate strong winds, cool temperatures, and occasional heavy rains. There are a few things you can do to moderate weather extremes and encourage fast plant growth.

Be water smart. Seedlings need about 1 inch of water per week for best growth. If it does not rain, water them gently with a watering can or hose fitted with a sprinkling nozzle.

Add a layer of mulch. After seedlings emerge from the soil and develop a second set of leaves, or shortly after setting out transplants, spread a 1-inch layer of finely shredded bark, leaves, or other organic mulch around plants. Keep mulch away from tender stems.

Thin plants. Although it might be difficult to discard some of your young seedlings, thinning is necessary for good growth. Thin seedlings by cutting off the weakest seedlings at ground level. Use scissors or pruners. Thin established plants by snipping them or gently pulling them, if doing so will not disturb the root system of nearby plants.

Consider row covers. If the threat of bad weather has the potential to harm tender seedlings, cover them with a floating row cover. Made of lightweight fabric resembling cheesecloth, floating row covers let sunlight, water, and air through while blocking insects and keeping the transplants slightly warmer. Simply drape fabric over the seedlings and anchor the sides. Or use wire to create half-circle frames. Sink the frames over the plants and drape the cloth over the frames. Floating row covers are so lightweight that vegetables will lift them as they grow.

Use cloches for warmth. Protect individual plants with mini greenhouses called cloches. Make your own cloche by cutting the bottom off gallon-size clear plastic jugs. Remove the bottom, make a V-shape slit in the handle's top, and set the jug over a plant. Insert a long stick through the handle and deep enough into the ground to keep the jug in place. Don't use the cap. Take off on days over 50°F to keep excess heat from building up inside; replace if you expect cold temperatures.

opposite Made of lightweight fabric, a floating row cover protects cold-sensitive peppers from extreme cold and wind. It also prevents insects from damaging plants. **above** Thinning carrots is especially important. A crowded carrot planting will produce small, odd-shape roots. Thin plants so they are 2 to 3 inches apart.

TOMATO TEPEES

To harvest the first tomato on the block, you'll need to place your seedlings out as early as possible, but you run the risk of a late frost killing plants. To protect the transplants from cold temperatures, place a water-filled frost protector over them. These commercially available plastic sleeves have cells that are filled with water. The water releases heat as it cools at night, significantly warming the enclosed seedling. This system protects seedlings of tomatoes and other warm-season crops down to 20°F. Remove the tepee once the weather is consistently warm.

CHAPTER SEVEN

Water Smart

Plant roots harvest water from the soil so you can harvest produce from the garden. Water smart to conserve this valuable resource.

85

86

91

Know when to water

Watering, like most garden chores, is not a one-size-fits-all kind of practice.

How much to water, when to water, and how to water all depend on your garden soil, weather, and the edibles you are growing.

Take cues from the soil

How much and how fast a soil can absorb water depends on its texture, namely the relative amounts of sand, silt, and clay it contains. Clay soils hold the most water for the longest time but absorb it slowly. Rain and irrigation may wash off and not soak into clay soil. Sandy soils are the opposite. They absorb water quickly but retain little of it. Most plants in sandy soils need more frequent watering. Mixing compost and other organic matter into clay or sandy soils helps compensate for the weaknesses of both.

Weather considerations

Generally, annual plants need about 1 inch of water a week to thrive. If nature delivers 1 inch of water or more, you likely will not have to supplement. If not, plan to water, especially early in the season when plants are establishing root systems.

Crop considerations

Annual plants, such as most vegetables, grow fast and need soil that is consistently moist. Young fruiting shrubs and trees also need water frequently compared with the same plants once their roots are established. Standard fruit trees need a lot of water. If this isn't supplied by rain, deep irrigation is necessary. Dwarf trees may not need as much water, but they do require a constant supply. A newly planted tree has a root spread of up to 2 square feet and needs a minimum of 2 to 4 gallons of water a week. Make appropriate adjustments for rainfall, high temperatures, and soil type.

BAG IT

BHG TEST GARDEN TIP

Use water bags, such as Gator Bags, to prevent runoff when watering newly planted fruit trees. These zippered bags have water reservoirs with holes in the bottom that allow water to seep out into the tree's root ball. It takes several hours for a water bag to drain, ensuring all the water percolates into the soil.

WATERING CUES

There are two ways to know when to water your plants. First, check the plants themselves. If you watch closely, you'll learn to tell when water is needed long before the obvious signal: wilting.

The soil also offers cues to water needs. Scratch the soil 1 to 2 inches below the soil surface. If it is moist, you don't need to water for at least two days. If it is dry, water deeply by soaking the soil to a depth of 6 to 8 inches below the surface.

opposite Lettuce and other spring crops generally receive plenty of moisture from rainfall, but if irrigation is necessary, a gentle spray from a garden hose is an easy way to deliver water.

left If you only have a few tomato plants or a very small garden, hand watering is the easiest way to deliver water to plants during prolonged dry spells.
above Soil basins are particularly effective around fruit trees and shrubs. They hold water, allowing it to seep into the soil.

Ways to water

There are many ways to deliver water to your vegetables, fruits, and herbs.

If your garden is like most, you'll likely use some combination of these most common watering methods regularly.

Hand watering: best for container gardens, watering one or two transplanted plants in a large garden, and watering seeds after planting. This simple method involves watering the garden with a handheld hose, usually with a spray head on the end, or a watering can. It involves no previous soil preparation or equipment installation. It is time-consuming and leads to underwatering because most gardeners do not have the patience to water plants for as long as needed.

Furrow irrigation: best for watering rows of plants; it is often used in large vegetable gardens. Furrows beside plant rows are filled with water and left to soak in. Plant foliage stays dry when furrow irrigation is used, helping to minimize disease development.

Basin irrigation: used mainly around fruit trees and shrubs. A ridge of soil is built to contain the water; then the basin that is formed by the ridge is filled with water, either from a handheld hose or a bubbler head on a permanent sprinkler system. A few basins can be filled quickly with water, but if many plants are irrigated by hand in this manner, watering can be time-consuming. Plant foliage stays dry when water basins are used.

Sprinklers: best for large, densely planted gardens. Hose-end sprinklers and underground installed sprinklers irrigate a large area at once. They are most effective when used to water heavily planted areas. Sprinklers are wasteful if they are used to irrigate sparsely planted areas. They are also hard to control in windy areas and they wet plant leaves, which may lead to disease problems. They are effective for delivering water over a large area and require less time than most other systems. Due to their drawbacks, choose alternative watering systems if possible.

Drip irrigation: best for any size garden and plants that require constant soil moisture. Drip irrigation systems apply water slowly, allowing it to seep into the soil. They are left on for a few hours at a time, often for 4 hours per day. Many types of delivery systems are available. If they are properly operated, drip systems do the best watering job because they keep the soil at a relatively constant state of moisture, without the wet-to-dry fluctuations of other methods. Drip systems work best in light soils and are a perfect solution to watering plants on steep slopes. They do not wet leaves.

LOW-WATER EDIBLES

A few edibles are drought tolerant after they have established a strong root system—about eight weeks after planting. For the most part, the vegetables in this group are warm-season plants. Cool-season plants are accustomed to frequent spring rain and balk at dry situations. Many perennial herbs and fruit trees, once established, are drought-tolerant.

VEGETABLES

Bean
Okra
Onion

HERBS

Chives
Lavender
Rosemary
Sage
Thyme

All about drip systems

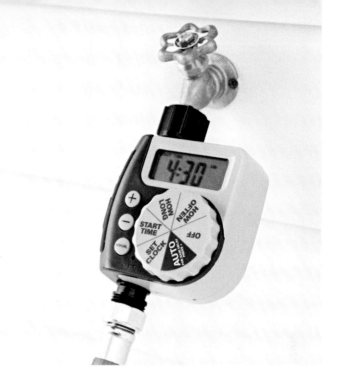

Easy on the environment and easy on you, drip irrigation is a smart way to deliver water to thirsty edibles.

A water-wise solution for drought-prone regions, drip irrigation prevents runoff by slowly delivering moisture to plant roots. This slow, steady application maintains a delicate balance of air and water in the soil, creating a nearly perfect environment for roots.

Easy to install and adaptable to any size or shape of garden, drip irrigation systems, also called micro-irrigation systems, can be purchased at most home improvement centers. You'll find kits that include necessary emitters, hoses, and other components. You can also purchase individual drip components that will allow you to customize your kit or create a system from scratch.

How it works

A drip system consists of a combination of hoses, emitters, and basic plumbing fixtures. A hallmark of this type of watering system is its simplicity. It does not need to be trenched into the ground, as is the case with sprinkler irrigation. The system's tubing is often laid on top of weed fabric and under mulch to keep it out of sight and to prevent a trip hazard.

The water source for a drip system is commonly a spigot. A backflow-prevention device is attached to the spigot to prevent contaminated water from flowing into the water system. A filter is then attached to trap small particles before they get into the system and clog emitters. A pressure regulator is installed next. This device reduces the household water system to 25 to 30 pounds per square inch. An automatic timer can be installed near the spigot to turn the system on and off.

A ½-inch polyethylene hose, a mainline, transfers water from the spigot to the garden site. The mainline should not exceed 200 feet for consistent water flow. Next, emitter tubing and emitters are attached to the mainline. Emitters can be placed every 12 to 24 inches to deliver water to a row-style garden or simply placed as needed in a garden with an irregular design.

EASY IRRIGATION

There are three basic parts to a drip irrigation system. You can add other features, available at home improvement stores, to customize your system.

MAINLINE As long as 200 feet, the mainline carries water from the spigot to the garden.

EMITTERS Place one emitter every 12 to 24 inches in a vegetable garden, or water shrubs or small trees using up to three emitters evenly spaced around the plants.

AUTOMATIC TIMER A timer turns a drip irrigation system on and off, handling the watering job for you.

Drip irrigation systems are easy to reconfigure, too. Goof plugs allow you to plug an emitter hole.

Getting started

The first step in installing a drip system is to take stock of your site. Measure the size of your optimal irrigation system by laying out a series of garden hoses in the anticipated location of the drip system. Measure the length of the hoses you used, and take the information with you to the home improvement store.

Maintenance

A drip system requires minimal care. During the growing season, check and clean emitters to ensure they are working properly. Remove and clean the filter from time to time.

opposite A simple drip system consisting of a single drip hose slowly delivers water to tender young lettuce.

Watering tips

TEST GARDEN TIP

WINTER HOSE CARE
Get a long and useful life from your garden hose by properly storing it in winter. First, disconnect and drain it. Coil hoses once they're drained, and connect the two ends to keep the coil neat. Store hoses flat, not hanging, ideally in a garage or basement where they will not freeze.

Be water smart with these simple tips about when and how much to water.

Make the most of every drop with efficient watering practices. These conservation strategies are especially important if your area's water is in short supply or expensive—or both.

Apply 1 inch per week. Most edible plants need 1 inch of water per week. Determine when to water by examining the soil. Gardens with sandy soil must be watered more often than gardens with clay soil. Generally, if the soil is dry 2 inches below the surface, it's time to water. If it is moist, you can delay watering for a couple of days.

Water deeply. Your goal whenever you water is to send moisture 6 to 8 inches into the soil to encourage greatest root growth. Well-established edible plants have roots that extend 6 to more than 36 inches deep. By watering deeply, you encourage roots to grow deep into the soil where they can mine their own water. If there is no rain, plan to water your garden deeply about once a week in summer.

Keep foliage dry. Discourage fungal disease from developing by keeping plant foliage dry when watering.

Deliver water directly to the root zone. If you must get the foliage wet, water plants in the morning so they dry quickly in the sun, as opposed to watering at night when the water will stay on the leaves for a longer period of time.

Water conservation

Mulch it. A 2- to 3-inch-thick layer of organic mulch reduces soil moisture evaporation and keeps the soil cooler in summer. In addition, mulch cuts down on weed growth.

Eliminate weeds. Weeds waste water. They compete with plants for water and nutrients. Get rid of weeds as soon as you spot them.

opposite Supplemental irrigation can prolong the harvest period of lettuce and other cool-season crops in early summer when temperatures rise. **above** Prevent soil-moisture loss by spreading a 2-inch-thick layer of finely shredded wood mulch or leaves around young edible plants.

Add organic matter. Mix compost, shredded leaves, and other organic soil amendments into the soil to promote water penetration and retention.

Try closer rows. A small area gardened intensely will produce more vegetables for every inch of water applied than a large garden that is not planted as densely. Most vegetables can be planted closer than the 2- to 3-foot row spacing indicated on seed packets. Radishes, onions, beets, and carrots are easy to grow in rows 1 foot apart. Stake tomatoes and grow cucumbers on trellises for a densely planted garden.

Choose a flat space. For the most efficient water penetration, plant on flat terrain. Planting squash, melons, and other vegetables on hills, as described on seed packets, is not the best practice for water conservation. Instead, plant those vegetables in a cluster on flat soil.

CHAPTER EIGHT

Garden Pests

Simple prevention strategies stop many garden pests before they cause problems. The following pages are stocked with quick prevention ideas and tips for managing pests if they get out of hand.

94

104

106

above Pest-resistant fruit and vegetable varieties make it easier than ever to grow blemish-free food without applying pesticides. *left* Keep pests at bay by planting a diverse garden. This roving herb planting includes thyme, chives, and bee balm. The cat keeps the vole population in check. *below* An insect pest is the cause of this foliage damage. Before using a chemical control, take time to accurately identify the pest.

All about pests

Insects, diseases, animals, and weeds are all considered pests in the garden. There are effective ways to handle and dissuade every interloper.

When you think of the word "pest," your mind might jump to insect pests—the cucumber beetles and tomato hornworms that munch on juicy produce and succulent leaves and stems. But "pest" encompasses more than insects. Diseases, animals, and weeds that cause problems for cultivated plants are also considered pests.

Natural balance

More often than not, insects, diseases, animals, and weeds do not reach pest status because you and nature control their population. The web of relationships in the garden seeks balance. If there is an overabundance of a disease or insect, most likely the environment will change slightly, knocking out the pest population before it becomes a problem.

For example, if aphids are sucking plant sap on tender new growth, watch carefully for a week or so. It is likely that green lacewings or ladybugs will soon appear. Their larvae feed voraciously on aphids, and the plants will probably recover.

Because a healthy garden relies on this intricate interaction between predators and prey, it is essential that you always observe pests in your garden before intervening; don't assume an unfamiliar insect is a pest.

In many cases, nothing is required of you when it comes to pest control. Nature will take care of the insect or disease before it becomes a significant problem. Weeds, on the other hand, require more vigilant monitoring and often require action. Because they will readily root in open soil, a 2- to 4-inch-thick layer of mulch will thwart weed seed germination, limiting weed growth most of the season.

Healthy plants

The best thing you can do to prevent pests from gaining the upper hand is to grow healthy plants. Research shows that healthy plants have strong immune systems. They react to pest outbreaks by releasing chemicals that help withstand the attack. The key to growing healthy plants is simple: Provide the sun exposure, soil conditions, moisture levels, and nutrients that the plants require, and they will reward you with vigorous growth.

Healthy plants are easy to grow in healthy soil. Poor soil conditions are among the most common challenges gardeners encounter. The soil around newly built homes and in urban areas can be particularly challenging. Before embarking on a garden adventure, take time to adequately prepare the soil. For soil-amending tips, refer to Chapter 5. If the native soil is unmanageable, build a series of raised beds or garden in containers filled with quality soil. The extra money and time required to garden this way will be well worth it when you are harvesting armloads of delicious produce.

BHG TEST GARDEN TIP

INVITE WORMS

Earthworms are great gardeners. Their tunneling and production of nitrogen-rich excrement keep the soil loose and fertile. They break up clay soils. They balance organic matter in the soil and make nutrients available to plants. Make your garden earthworm-friendly by annually incorporating a 2-inch-thick layer of compost and limiting the use of pesticides.

above Simple to apply and inexpensive, a layer of weed-free straw mulch applied in spring will suppress weeds until fall.

left Accurate identification of a pest is essential for managing it. Keep an inexpensive magnifying glass nearby for identifying pests.

Integrated pest management

Good gardening practices help deter pests and keep crops healthy.

Integrated pest management (IPM) is a gardening approach that promotes good practices to combat pest problems. The goal of IPM is to solve a problem with the least toxic effect on the environment. Chemical pest control methods are the last option and rarely used in IPM.

If a problem does arise, IPM encourages a gardener to look at all of the options for control. Blending a variety of plant-care and pest-control techniques is more effective over the long term than reliance on pest-control chemicals alone. IPM uses commonsense gardening practices, most of which you probably do already. Here are the steps of IPM.

Prevent problems. Healthy plants and sound gardening habits are the first steps in an effective home-garden IPM program. Provide plants with the sun exposure, moisture, and nutrients they require for strong, healthy growth.

Identify symptoms and pests. As you work in the garden, look for signs of stress or disease, such as yellowing, wilting, puckering, discoloration, and holes in or chewed edges on foliage. Identify the cause. For tiny insects, such as mites, aphids, and the crawler stage of scales, hold a piece of white paper under a leaf and tap the leaf. Then look for specks crawling on the paper. You'll find that a magnifying glass is helpful.

Use reference books and Internet sources to identify what you find. The pest may be short-lived or the damage it causes is inconsequential and no control tactics are needed.

Monitor the situation. If you think a plant has a pest, watch to see what changes take place over the following days or weeks. Are the edible parts of the plant damaged? Does the entire plant or just a portion of the plant show signs of decline? Has another insect arrived on the scene, perhaps to consume the first?

PROMOTE HEALTHY PLANTS

A key component of integrated pest management is to start with healthy plants. Robust, vigorously growing plants will withstand pest problems with greater ease than plants that are struggling to survive. Promote healthy plants with these tactics.

Choose insect- and disease-resistant plant varieties. The encyclopedias at the back of this book highlight varieties with notable pest resistance.

Buy healthy, sturdy transplants with well-developed root systems. Wind, intense rain, and cold temperatures work against transplants in spring. Vigorous, well-rooted transplants will withstand difficult conditions.

Buy plants from reputable growers or grow your own plants from seeds. Diseases and insects are easily transferred from the greenhouse to the garden.

Is the damage cosmetic and not harming the plant? Depending on the type of insect, the damage, the weather conditions, and your goals for the plant, you may not need to intervene at all.

Decide if control is required. Only a small percent of insects are potential pests. Determine if the damage is sufficient to warrant control.

Choose control methods. Choosing which (if any) control methods to use is the backbone of an effective IPM program. A successful solution integrates all factors, including the pest, plant, growing conditions, weather, gardener's needs, potential control methods, and cost. This is where you can have a significant impact on your surroundings by starting with the least toxic control methods before advancing to other options, using chemical pest controls as a last resort.

above Handpicking insects and dropping them into a container of soapy water is a simple way to knock down a pest population. **left** A chemical control product might eliminate a troublesome pest, but it might also harm beneficial insects such as this Monarch butterfly. Choose nonchemical control methods whenever possible.

All about insects

Pest populations can be controlled by a variety of methods.

When insect pest populations appear to be on the rise and threatening your crops, take a hard look at the damage. Are the pests feeding directly on the harvestable parts of the plant? If so, they might warrant control. Many insects feed on nonedible plant parts. In most cases these pests do not need control. In fact, they might serve a useful purpose by attracting predatory insects that will then feed on more damaging insect pests in the future. When control is necessary, here are the three main ways to outmaneuver pests in your garden.

Physical

Use physical controls to prevent insects from accessing plants or to remove insects that reach plants.

Your fingers Remove leaves that are heavily infested with insects or larvae. Handpick larger insects such as beetles, tomato hornworms, or cabbage loopers. Toss the infested foliage and insects into a bucket of soapy water before discarding them.

Water Dislodge insects from infested plants with a sharp blast of water from a hose. Be sure to spray the entire plant, including the undersides of foliage. This works well against small insects, such as white flies and aphids, as well as spider mites. Repeat treatment as often as needed.

Barriers Floating row covers are lightweight woven materials that keep flying insects, such as leafhoppers and moths, from landing on plants to feed or lay eggs. Cardboard collars around seedlings prevent cutworms from reaching and chewing through stems.

Traps Commercial sticky traps attract insects such as leafhoppers, flea beetles, and whiteflies. Note that many insect traps perform best as monitoring devices, alerting you when pests arrive in the neighborhood; they are less effective at killing sufficient numbers to make a noticeable dent in pest populations.

CALLING ALL BENEFICIAL INSECTS

The adults of many beneficial insects require a diet of carbohydrate-rich nectar and pollen. Herbs in the parsley family are among the most attractive plants to various beneficial insects. Plant several clusters of cilantro, dill (shown above), fennel, and parsley around your garden to beckon beneficial insects. After they take up residence in your garden, they'll get to work eliminating troublesome pests.

Biological

Biological control is what nature does all by itself. Beneficial or predator insects carry out most biological control by dining on pest insects. Some common beneficial creatures include green lacewings, ladybugs, praying mantis, predatory mites, and spiders. Beneficial parasites, such as nematodes, use garden pests as hosts, eventually killing the pest.

You can augment nature's efforts by making your garden inviting to beneficial insects. Create a vibrant community of beneficial organisms in the soil by regularly mixing compost into the planting area. Avoid using pesticides, which kill beneficial insects along with the pests. And include predator-friendly plants in your garden.

Chemical

Chemical controls are typically used as a last resort, after a combination of other control strategies have failed. There are many types of pest-control products, including organic options. Select the appropriate product for each situation. If you have a choice, select a target-specific product that acts against a limited number of species.

All about diseases

Diseases are caused by a variety of things including fungi, bacteria, and viruses.

Fungi, bacteria, and viruses are tiny, often microscopic organisms responsible for plant problems that range from powdery white film on foliage to fungus-riddled, mushy fruits. Fungi are miniscule organisms that live on plants, causing visible symptoms. Insects, water, and wind are typical ways they spread. Bacteria are single-cell organisms that live on various kinds of organic matter. Unable to survive in the open, they live inside plants and are transferred from plant to plant by insects, water, and hands. Viruses are the smallest of the three and the most difficult to control. They are usually spread by insects, though some are spread by seeds and tools.

Generally, for a disease to occur, organisms must be transported to a susceptible host. This is often done unintentionally. After the disease is transported to the host, the perfect environmental conditions must be in place for the disease to thrive. Your best line of defense against diseases is prevention. Embrace these practical garden hygiene and prevention tips, and diseases will have trouble getting a toehold in your garden.

Select a great site. Site your garden in a sunny location with well-drained soil and good air circulation. Remove weeds not only from the garden area but also from surrounding areas because weeds harbor many disease organisms. Choose plant varieties bred to be resistant to diseases.

Cultivate deeply. Whether by hand or with equipment, cultivate as deeply as possible in order to completely bury remnants of the previous crop or any disease organisms. Till to a depth of 10 to 12 inches.

Control weeds. Certain weeds, particularly those botanically related to the fruits and vegetables in your garden, may harbor viruses or other diseases.

Start disease-free. Shop at a reputable nursery for healthy, disease-free transplants and certified disease-free seed potatoes.

ALWAYS ROTATE

The simple practice of rotating crops, or planting them in a different location every year, will help minimize pest problems. A rotation strategy confuses pests. Many insects and diseases overwinter in the soil and spring forth the following year to attack plants in the same location. If their preferred host plants are not in the immediate vicinity, the pests are much less likely to reach problem status.

Crop rotation is especially critical for members of the cabbage family (broccoli, cabbage, and related plants) and the tomato family (tomato, pepper, eggplant, and related plants). Members of this group should not be planted in the same space more than once every three years.

THE FIVE-MINUTE INSPECTION

Spend time in your garden inspecting your plants. You'll spot problems while they're small and easy to manage. Try this: Spend five minutes in the garden on your way to the mailbox every day.

opposite Healthy, disease-free transplants, such as this lettuce seedling, are a great way to combat disease problems. For added protection, choose a cultivar with notable disease resistance.

All about weeds

Weed prevention starts in spring before the pests have a chance to get a roothold.

Weeds are divided into two categories. The first includes weeds that produce enormous quantities of seeds. These weeds are often easy to kill, either with weed-control products or with a hoe, but new ones keep appearing. Weeds in the second category are hard to kill, often because they have persistent underground parts that can sprout into new plants. A few especially troublesome weeds, such as dandelions, have both of these characteristics.

War on weeds

When removing weeds by hand or using a tool, work to remove as much of their roots as possible. Use a small trowel or taproot weeder to pry pesky roots out of the ground. Dedicate a few minutes every other day to weeding. Regular weeding keeps weeds small and easy to pull and prevents weeds from setting seed and creating hundreds of new seedlings.

Weed-control products are rarely used in food gardens. Toxicity to crops, difficulty in applying chemicals accurately, and potential for toxic residues are the main reasons for avoiding them. Weed prevention begins in early spring before weeds have a chance to get a strong foothold in the garden. Follow these prevention strategies.

Mulch, mulch, mulch. An organic mulch, such as grass clippings or shredded bark, is one of the easiest ways to suppress weeds. A 2-inch-thick layer of mulch blocks light and prevents weed seed germination.

Plant a cover crop. Cover crops provide many benefits, among them reducing weeds. Because they grow fast, cover crops outcompete weeds in the struggle for light and nutrients. Once the cover crop is cultivated and near the soil surface, it acts as a mulch to shade the soil and to prevent germination of weed seeds. Cover crops can be planted anytime during the growing season.

HANDY TOOLS

Your hands are likely the best all-purpose weeding tools, but when you need a little more power to pry up deep-rooted dandelions or scuffle out a large patch of lamb's quarters, turn to one of these reliable tools.

Oscillating hoe The stirrup-shape blade of this long-handle garden weeder is sharp on both sides. Eradicate weeds by moving it back and forth in the soil. It is a pro at severing the roots of seedlings and young weeds.

Taproot weeder (above) Many kinds of taproot weeders are available on the market. This short-handle tool with a fork at the business end works as a fulcrum, giving you leverage to pull the entire root of an obstinate weed.

BHG ASK THE GARDEN DOCTOR

I have little time to weed. Are there any crops that are nearly weed-free?

ANSWER: Some vegetable crops take care of many weed chores for you by shading the soil so much that they prevent weed seeds from germinating. Squash, beans, pumpkins, cucumbers, melons, and corn suppress weeds well after they establish a dense canopy of foliage.

opposite Pulling weeds when they are young and before they set seed or ramble out of control saves hours of weeding later in the season.

left Combat poor-draining or rocky soil by growing edibles in raised beds. When filled with nutrient-rich compost and topsoil, raised beds produce healthy plants that fend off pests with ease. **top** Harvest vegetables after the morning dew has dried, typically by midmorning, to avoid spreading disease. **above** A layer of cocoa-bean mulch prevents soil and disease-causing organisms from splashing onto the leaves of young pepper plants. **below** Greens and rhubarb, along with other spring crops, are best planted and harvested in cool weather. In spring they have better flavor and are less likely to succumb to pests.

Garden smart to prevent pests

The old adage "an ounce of prevention is worth a pound of cure" is true when it comes to preventing pests.

More often than not, it is much easier to prevent an insect from taking hold or disease from infecting plants than it is to eliminate the pest once it has invaded the garden. These simple tips and techniques will discourage pests from calling your garden home and send them packing if they do try to take up residence.

Plant crops and varieties that are well suited to the soil and climate in your garden. Your local extension service or garden center might be able to provide area-specific plant and variety recommendations.

Choose pest-resistant varieties when possible. Plant breeders have developed many crop varieties that withstand pest damage and even discourage pests.

Water plants in the morning so they have time to dry before evening. A drip irrigation system is especially beneficial because it prevents foliage from getting wet when watering.

Space plants properly to prevent overcrowding. Often a too-dense planting scheme causes weak growth and reduced air movement, resulting in increased insect and disease problems.

Keep weeds out. Weeds often harbor pests and compete with crops for nutrients and water. Organic mulches are extremely effective for weed control and soil improvement.

Spread a 2- to 4-inch layer of mulch to keep soil from splashing onto leaves, which may bring soilborne diseases in contact with the plants. Mulch also conserves valuable soil moisture.

Rotate your garden plot if you can. Do not grow the same kind of produce in the same place each year. Plant related crops (such as broccoli, cabbage, Brussels sprouts, and cauliflower, which are all in the cabbage family) in one site only once every three years.

Stay out of the garden when the plants are wet with rain or dew to prevent spreading disease.

Avoid injury to plants. Broken limbs, cuts, bruises, cracks, and insect damage are often sites for infection by disease-causing organisms.

Remove and dispose of infected leaves from diseased plants as soon as you observe them. Remove severely diseased plants before they contaminate others.

Plant warm-season crops after the soil has warmed to avoid problems with seed and root rot and to promote vigorous growth. A general guideline is to plant warm-season crops two weeks after the last average frost date.

Inspect plants for egg clusters, beetles, caterpillars, and other insects as often as possible. Handpick as many pests as you can. Avoid sprays until the population of insects has reached a critical threshold level.

Enlist the aid of birds in pest control. Overall, they do more good than harm in the garden. Consider planting trees and shrubs with fruits that attract birds.

Encourage beneficial insects. Naturally occurring predators and parasites are found throughout the landscape. Learn to properly identify these species and avoid using pesticides around them.

Insect pests

Aphid
Aphids do little damage in small numbers, but their population can build rapidly to damaging numbers. They use their piercing mouthparts to puncture plant tissue and remove sap and cell contents.
PREVENTION/MANAGEMENT: Wash aphids off plants with water. Encourage beneficial insects, many of which feed on aphids. Spray plants with insecticidal soap, or if it is safe for the plant, apply horticultural oil.

Borer
These larvae of beetles or moths tunnel into stems, twigs, and branches.
PREVENTION/MANAGEMENT: Maintain plant health by watering and fertilizing regularly. Cut out and destroy dead or dying branches. Inspect vining plants for borers. If you find damage, slit the vine open with a sharp knife to remove the borer. Drop the borer into soapy water.

Cabbageworm
Cabbageworms and cabbage loopers munch crops in the cabbage family and lettuce foliage and are prevalent in spring.
PREVENTION/MANAGEMENT: At the end of the season, remove infested plants from the garden to prevent pests from overwintering. If white moths hover near plants, cover the crop with row covers. Spray or dust plants with bacterial *Bacillus thuringiensis* (Bt) while the caterpillars are small.

Colorado potato beetle
Both larvae and adult Colorado potato beetles devour the leaves and stems of potatoes, tomatoes, and related crops.
PREVENTION/MANAGEMENT: Choose an early-maturing variety and plant earlier or later than normal to avoid peak beetle activity. Rotate crops, planting a new crop as far away from the previous year's crop as possible. Handpick adults, larvae, and eggs. Destroy them by dropping them in a bucket of soapy water. Use *Bacillus thuringiensis tenebrionis*.

Cucumber beetle
Cucumber beetles chew holes in aboveground plant parts, and their white grub larvae destroy roots and stems below the soil line. They carry two serious diseases that kill cucurbits: mosaic and bacterial wilt.
PREVENTION/MANAGEMENT: At the end of the season, remove infested plants from the garden to prevent pests from overwintering. Rotate crops, planting a new crop as far away from the previous year's crop as possible. Handpick adults and destroy.

Cutworm
As their name indicates, cutworms cut down young plants at their base and are most problematic in early spring when they attack young, tender plants. They rarely cause problems later in the season
PREVENTION/MANAGEMENT: Cultivate the soil thoroughly in late summer and fall to expose and destroy cutworm eggs, larvae, and pupae. Place a cardboard collar around each individual seedling, as shown above, to prevent the cutworm from reaching the stem. Dust the soil around seedlings with diatomaceous earth.

Japanese beetle
Iridescent beetles devour plant foliage, reducing yield and killing perennial crops.

PREVENTION/MANAGEMENT: Watch for beetles daily, picking those that you see and dropping them in a bucket of soapy water. Most Japanese beetles overwinter in turfgrass, so treating your lawn for grubs may help.

Leafhopper
Leafhoppers attack plants by piercing foliage and drawing out plant sap. Plants may become weak and produce few, if any, fruits.

PREVENTION/MANAGEMENT: Clean up and compost plant debris in fall after harvest to prevent leafhoppers from overwintering. Eliminate nearby weeds. Use floating row covers to protect plants. Diatomaceous earth and insecticidal soap will reduce populations.

Scales
Scales are common tiny pests on citrus trees and, to a lesser degree, other fruiting trees and shrubs. Scales do not affect vegetable plants or nonwoody fruits.

PREVENTION/MANAGEMENT: Scales attack weak plants. Water and fertilize as needed to promote healthy plants. Promote beneficial insects. Some ladybugs and parasitic wasps attack scales. Spray plants with horticultural oil.

Snails and slugs
Thriving in moist, shaded places, snails and slugs feed on a wide variety of plants. They are similar except that snails have a hard shell they can retreat into and slugs do not. Both are nocturnal.

PREVENTION/MANAGEMENT: Avoid spreading mulch more than 2 inches thick; deep mulch is an optimal snail and slug habitat. Inspect the garden for them at night by flashlight and remove them by hand. Traps are also effective. Surround garden beds with strips of copper or diatomaceous earth.

Squash bug
Squash bugs pierce plant parts and kill or injure plants by sucking sap from cells. Young plants are susceptible.

PREVENTION/MANAGEMENT: Clean up and compost plant debris in fall after harvest to prevent squash bugs from overwintering. Rotate crops, planting a new crop as far away from the previous year's crop as possible. Plant varieties that are resistant to squash bug. Handpick and crush adults and eggs. Trap squash bugs by laying boards on the ground and destroy bugs beneath them.

Wireworm
Wireworms feed by drilling holes into the base or roots of plants. They are most common in soil where lawn grass was previously grown, in poorly drained soil, and in soil that is high in organic matter.

PREVENTION/MANAGEMENT: Plant after the soil is fully warmed as larvae are more active in cool soils. Use carrots and potatoes as traps. Place a carrot or half a potato in garden soil as though it were growing. Check it every other day or so and discard any wireworms attached to it.

Anthracnose
Anthracnose is a fungal disease that is spread by water. Tiny spores land on fruits, vegetables, and leaves and can render a bountiful harvest into a rotted mass of foliage or fruit in a few days during hot, humid weather.

PREVENTION/MANAGEMENT: Mulch plants to limit disease spread. Avoid overhead watering. Rotate crops. Clean up end-of-season plant material. Remove and destroy infected plant parts; do not compost them.

Bacterial blight
Most common in moist, humid weather, this bacterial disease is easily controlled by not working around wet plants.

PREVENTION/MANAGEMENT: Plant disease-free seeds. Don't touch or work around wet plants. Rotate plants by planting in an area only once every three years. Clean up end-of-season plant material. Spray *Bacillus subtilis*.

Blossom drop
Caused by environmental factors rather than a disease, blossom drop is grouped here with diseases for convenience. Some plants drop their blossoms when nighttime temperatures dip below 58°F or rise above 85°F.

PREVENTION/MANAGEMENT: Use row covers to raise night temperatures. Promote healthy plants by supplying them with approximately 1 inch of water per week.

Blossom-end rot
Blossom-end rot is caused by a lack of calcium in the soil. Exceptionally dry conditions can make calcium unavailable to plants. Excessive amounts of high-nitrogen fertilizer can do the same thing.

PREVENTION/MANAGEMENT: Provide plants with at least 1 inch of water per week. Spread a 2-inch-thick layer of mulch around plants to conserve soil moisture. Don't cultivate too close to plants. Avoid using high-nitrogen fertilizers and fresh manures; well-decomposed compost is a good choice.

Damping off
This fungal disease causes sudden collapse of seemingly healthy seedlings or failure of seeds to germinate.

PREVENTION/MANAGEMENT: Prevent damping off by using by good seed-starting practices. Plant when the soil is at the optimum temperature for the crop. Presoak seeds to speed germination. Use sterile potting mix and containers. Allow the soil to dry between watering. Encourage air circulation near seedlings.

Downy mildew
Downy mildew is a fungus that thrives in cool, wet conditions and high humidity.

PREVENTION/MANAGEMENT: Water plants in the morning so they can dry before nightfall. Promote good air circulation around plants by thinning to proper spacing and abiding by plant-spacing recommendations. Spray *Bacillus subtilis*.

Fire blight
A fungus that is most common in spring when the weather is moist, fire blight is spread by insects and wind.
PREVENTION/MANAGEMENT: Plant resistant varieties. Remove dead stems 8 inches beyond the symptom, and disinfect pruners with bleach between cuts. Spray plants with *Bacillus subtilis*.

Mosaic
A frustrating virus, mosaic is spread by aphids and cucumber beetles. Control large populations of aphids and cucumber beetles, and you will reduce the chances of plants being infected by mosaic.
PREVENTION/MANAGEMENT: Plant resistant varieties. Remove and destroy infected plants. Control aphids and cucumber beetles. Attract beneficial insects to control aphids. Control weeds; mosaic lives in many kinds of weeds.

Nitrogen deficiency
Nitrogen deficiency is an environmental problem occurring in poor soil. Poor or slow plant growth is an indication of nitrogen deficiency, as is yellowing foliage.
PREVENTION/MANAGEMENT: Incorporate a 2-inch-thick layer of compost into the garden every year to replenish nitrogen. However, too much compost can cause nitrogen deficiency. Spray affected plants with a foliar fertilizer.

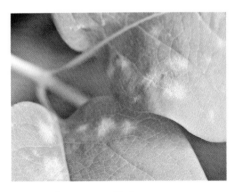

Powdery mildew
Powdery mildew is a fungus that thrives in both humid and dry weather. Leaves appear as if they were dusted with flour and can become stunted or distorted.
PREVENTION/MANAGEMENT: The best defense against this disease is to plant disease-resistant varieties. Promote good air circulation by spacing and thinning plants appropriately.

Scab
More unsightly than destructive, this fungal disease disfigures leaves and fruits. The fruits are edible after peeling. Trees that lose most or all of their leaves are likely to survive and produce new leaves the following year. However, trees that lose foliage for several consecutive years may stop producing fruit.
PREVENTION/MANAGEMENT: Remove fallen fruit and leaves. Plant resistant varieties. Apples are susceptible; search out resistant varieties for long-lasting, healthy apple trees.

Sunscald
Caused by environmental factors, sunscald occurs on fruits when they are suddenly exposed to excessive sunlight and their skin is damaged. Sunscald can also affect tree bark.
PREVENTION/MANAGEMENT: Limit pruning when fruit is forming. Provide shade if fruits are exposed to sunlight after pruning. Prevent sunscald on tree bark due to intense winter sunlight by wrapping the trunk with paper tape or burlap to the lowest branch.

Common weeds

Bermudagrass *(Cynodon dactylon)* is a perennial grass with a vigorous creeping habit. The roots may grow several feet deep, making the plants drought- and heat-tolerant and also difficult to kill. Bermudagrass spreads by seeds as well as above- and below-ground stems.
MANAGEMENT: Smother leaves with a heavy layer of fabric or black plastic for several months. Apply glyphosate anytime the grass is actively growing. If your garden is surrounded by a Bermudagrass lawn, prevent the grass from creeping into your edibles by burying vinyl edging at least 6 inches deep or by gardening in raised beds.

Common chickweed *(Stellaria media)* prefers damp, shady areas with rich soil. It is a winter annual that grows from seeds sprouting in the fall. The ½- to 2-inch heart-shape leaves are attached to the stem by a slightly hairy stalk. The creeping stems root at their joints wherever they touch the soil. Small, white, starlike flowers bloom in clusters on the ends of the stems from spring through fall.
MANAGEMENT: Hand cultivation and a 2-inch-thick mulch layer together provide most of the control needed.

Crabgrass *(Digitaria* spp.) is an annual weed that grows fast in hot, dry weather. The blades are 2 to 5 inches long and ⅓ inch wide. Seed heads are 1 to 3 inches across (smooth crabgrass) or 4 to 5 inches across (large crabgrass). The seeds remain dormant over the winter and then sprout in the spring. The plants are killed by the first fall frost.
MANAGEMENT: Use a mulch and spread out irrigations, watering only as often as necessary. Frequent cultivation and weed-control products that contain acetic acid also can control crabgrass. Use a preemergent weed-control product containing corn-gluten meal. Note: Do not use a preemergent at the same time you are planting seeds in the garden. It will prevent the seeds you sowed from germinating.

Dandelion *(Taraxacum officinale)* is a rosette-shape perennial with a thick, fleshy taproot that may grow 2 to 3 feet deep in the soil. Its yellow flowers bloom primarily in spring but continue sporadically until frost. Wind carries the seeds. The taproot survives winters.
MANAGEMENT: Pull roots from moist soil. Take care to extract the entire taproot; even a small piece is enough to regenerate the plant. A 2-inch-thick layer of mulch will prevent seeds from germinating and make any that do manage to grow easier to pull.

Lamb's quarters (*Chenopodium album*) grows 1 to 4 feet tall from a short, branched taproot and is common in gardens. The plant is a host for the beet leafhopper, which transmits curly top, a virus disease of beets. Leaves are 1 to 3 inches long with toothed edges. Seeds remain dormant over the winter and sprout in the spring.

MANAGEMENT: Hand-pull or remove plants by hoeing. A 2-inch-thick layer of mulch will prevent seeds from germinating. Stop seeds from germinating in a vegetable garden with a preemergent weed-control product containing corn-gluten meal. Note: Do not use a preemergent product at the same time you are planting seeds in the garden. It will prevent edible plant seeds, as well as lamb's quarters, from germinating.

Nutsedge (*Cyperus* spp.) includes two troublesome species— yellow nutsedge and purple nutsedge. Yellow nutsedge is found throughout the United States, and purple nutsedge is primarily a problem in the southeastern United States and coastal California. All nutsedges prefer poorly drained, rich soil. They thrive in frequently watered garden areas. The grasslike, yellow-green leaves grow on erect triangular stems. Seed heads are purple or yellow, appearing from July to October. Nutsedges reproduce by seeds, underground stems, and tubers.

MANAGEMENT: If there are only a few clumps of nutsedge in your garden, dig up the plants, taking care to dispose of the soil in order to also dispose of the tubers. Glyphosate applied when the plant is actively growing is effective.

Purslane (*Portulaca oleracea*) is a common annual weed in vegetable gardens. It thrives in hot, dry weather. Purslane leaves are ½ to 1½ inches long, succulent, and wedge shape. Small yellow flowers open only in full sunlight from midsummer to frost. The seeds may remain viable in the soil for many years and will sprout in warm weather when brought to the surface during tilling or cultivating.

MANAGEMENT: Because purslane grows low to the ground, an oscillating hoe is often effective, though uprooted plants left in place may reroot. A 2-inch-thick layer of mulch effectively prevents seeds from germinating.

Quackgrass (*Agropyron repens*) is a perennial grass weed in the northern United States. Its extensive fibrous root system consists of long, yellow-white roots that may grow 5 feet or more in a single growing season. The narrow, bluish-green leaves grow on stalks 1 to 3 feet tall. Wheatlike spikes produce seeds from May to September. Seeds may survive in the soil for up to four years. The underground creeping rhizomes also send up new shoots, increasing the infestation. Quackgrass tolerates any type of soil.

MANAGEMENT: If there are only a few clumps of quackgrass in your garden, dig up the plants. Glyphosate is the quickest way to kill quackgrass.

While animals are intriguing to watch in nature, gardeners don't usually roll out the welcome mat for them in the garden. Deer can mow down a row of lettuce in minutes, and raccoons are known to have a midnight feast in the sweet-corn patch.

Gardeners have developed several ways to repel animals, but often the results are inconsistent. They work one year but not the next. Deer in populated areas even learn which dogs to fear and which are harmless nuisances. Deer and rabbit populations are so large in some areas that growing an edible garden is almost impossible without a sturdy fence. Barriers—a fence around the garden to a sheet of hardware cloth laid over a vegetable bed—are usually the most effective ways to control animal pests.

When animal pests need to be removed, traps are usually more effective than poisons. Traps let you see you've caught the animal. If you don't want to kill the animal, catch it in a live trap and release it in a nearby wilderness area. Local regulations may govern this. Consult your county agricultural commissioner's office about the rules in your area.

Birds of all types feed on seeds, seedlings, fruit, and berries in the garden. Birds scratch away at soft soil to unearth newly planted seeds. They peck at seedlings and young leaves. The creatures are especially damaging to berries, grapes, and soft fruit.
MANAGEMENT: Once birds develop the habit of feeding in your garden, you'll probably have to exclude them with wire or fabric cages. If they have not yet developed that habit, you may be able to repel them. Set up stakes around the plantings you wish to protect, and tie crisscrossing strings between the stakes. Attach strips of aluminum foil to the strings. Birds will not readily fly through the crossing string and will avoid the shiny aluminum. To prevent birds from digging up seeds, lay hardware cloth (¼-inch mesh) over the seedbed. Remove it before the plants are too large to slip through.

Deer cause severe damage to gardens and landscaping. They eat fruit and vegetable plants and graze on bark, twigs, and leaves of trees and shrubs. Males damage trees by rubbing their antlers on the trunks and branches.
MANAGEMENT: Prevent deer damage by fencing out the animals. Deer are strong and agile jumpers; a fence must be at least 8 feet high to keep them out. To protect a single tree, loosely wrap the trunk with a 3-foot-tall piece of chicken wire or a drainage tile that is slit down one side. Look for repellent sprays containing tetramethylthiuram disulfide, egg solids, and hydrolyzed casein protein powder.

Gophers are burrowing rodents that live and feed primarily underground. They eat roots, bulbs, and plants that they pull down into their burrows.
MANAGEMENT: Trapping is the best way to control gophers. Find traps at your local garden center or online. Protect plants where gophers are present by planting them in a cage of hardware cloth. If you garden in raised beds, line the bottom of the raised bed with hardware cloth for added gopher protection.

Rabbits are one of the most damaging garden pests. In the summer they feed on tender young plants, especially vegetables. During the winter they gnaw on bark, twigs, and buds. They are especially destructive to young fruit trees in the winter. Rabbits bite off twigs cleanly as if with a knife. They can also clip off twigs on older trees up to 2 feet above snow or ground level.
MANAGEMENT: The best way to keep rabbits out of a vegetable garden is to enclose it with a 1½-inch mesh chicken wire fence. The fence should be 2 feet tall or above the snow level. The bottom should be buried 3 to 4 inches in the soil. To protect a single tree, loosely wrap the trunk with a 3-foot-tall piece of chicken wire or a drainage tile that is slit down one side. Live traps, chemical repellents, cats, and dogs may also be effective.

Raccoons forage at night and are especially fond of sweet corn. These agile climbers also climb trees to feed on fruit, often knocking many fruits to the ground.
MANAGEMENT: Raccoons are intelligent and can be difficult to exclude. Discourage them from raiding your vegetable garden by erecting a 4-foot-tall chicken wire fence, with its top extending 18 inches above the fence post. As the raccoon climbs up to the unattached portion of the fence, its weight will pull the fence down to the ground. Low-voltage electric fences are also popular and effective.

Voles are mouselike with compact, heavy bodies and short legs. They create short, shallow burrows and damage fruit trees by eating bark at or near ground level during winter. When voles gnaw off bark completely around the main stem of a plant, the plant will die.
MANAGEMENT: Limit vole damage by exclusion and habitat modification. Eliminate tall weeds in which they hide, and create weed-free strips around fruit trees. Voles will quickly diminish when their habitat disappears. Limit damage in winter by encircling the lower trunk of trees with a 1-foot-tall cylinder made with ¼-inch hardware mesh.

Woodchucks live in underground burrows and feed on tender vegetables in the early morning and late afternoon. Primarily a problem in the North and Northeast, woodchucks also gnaw on tree bark. They don't tunnel for their food; they eat aboveground.
MANAGEMENT: The best way to eliminate damage is to fence out woodchucks. Surround the area you wish to protect with a woven-wire fence about 3 feet high. To prevent woodchucks from burrowing under the fence, bend the bottom 12 inches of the wire mesh outward before burying it a few inches deep in the soil.

CHAPTER NINE

All About Pruning

A few simple pruning practices will ensure that your fruiting trees and shrubs produce bushels of fruit year after year.

116   121   122   124

above Most raspberries spread by sending out underground shoots. Annual pruning prevents the plant from ranging out of its planting area. **left** Most citrus trees require little pruning other than removing dense growth to open the center of their canopy.

Getting started

Pruning and training is part of growing healthy fruit crops.

While it might seem counterintuitive that snipping branches off a newly planted cherry tree or sawing limbs off an established heirloom apple will make it produce more fruit, pruning increases fruit production in time.

Don't be overwhelmed by pruning. A backyard fruit tree and shrub planting is a cinch to prune in 60 minutes or less on a crisp winter day. And don't let the fear of pruning stop you from planting fruiting trees and shrubs. Pruning is simply the removal of plant stems and branches to benefit the plant as a whole. More often than not, if you make a wrong pruning cut, there will be few repercussions and the plant will push out new growth in short order.

Why prune?

Pruning is preventive maintenance. Trees and shrubs will live, grow, and bear fruit without ever being pruned, but experience has shown that good pruning and some training can prevent or remedy many of the problems that arise in fruit growing.

Pruning mature trees can spur them to produce more fruit and improve their fruit quality. Removing branches allows sunlight to filter into the tree canopy, which will promote uniform ripening, increase the fruits' sugar content, and decrease disease problems because fruit and foliage will dry quickly after rainfall. Pruning shrubs has similar benefits.

Annual pruning also keeps the size of a tree or shrub under control. Thoughtful pruning strengthens a tree by encouraging the growth of strong branches that can support mature fruit.

What to prune

Fruit Trees Dwarf fruit trees naturally retain their short stature, but annual pruning will ensure that light can easily reach the center of the tree. Occasional pruning at the top of the tree will limit its height. When to prune fruit trees depends on the

type of tree and the climate, but in general, fruit trees are pruned in the dormant season.

Brambles Cane fruits produce berries on one- and two-year-old canes. When the canes finish fruiting, they die back to the ground. Pruning removes these unnecessary canes and also thins any spindly new growth to promote big berries and healthy plants.

Grapes Extensive pruning and training is required to produce top-quality grape clusters. They are pruned after the leaves fall off in fall and before new growth emerges in spring.

PRUNING LINGO

Understanding pruning instructions is simple when you can talk the talk. Brush up on your pruning vocabulary with the help of these illustrations.

1 TERMINAL BUD This large bud is on the tip of a branch. Terminal buds grow much faster than buds behind the tip. If the terminal bud is removed, several buds behind it will begin to grow.

2 LATENT BUD Small latent buds are usually located above the scar left by last year's leaf. Latent buds begin to grow when the terminal bud is removed, creating shrubby, dense growth.

3 FRUITING SPUR These short shoots produce the fat flowering buds that become fruit. Apples, apricots, pears, and plums have long-lived fruiting spurs.

4 LEAF SHOOTS OR BUDS Small flat leaf shoots produce leaves and stems. Make a pruning cut just above a leaf shoot to force the branch's growth in the direction the bud points.

Pruning
fruit trees

Most fruit trees are pruned when they are leafless. Early spring is pruning time.

In freezing climates, prune apples and pears in early spring just as the buds begin to swell, but prune stone fruits (such as peaches and cherries) after they bloom. Avoid pruning early in the dormant season, in November or December, in climates with severe weather. In moderate climates, prune all but stone fruits anytime during the dormant period, which is between leaf fall and the beginning of bud swell in spring.

Don't leave stubs

When pruning limbs and small branches, make a pruning cut just beyond where the offending limb attaches to the larger branch or tree. This area is called the branch collar; it contains tissue that prevents decay.

When pruning branches more than 1½ inches in diameter, use a three-part cut. The first step is to saw an undercut from the bottom of the branch to about 6 to 12 inches out from the trunk and about one-third of the way through the branch. Make a second cut about 3 inches beyond the undercut, cutting until the branch falls away. Cut the resulting stub back to the collar.

Types of pruning cuts

The two basic types of pruning cuts are heading and thinning cuts. Heading is the process of shortening a branch, not removing it entirely. It encourages buds on the remaining portion of the branch to sprout new growth. Thinning removes a branch entirely and puts an end to growth. All thinning cuts are made to the base of the branch or watersprout (strongly upright growing shoot) so there are no buds left to sprout new growth.

When you cut a plant, you leave a wound that is susceptible to pests and diseases; make wounds as small as possible. Always make cuts close to a node (point of leaf attachment or branching). Make cuts at a slight angle. A horizontal surface that holds water is more attractive to diseases and burrowing pests.

HOW TO PRUNE A FRUIT TREE

1. Prune away dead, diseased, or damaged branches.

2. Remove branches that cross or rub against other branches. Rubbing branches cause wounds, making the tree susceptible to infection.

3. Thin especially dense growth in the top of the tree to allow sunlight to reach the center.

4. Reduce the height of excessively tall trees by cutting limbs out of the top, making cuts near the bark of a lower limb.

5. Remove all fast-growing shoots, called suckers, that arise near the base of the tree.

TOOLS OF THE TRADE

Good pruning equipment ensures smooth cuts that are less likely to be invaded by insects. When you have these tools on hand, pruning will be a breeze.

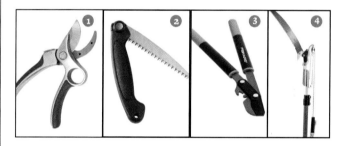

1 HAND PRUNERS
You'll use these more often than any other tool. Invest in a high-quality, ergonomically designed pair.

2 FOLDING PRUNING SAW
Small enough to tote around with ease but sharp enough to make quick work of cutting off limbs, a folding pruning saw is essential.

3 LONG-HANDLE LOPPERS
Thanks to the leverage provided by long-handle loppers, you can easily cut through 1-inch-thick branches. They are also indispensable for reaching into thorny brambles and dense shrubs.

4 POLE PRUNERS
Reach the top of a dwarf fruit tree from ground level with pole pruners. The handle can extend 10 to 15 feet high.

opposite The branch collar is the optimal place to make a pruning cut. This swelled region where a branch attaches to the trunk of the tree has tissue that prevents decay.

Training fruit trees

Training is essential to good growth and fruiting and keeps trees balanced.

There are three main training methods: open center, central leader, and modified central leader. Each method has its own advantages for the tree and the gardener.

Open center
Training to an open center creates a broad, vase-shape tree with sturdy, thick branches. Cut back at planting time to 2 feet above the ground for a dwarf and 3 feet for a standard tree. Cut just above a bud and prune any side branches back to two buds.

After the tree has grown into its first winter dormancy, choose three or four branches, called scaffolds, attached to the trunk. Choose branches that radiate evenly around the trunk with almost equal distance between them. Maintain at least 6 inches of vertical distance between branches.

If there are three such branches, cut off the vertical stem above the top branch. If there are fewer than three good branches, leave the vertical stem and choose the remaining scaffold branches during the next dormant season, cutting off the vertical stem just above the highest selected scaffold. Remove the weakest side branches from the scaffolds from the first dormant season.

During the third dormant season, thin surplus shoots and branches. Select the strongest and best-placed terminal shoot near the tip of each scaffold branch as well as one or two other side shoots on each branch. Remove all other branch shoots.

Central leader and modified central leader
Train to a central leader to produce a tree with tiers of branches and a pyramidal outline; this allows all branches to intercept sunlight. Trees trained to a central leader have a strong trunk; this is good for weighty fruit, such as apples.

A modified central leader system produces the strength of a central trunk and the sun-filled center of a vase shape. A single trunk is allowed to grow vertically with whorls of branches in the same manner as a central leader form. At the end of the third or fourth growing season, when the tree is 6 to 10 feet tall, cut off the main leader at 3 or 4 feet. Then select main scaffold branches and prune to form a vase shape.

opposite A mature tree that has been trained to an open center has several main branches that originate low on the trunk and radiate out evenly around the tree. **above** Training to a central leader creates a strong structure that is especially good for trees producing heavy fruit, such as apples.

THINNING FRUITS

Reducing the number of fruits on a tree is a form of pruning. Most common fruit trees require thinning in order to produce large, sweet, top-quality fruits. Thinning also moderates a tree's production, which encourages steadier production from year to year.

It is generally best to thin fruit before the natural fruit drop that occurs three to six weeks after bloom. When fruits are about the size of a quarter, select the largest fruits and remove nearby fruit so there is a distance of twice the expected diameter of the mature fruit between all remaining fruits on the tree.

Pruning brambles

Bring order to the bramble patch (and increase fruit production) by removing nonproducing and dead canes.

Red, purple, and black raspberries and other cane fruits in the *Rubus* genus of plants are collectively called brambles. Brambles produce fruit on biennial canes; the canes grow, produce fruit, and die within two years.

Pruning brings order to the bramble patch by removing second-year canes after fruiting and dead canes later in the season. Pruning is also a good way to control brambles' tendency to creep out of garden beds and become dense thickets.

While pruning practices vary slightly among the specific types of brambles, there are a few basic tasks. Remove all dead, diseased, or damaged canes whenever you notice them in the garden. Prune the canes back to ground level.

Blackberries
When: late winter or early spring

First, remove injured and diseased canes as well as canes that fruited the previous year. Thin the remaining canes to two per linear foot of row. Shorten side branches to about 15 inches long. Trim the side branches of trailing types to about 18 inches long and thin them to six to eight canes per hill in northern regions, four to six in southern regions. Heaviest fruiting may occur at the stem tips, so avoid cutting canes back severely. When new canes reach about 36 inches, prune the shoot tips back by 3 or 4 inches to encourage side-branch development.

opposite left Red raspberries have a tendency to spread, creating a dense thicket if they are not kept in check with annual pruning. Snip off wayward canes at ground level. *opposite top:* Stem tips often produce the most blackberries. Avoid pruning them severely after early spring. *opposite right, middle:* Cutting back the tips of black and purple raspberries in early summer spurs plants to produce side branches and more fruit. *opposite right, bottom* Everbearing and summer-bearing red raspberries are pruned differently. If you don't know what type of raspberries you are growing, it is simple to figure out. When does the fruit ripen? If all of your berries ripen over a couple of weeks in summer, your plants are summer-bearing. If some fruit ripens in fall, the plants are everbearing.

Everbearing (fall-bearing) red and yellow raspberries
When: early spring and late summer, after harvesting summer crop

To prune for a summer crop and a fall crop: In spring remove any two-year-old canes along with any damaged, diseased, or dead canes. Then pinch the tips of canes where the previous fall crop was borne. The summer crop will fruit on the lower buds of these canes. Immediately after harvesting the summer crop, remove the two-year-old canes entirely.

To prune for one large late-summer crop: In early spring, prune all canes back to ground level. This eliminates a summer crop, but the fall crop matures two weeks earlier—typically by late summer. Maintain the plants in a 1- to 2-foot-wide hedgerow, pruning wayward canes as necessary. No summer pruning is needed.

Summer-bearing red and yellow raspberries
When: early spring and late summer

Remove all weak, diseased, and damaged canes at ground level. Leave the most vigorous canes, those approximately ¼ inch in diameter when measured 30 inches from the ground. Cut as needed so remaining canes are spaced 6 inches apart. After the last harvest of summer, prune off the old fruiting canes at the soil surface.

Black and purple raspberries
When: early spring and early summer

Remove all the small, weak canes, leaving only four or five of the largest, most vigorous canes per clump or plant. Cut back the side branches to 12 inches long for black raspberries and 18 inches for purple raspberries.

Starting in late May or when the new growth reaches a height of 3 to 4 feet, cut the shoot tips back by 3 to 4 inches. This pruning encourages side shoots, which will increase yield. Because not all the new shoots will reach the desired height at the same time, go over the planting about once a week until midsummer to remove shoot tips.

Pruning fruiting shrubs and grapes

Grab a pair of sharp pruners and increase plant production.

When riddled with leafy, excess growth and dead stems, fruiting shrubs and grapes produce a fraction of the fruit that they will when they are pruned annually.

Fruiting shrubs

Blueberries, currants, gooseberries, and other small shrub fruits thrive when sunlight and air can easily reach the center of the shrub. Depending on the shrub's growth rate and age, annual pruning to create an open form will range from removing a few stems to snipping away what seems like half of the plant.

In early spring, cut out all diseased, damaged, crossing, or rubbing stems. If the center and top of the plant are dense with growth, remove two or three of the largest stems to encourage air and sunlight to reach the center of the shrub. Annually remove one or two of the oldest stems to promote new, vigorous growth. In general, one-, two-, and three-year-old stems produce the most fruit.

Grapes

Train the vines to grow on a trellis to maximize production. The most common trellis system for a home garden is the Kniffin system. A four-cane Kniffin consists of four fruiting canes, two on each side of the grape's trunk; a six-cane Kniffin contains six fruiting canes on three trellis wires.

The best time to prune grapes is late in the dormant season, in late winter or early spring. Vines that are pruned after early spring are likely to bleed heavily, but the bleeding will not harm the vines.

opposite Mature blueberry bushes produce the most fruit when they are pruned to contain 15 to 25 canes of varying ages. Annually remove the oldest canes at ground level.

THIN GRAPE CLUSTERS

Vigorous vines tend to overproduce; thinning fruit bunches helps the remaining grapes to grow large and sweet. Table-grape clusters must be thinned to produce large grapes free from rot and insect damage. Thin clusters to one or two bunches per shoot by removing clusters when the grapes are no more than $\frac{1}{8}$ inch in diameter.

PRUNING GRAPES

SELECT the appropriate number of fruiting canes. These are the canes that will run along the wires on the training system. Select four canes for a four-cane Kniffin and so on. Tie a colorful piece of cloth to each cane you are saving to make it easy to identify when you are pruning off other canes.

LEAVE an equal number of renewal spurs or short canes; usually one renewal spur is left on each main cane. Remove all other canes.

WEIGH the pruned canes. The weight of the canes is used to determine the number of buds to leave on the grapevine.

A SIMPLE FORMULA called "30 plus 10" is a guide for how many buds to leave on the fruiting canes. For the first pound of canes removed, leave 30 buds. For each additional pound, leave an additional 10 buds. When counting the number of buds to be saved, include the buds on the fruiting canes and the renewal spurs.

PRUNE remaining canes and renewal spurs so the plant has the appropriate number of buds.

CHAPTER TEN

Garden Plans

Easy-to-follow planting plans make quick work of designing and planting your garden feast. You'll find planting plans for petite patios and large landscapes.

128   132   134

Salad bowl

Toss together a big bowl of cool-season edibles including tender lettuce, violas, and pansies for garden-fresh spring salads. Sow lettuce seeds for a harvest in about 50 days, or go with nursery-started seedlings to enjoy your first harvest in half that time.

Essentials

Container: 16-inch glazed ceramic bowl
Light: sun
Water: keep soil moist

Ingredients

- **A.** 3 pansy ('Ultima Baron Merlot')
- **B.** 4 lettuce ('Esmeralda')
- **C.** 3 ornamental cabbage ('Pigeon Red')
- **D.** 3 viola ('Sorbet Primrose Babyface')
- **E.** 3 viola ('Sorbet Yellow Delight')
- **F.** 1 chives

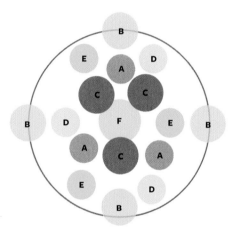

BHG ASK THE GARDEN DOCTOR

HOW CAN I HAVE SALAD GREENS ALL SUMMER?

ANSWER: Hot weather typically spells an end to cool-season greens. Plant varieties that are heat-tolerant or slow to bolt (set seed). Move the container to a shadier, cooler location when temperatures warm.

Essentials

Container: 1 each: 12×12-inch, 15×24-inch, 20×32-inch, and 24×40-inch lightweight pots

Light: sun

Water: when soil begins to feel dry

Ingredients

15×24 lightweight pot
A. 1 nasturtium ('Jewel Mix')
B. 1 cantaloupe ('Sweet 'n Early')
C. 1 bush sweet potato ('Porto Rico')

24×40 lightweight pot
D. 1 tomato ('Health Kick')
E. 1 tomato ('Patio Princess')
F. 1 sweet pepper ('Red Delicious')
G. 1 hot pepper ('Mariachi')

20×32 lightweight pot
H. 1 kale ('Dwarf Blue Curled Vates')
I. 1 kale ('Red Winter')
J. 1 Italian parsley
K. 1 basil ('Summerlong')
L. 1 oregano
M. 1 marjoram

12×12-inch lightweight pot
N. 1 basil
O. 1 Italian parsley

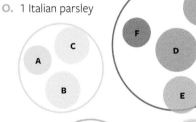

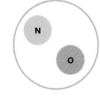
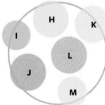

Small wonder

The best flavors of summer are contained in these four action-packed pots. Cultivar selection is key to the success of this patio-friendly container garden. If you cannot find the cultivars listed below, choose bush-form or dwarf varieties.

BHG TEST GARDEN TIP

SNIP FLOWERS

Flower stalks on basil and parsley are signs that these plants are slowing production of their flavorful foliage. Snip away the flower stalks as soon as they appear to encourage plants to continue unfurling fresh new leaves that you can use to flavor your favorite dishes.

Taste of summer

Repurposed baskets are the perfect home for this collection of essential kitchen herbs and summer vegetables. Begin harvesting the herbs shortly after planting in late spring or early summer. The vegetables will begin ripening in midsummer and produce succulent fruits through early fall.

Essentials

Container: repurposed wooden crates (produce or wine boxes) and baskets; line the crates or baskets with landscape fabric

Light: sun

Water: when soil begins to feel dry

Ingredients

Container #1
A. 1 thyme
B. 1 chives
C. 1 pepper

Container #2
D. 1 tomato ('Patio')
E. 1 basil
F. 1 parsley

Container #3
G. 1 bush cucumber
H. 5 onion

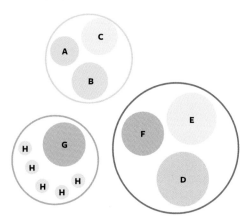

CAN I GROW ANY KIND OF TOMATO IN A CONTAINER?

ASK THE GARDEN DOCTOR

ANSWER: You can, but tomatoes bred for growing in pots are easier to manage. Most tomatoes, including heirlooms, are tall and sprawling, making them tough to grow in a container. Go with a short, stocky container variety such as 'Patio', 'Tiny Tim', or 'Bush Big Boy'.

Essentials

Container: 20×24-inch lightweight pot

Light: sun

Water: when soil begins to feel dry

Ingredients

A. 1 eggplant ('Little Fingers')

B. 1 *Verbena bonariensis*

C. 1 floss flower (*Ageratum*)

D. 1 Bacopa

E. 1 sage

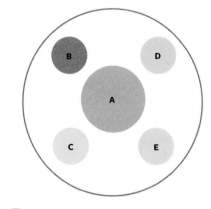

BHG TEST GARDEN TIP

STAND TALL

Many tomato, pepper, and eggplant cultivars need extra support when grown in containers. At planting time, sink a sturdy stake into the container alongside the plant. Use strips of cloth or plant ties available at your garden center to loosely but securely tie the main stem to the stake.

Flowers and fruit

When this container combination is decked with glistening eggplants, you'll hesitate to harvest the meaty fruit. Rest assured that the more you pick, the more eggplants you'll get. Long-blooming annuals provide color from spring through fall.

Seasonal harvest

Keep your pantry full with a succession garden where past-their-prime plants are regularly replaced with fresh varieties. This hardworking garden plan packs many vegetables in a tiny space, making it perfect for a small yard, a courtyard, or a community garden plot.

Essentials

Plot: 8 feet long by 4 feet wide; build a raised bed using 2×6 lengths of untreated lumber if you like

Light: full sun

Water: water when the soil feels dry 1 inch below the surface

Ingredients

Spring
A. 7 kale
B. 4 chives
C. 12 lettuce
D. 6 sweet alyssum (*Lobularia maritima*)

Summer
E. 1 tomato
F. 2 pepper
G. 1 basil
H. 1 bush cucumber
I. 8 bean
J. 28 onion
K. 1 eggplant

Fall
L. 9 spinach
M. 8 pea
N. 20 lettuce
O. 2 broccoli

COMPOST ANNUALLY

The soil supporting this long-season garden works overtime supplying valuable nutrients to plants. Replenish lost nutrients by annually blanketing the soil with a 2-inch-thick layer of compost in fall and mixing it into the top 6 to 8 inches of soil. If you forget to add compost in fall, spread a 2-inch-thick layer in spring.

SPRING
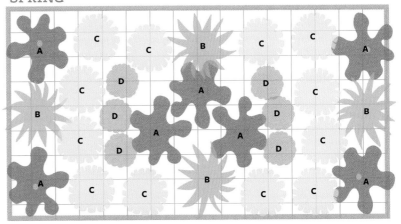

SUMMER
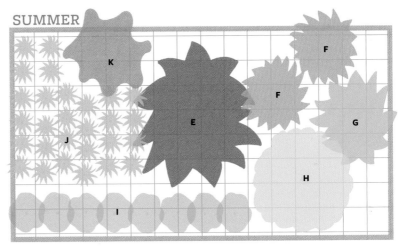

FALL
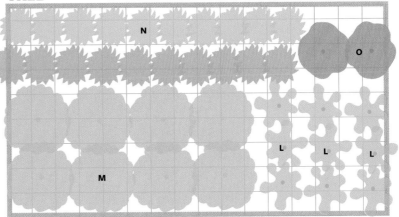

Patio garden

Garden patioside with this bountiful plan that includes nutrient-rich spinach and broccoli and a host of tender lettuces. Enjoy the cool-season crops into summer by planting the garden on the east side of the house or in dappled shade to protect the plants from extreme heat.

Essentials

Plot: 7×7-foot garden; 5×4-foot garden

Light: part shade

Water: keep soil moist

Ingredients

A. 7–10 romaine lettuce
B. 20–30 mesclun lettuce
C. 15 spinach
D. 15–30 carrot
E. 6 chives
F. 1 dwarf apple
G. 12 looseleaf lettuce
H. 7 broccoli
I. 5 pole bean
J. 1 cardoon

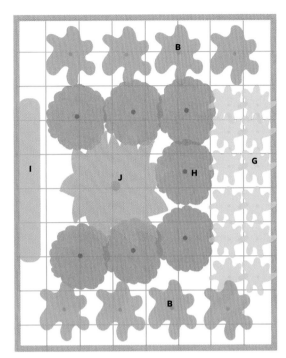

 DWARF TREES

Petite versions of their standard-size cousins, dwarf fruit trees produce regular-size fruit on trees that stand 10 feet tall or less. Easy to grow and maintain in courtyards, patios, and other small spaces, dwarf fruit trees respond well to pruning and shaping and can even be pruned so they grow against a wall or fence. This intense method of training is called espaliering.

BESIDES SPINACH AND LETTUCE, WHAT OTHER VEGETABLES GROW IN PARTIAL SHADE?

ANSWER: Vegetables that are grown for their foliage rather than for fruits or roots grow best in low-light areas, but there are a few exceptions. Try chard, cabbage, kale, leek, parsnip, pea, radish, and turnip. Most herbs will withstand a few hours of shade. Parsley, mint, and sage do well in partial shade.

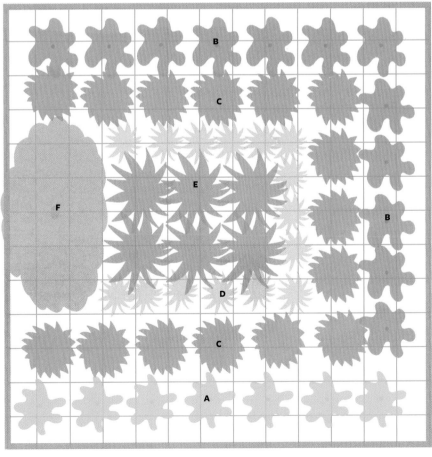

CHAPTER ELEVEN

Vegetable Encyclopedia

Stock your garden with a variety of spring, summer, and fall vegetables, and you'll enjoy months of garden-fresh flavor.

147

151

172

Artichoke
Cynara scolymus

This thistle-family member produces large, attractive plants. If the edible flower buds are not harvested, they bloom into fuzzy purple flowers. Artichokes are valuable members of edible landscapes.

Planting & Growing

Plant in full sun and moist, well-drained soil. Artichoke requires ample, consistent moisture for best growth. It survives drought but will not produce well. Start artichoke from root divisions or seeds. Root divisions do better, however, because seeds often produce inferior plants. Plant root divisions after the last frost, 24 to 36 inches apart in rows that are about 36 inches apart. Amend the soil prior to planting by mixing in a 2-inch-thick layer of compost.

Artichokes grow best in fertile, well-drained soil. If your soil doesn't fit that description, try planting on 6-inch-tall mounds or in raised beds. Fertilize plants monthly with a high-nitrogen fertilizer. Keep the soil consistently moist by watering and mulching with organic mulch, such as straw. When growing artichoke as a perennial, amend the soil around plants each spring with a 1- to 2-inch-thick layer of compost. In Zones 6 and 7, where artichokes are marginally hardy, cut back the plant in fall and cover with a 6-inch-thick layer of straw.

Harvesting

Where artichoke is grown as a perennial, the main harvest is in spring. Plants continue producing throughout the growing season with a secondary peak in fall. Where artichoke is grown as an annual, harvest from midsummer through fall from a spring planting. Harvest flower buds when the stalk has fully extended but the bud has not opened. Err on the side of early harvest rather than late harvest to avoid the delectable heart becoming woody. Harvest buds with a sharp knife, cutting 1 to 2 inches below the bud base. Some blackening of the outer leaves may occur if the buds are exposed to frost. After removing all the buds on a stalk, cut it back to the ground. Store harvested artichokes in the refrigerator.

VARIETIES

1. GREEN GLOBE IMPROVED is a widely grown variety that produces globe-shape, thick buds with a purple tinge on the leaf bracts.

2. IMPERIAL STAR is an excellent plant, producing fruit in midsummer.

3. VIOLETTO bears slightly elongated violet or green flower buds. It tolerates cold temperatures well and is a good choice for northern gardens.

Asparagus
Asparagus officinalis

Asparagus is one of the first vegetables to the table in early spring. The spears can be harvested for up to eight weeks. This hardy crop lasts for decades in the garden.

Planting & Growing

Plant in full sun and moist, well-drained soil. Fertile soil is key. Mix a 2-inch-thick layer of compost into the planting site. Because asparagus is long-lived, it is important to adequately prepare soil before planting. Grow asparagus from rooted crowns. Find them at garden centers and through online sources. A month before the last frost in early spring, dig trenches 6 inches deep in clay soil or 8 to 10 inches deep in sandy soil. Space the trenches 36 inches apart.

Young asparagus plants benefit from phosphorus, so add a phosphate fertilizer to the planting trench according to package directions. Avoid fertilizers high in nitrogen. Set root crowns 12 inches apart in the trenches. Cover the crowns loosely with about 3 inches of soil. After the new plants grow for six weeks, add another 3 inches of compost-enriched soil. Finish filling the trench in fall.

Each spring, spread a 2-inch-thick layer of compost over the planting bed. Weeding is critical to keep an asparagus bed productive. Hand-weeding is the best option to avoid damaging roots. Water young asparagus plantings until established. Allow fernlike shoots to develop after the last spring harvest, but cut them back to the ground in fall after a hard freeze.

Harvesting

Leave asparagus unharvested the year of planting. In the second year after planting crowns, harvest for only two weeks. In the third year, harvest for the usual five to eight weeks in midspring. Start harvesting when the spears are ½ inch in diameter. In the morning when it is still cool, cut or break off 7- to 9-inch-long spears with tightly closed tips. To store, wrap asparagus in damp paper towels and place in a plastic bag in the refrigerator for up to one week.

YOU
_ SHOULD KNOW _
Tender asparagus spears are tastiest when eaten as soon as possible after harvest. Try these flavor- and vitamin-packed vegetables roasted or blanched.

VARIETIES

1. UC 157 is a great choice for warm-winter regions. Developed in California, it's better suited to hot, dry conditions.

2. JERSEY SUPREME has higher yields than others in the Jersey series, with good disease resistance.

3. JERSEY GIANT is the most widely available variety and features green spears with purple bracts.

Bean

Glycine, Phaseolus, Vicia, Vigna species

Beans are some of the easiest vegetables to grow. Perfect for a first-time gardener or a child's vegetable garden, beans quickly germinate and produce copious amounts of tasty treats.

Planting & Growing

Several types of beans are a snap to grow in home gardens. Beans come in many colors, shapes, and sizes. Pods may be green, yellow, purple, or speckled. The plants range in size from 2 feet tall for bush types to pole types that may climb to 12 feet. A bean harvested when young, before the seeds fully develop, is called a snap bean. Once the seeds have reached full size, but pods have not turned brown, it's called a shelling bean. After the pod dries and seeds mature, it's called a dried bean.

Snap beans (*Phaseolus vulgaris*) are harvested when young, before the seeds mature. Plants may be bush or vining in form. Once called string beans, snap beans received a new name when plant breeders eliminated the fibrous seam along one side of the pod. This group includes green beans, wax, and purple-pod varieties.

Shelling beans are harvested after the seeds mature but the pods are still green.

Dried beans are harvested after the pod is dried and the seeds mature. While some beans can be harvested at any stage, most varieties are best at only one stage. If you would like to grow beans for drying, select a dried-bean variety rather than allowing snap beans to remain on the bush until they are dry. Dried beans vary widely by color and size.

Pole beans are the vining form of snap beans and often require a slightly longer growing season than snap beans. Grow them on a sturdy trellis that is at least 6 feet tall.

Lima beans (*Phaseolus lunatus*) develop flat pods with several seeds in each that may be harvested as shelling beans or as dried beans. The plants may be either bush or vining.

Asparagus beans (*Vigna unguiculata*) climb 8 to 12 feet tall and need support. They produce beans that grow more than 10 inches long.

Fava beans (*Vicia faba*) grow into majestic 5-foot-tall plants. They grow best in cool climates. Or grow them as a winter crop in warm climates.

BHG
TEST
GARDEN
TIP
LOOK FOR RUST

Rust is a serious disease of beans. This fungus causes rust-orange spots on leaves and bean pods. To avoid spreading this disease, don't weed after a rain or early in the morning when the foliage is still wet from dew. Grow disease-resistant bean varieties to avoid rust.

Edamame (*Glycine max*), also called soybeans, grow on shrubby plants that are 2 to 3 feet tall.

Southern peas (*Vigna unguiculata*), also called cowpeas, come in bush and vining varieties.

Plant beans in full sun. They prefer moist, well-drained soil. Beans are adaptable to many soil types as long as the soil drains readily. They can also be grown in almost any climate.

Plant seeds in the garden after the danger of frost passes in spring. Daytime temperatures between 70ºF and 80ºF are ideal. Before planting, mix a 1-inch-thick layer of compost into the soil. Sow snap-bean seeds 1 inch deep and 2 to 3 inches apart in rows 24 inches apart. Thin seedlings to 4 to 6 inches apart after they form true leaves.

BUSH BEAN VARIETIES *RIGHT*

1. DERBY produces tender, easy-to-harvest beans. It's an exceptional producer. Good disease resistance. 7 inches long. 57 days.

2. ROC D'OR has thin, yellow pods and is very productive. 6 inches yellow. 52 days.

3. BLUE LAKE 274 is widely adapted and a reliable producer in all climates. 6 inches green. 58 days.

PROVIDER is known for fast growth. Expect beans to ripen about one week before other green varieties. 5 inches green. 50 days.

VENTURE is another quick grower that is a great choice if you would like to harvest beans over a couple of weeks. Harvest as many as you would like, and leave others to ripen a bit longer; they'll remain tender for days. 5–6 inches green. 55 days.

EDAMAME VARIETIES *LEFT*

4. SAYAMUSUME is one of the highest-yielding edamame. Expect three or four light green beans per pod. 85 days.

ENVY is a very early-maturing edamame variety. Expect two or three flavorful beans per pod. 75 days.

Plant pole and asparagus beans so they can climb 6- to 8-foot-tall poles arranged in a tepee. Plant three to five seeds 2 to 3 inches apart. Plant southern peas 6 to 12 inches apart in rows that are 24 to 36 inches apart.

For a continuous harvest, sow snap beans every two to three weeks until midsummer. Beans will ripen into fall.

Fava beans are the exception in the heat-loving bean family. They require cool temperatures to grow and produce best. Staking or trellising is also recommended. Plant favas in early spring, about two to four weeks before the last frost. In warm areas, plant fava beans in fall for a winter harvest. Plants can survive temperatures down to 15°F. Space the seeds 4 to 6 inches apart in rows 24 to 36 inches apart. Thin seedlings to 12 inches apart.

Shallowly weed around the rows and poles, being careful not to disturb the tender bean roots. When the bean plants are 3 to 4 inches tall and the planting is free of weeds, mulch the area with a 2- to 3-inch-thick layer of straw, pine needles, chopped leaves, or grass clippings to conserve soil moisture and prevent weeds.

Keep beans evenly watered, especially during flowering and fruiting. Aim to provide about 1 inch of water per week. Apply fertilizer only if the soil is poor, in which case incorporating a 3-inch-thick layer of compost at planting time often provides all necessary nutrients. Beans can also be fertilized with a balanced liquid fertilizer during watering.

Harvesting

Harvest snap bush beans 40 to 60 days after planting, when the pods are full and 5 to 8 inches long, before pods and seeds reach full size. Modern varieties are considered stringless, but pick beans before the seeds reach full size or the pods will become tough and chewy. Specialty bush beans, called filet beans or flat pod beans, should be harvested when they are very slender—about ¼ inch in diameter.

Snap bush beans tend to produce all at once, making them perfect for canning or freezing. After two or three pickings, bush beans are mostly finished producing and can be pulled out. Plant another bean crop, or if it is late in the season, a cool-season vegetable such

LIMA BEAN VARIETIES

1. FORDHOOK 242 is an adaptable variety, tolerating cold, heat, and drought. It has a bush habit and produces three or five white beans per pod. 85 days.

2. JACKSON WONDER is a baby lima bean that is good for cool-summer areas. It has a bush habit and produces three or four light brown seeds per pod. 75 days.

POLE SNAP BEAN VARIETIES *LEFT*

3. ROMANO is an Italian bean, known for its flat pod. It has a distinctive, full flavor and produces heavy yields. Expect it to produce tender, stringless beans until frost. 6 inches flat green. 70 days.

4. KENTUCKY WONDER is an old-fashioned, vigorous variety that is a favorite of many gardeners. This disease-resistant variety also comes in bush form. 8 inches green. 67 days.

as spinach, where the beans were growing. To avoid a glut of bush beans, stagger your plantings, sowing short rows every two weeks.

Snap pole beans and asparagus beans begin producing 60 to 80 days after planting and produce handfuls of 6- to 12-inch-long beans until frost.

Store freshly harvested beans unwashed in plastic bags in the refrigerator for several days.

Harvest shelling beans once the seeds have reached full size, about 80 days from seeding but before the pods dry. Harvest dried beans 100 to 120 days after planting, when the pods have changed color and are fully mature. Because pods split and can drop beans onto the ground when dry, set a wide and large pan or bucket beneath the plants when picking. In humid climates, pull out the plants when the pods have matured and suspend plants upside down to dry in a shady, dry room with good air circulation. Store dried beans in an airtight jar in a cool, dry location.

Harvest lima beans, edamame, and fava beans 70 to 85 days after sowing the crop, when the seeds have reached full size and the pods are plump. Store shelled beans unwashed in plastic bags in the refrigerator for a few days.

FOUR-LEGGED BEAN LOVERS

Humans aren't the only creatures who love the taste of fresh garden beans. Animals such as woodchucks, deer, and rabbits can quickly decimate a bean crop. Erect animal-proof fencing. Or use animal repellents to deter these pests. Insect pests include the Mexican bean beetle. This brown beetle has black spots and is sometimes confused with the beneficial ladybug beetle. The soft-bodied yellow Mexican bean beetle larvae eat bean foliage, reducing the bean harvest. Crush eggs and larvae by hand, and spray adults with a pest-control product.

SHELLING AND DRIED BEAN VARIETIES

1. BLUE SPECKLED TEPARY is a good choice for the Southwest, especially desert climates. It has brown seeds with red speckles. 90 days dried.

2. CANNELLINI is a white kidney-shape bean with mild flavor. Plants have a bush habit. 80 days shelled; 100 days dried.

3. SCARLET RUNNER produces lima-shape beans and is commonly grown for its showy red flowers. The seeds of this pole bean are red with black blotches. 70 days shelled; 115 days dried.

PINTO produces buff-color seeds that are speckled with brown. It has a bush habit. 90 days dried.

Beet
Beta vulgaris

Beets do double duty in the kitchen. Both their roots and shoots are edible. The roots come in striped, yellow, pink, and red, and the greens sometimes have red stems.

Planting & Growing

Plant in full sun or part shade and loose, well-drained soil. Beets tolerate low fertility, growing well in sandy loam soil, but they require consistent moisture. Mix a 1- to 2-inch-thick layer of compost into the soil before planting. Beets need loose, stone-free soil. Remove any debris before planting, and if your soil is poorly drained or heavy, build a raised bed for growing beets.

Sow seeds in the garden in spring two weeks before the average last frost. Sow seeds ½ inch deep and 1 inch apart in rows 15 inches apart. Keep the seedbed well-watered to increase germination. The ideal temperature for growing beets is 60°F to 65°F. In cool-summer areas, sow every three weeks into the summer for a continual harvest. In warm-summer areas, sow in spring and again in fall so the roots mature during cool periods. Beets are closely related to Swiss chard and spinach. Avoid planting in a site that hosted either of these crops during the previous year.

When beets are 4 inches tall, thin to 4 inches apart. Cut rather than pull plants when thinning, to avoid disturbing nearby roots. Save the thinnings for salads. Hand-weed carefully until the beets are established in the bed. Mulch around plants with a 1- to 2-inch-thick layer of organic material to deter weeds and conserve soil moisture. Keep beets well-watered so that sweet, blemish-free roots develop.

Harvesting

Collect beet greens when they are 4 to 6 inches tall. Beet roots can be eaten at any time during their development, but they are best harvested 55 to 80 days after seeding or when they are 1 to 2 inches in diameter. When harvesting, leave 1 inch of foliage on the root to keep it from bleeding during cooking. Beets can be stored for three to four months in conditions similar to a root cellar.

VARIETIES

1. LUTZ GREEN LEAF/WINTERKEEPER features green leaves, pink stems, and purplish-red roots; its roots stay tender even when allowed to grow large. 80 days.

2. GOLDEN has green leaves with yellow stems and sweet golden roots. 55 days.

Broccoli

Beta oleracea Italica group

Easy to grow and packed with nutrients, broccoli is one of the first vegetables to mature in late spring. This cool-season crop grows best when daytime temperatures are around 60°F.

Planting & Growing

Plant in full sun and rich, well-drained soil. Work a 2-inch-thick layer of compost into the soil before planting. To help reduce diseases, do not plant broccoli or other cole crops, such as cabbage and Brussels sprouts, in the same location more than once every three years. Direct-sow seeds in spring two weeks before your last frost date, or start transplants indoors four weeks before setting them in the garden. Plant a fall crop in late summer or early fall. Where winters are mild, such as along the Pacific and Gulf coasts, grow overwintering varieties in fall to mature the following spring.

Sow seeds ½ inch deep and 3 inches apart in rows 36 inches apart. Thin seedlings to 18 inches apart when the second set of leaves appears. Hand-weed established plants, being careful not to disturb their shallow roots. Keep the soil evenly moist by applying 1 inch of water per week. Mulch the broccoli bed with a 2- to 4-inch-thick layer of organic material to prevent weed growth.

Ten or more days with high temperatures reaching only about 40°F causes some cultivars to flower prematurely, producing small heads called buttons. Cover transplants with a floating row cover during periods of cool weather.

Harvesting

Most varieties of broccoli produce one main head and then smaller side heads after the main head is cut. Sever heads with a sharp knife when they're tight and firm, keeping a 6-inch stem. Slice the stem at an angle to reduce the likelihood of the stem rotting. Heads with buds beginning to separate into yellow flowers indicate the broccoli is past its peak. Harvest smaller side heads as they mature. The flavor is best right after harvest, but broccoli heads can be stored unwashed in open plastic bags in the refrigerator's crisper drawer.

YOU
— SHOULD KNOW —
A rich source of antioxidants, broccoli packs more nutrients than any other vegetable. Delicious raw or blanched for three to four minutes, it is a quick and easy side dish.

VARIETIES

1. PACKMAN bears a 9-inch-diameter main head and is ideal in the South because it produces early and tolerates heat. 52 days.

2. GREEN GOLIATH is a widely adapted hybrid that produces a tight, 8-inch-diameter head good for freezing. 55 days.

3. ARCADIA is a disease-resistant variety for wet areas such as the Pacific Northwest. It produces an 8-inch-diameter main head. 69 days.

Brussels sprout
Brassica oleracea Gemmifera group

Brussels sprouts look like tiny cabbages clustered on a stalk. This cool-season plant is often planted in summer for a late-fall harvest because sprouts take on a pleasing, sweet flavor after light frost.

Planting & Growing

Plant in full sun or light shade and moist, well-drained soil. Work a 2-inch-thick layer of compost into the soil before planting. To help reduce diseases, do not plant Brussels sprouts or related crops, such as collards, cauliflower, and broccoli, in the same location more than once every three years.

Plant transplants or sow seeds in the garden in early summer, at least 100 days before the first average fall frost. Brussels sprouts that mature in cool fall weather have a flavor that is much sweeter than those that mature in the summer. Avoid bitterness by delaying planting until early to midsummer. Space plants 18 inches apart in rows 24 inches apart.

Plants do best when they receive about 1 inch of water a week. Hand-weed these shallow-root plants to avoid damaging their delicate surface roots, then mulch around plants with a 2- to 4-inch-thick layer of organic material, such as straw, pine straw, or grass clippings. Stake mature plants to prevent them from blowing over during storms.

Harvesting

Brussels sprouts' flavor sweetens with a touch of frost. After a few light frosts and the sprouts are 1 to 1½ inches in diameter, harvest them with a sharp knife. First remove the leaf under the sprout, then the sprout. To hasten maturity, remove the growing tip (top of the stalk) when the bottom sprouts measure ½ inch in diameter; sprouts should be ready about two weeks later.

The fresher the sprouts, the better the flavor, so do not let refrigerator storage exceed one or two days. To store, remove damaged outer leaves and store unwashed sprouts in a plastic bag in the refrigerator's crisper.

VARIETIES

1. DIABLO HYBRID is a late-maturing variety with sprouts that keep well on the plant once they've matured. 110 days.

2. JADE CROSS E produces uniform sprouts all the way up the stalk. 90 days.

3. RED RUBINE is an heirloom variety with purplish-red sprouts that hold their pretty color even after cooking. 95 days.

Cabbage

Brassica oleracea Capitata group

Cool weather and cabbage plants partner to create dense, vitamin-packed green or red cabbage heads in early summer and late fall. Plant in early spring so the crop matures before summer's heat.

Planting & Growing

Plant in full sun or light shade and moist, well-drained soil. Cabbage is an exceptionally heavy feeder; work a 2-inch-thick layer of compost into the soil before planting. To help reduce diseases, do not plant cabbage or related crops, such as Brussels sprouts and broccoli, in the same location more than once every three years.

Start from transplants or seeds. For a spring crop, plant frost-tolerant transplants outside as soon as the soil can be worked. Or start from seeds planted ½ inch deep and thinned to 12 to 24 inches apart in rows about 32 inches apart. Plant small-head varieties closer together. For a fall crop, set out transplants or sow seeds in midsummer. If possible, select a site where young plants will have some shade from the intense summer sun.

Cabbage needs ample water to thrive. Provide about 1 inch of water a week. Carefully weed around shallow-root cabbage plants. Spread a 2- to 4-inch-thick layer of mulch around plants to prevent weeds and conserve soil moisture. Apply high-nitrogen fertilizer about four weeks after transplanting. Avoid fertilizing during head formation; fertilizing at this time causes fast growth, which can lead to cracked heads.

Harvesting

Harvest cabbage anytime after heads form. For greatest yield, cut heads when they feel solid. Harvest by cutting heads at their base with a sharp knife. After the first head is harvested, small cabbage heads or sprouts may form at the plant base. Allow them to grow and form 2- to 4-inch-diameter baby cabbages. Unwashed smooth-leaf cabbage can be stored for as long as two months in the refrigerator. Store savoy (crinkled-leaf) varieties for only a few days.

YOU _ SHOULD KNOW _ The top half of a head of cabbage is more tender than the bottom half. Slice the head horizontally and use the top raw in salads and slaw, and the bottom half in cooked recipes.

VARIETIES

1. DANISH BALL HEAD is a green cabbage that is best for late-season planting. This heirloom stores well in winter. 100 days.

2. SAVOY QUEEN produces deep-green crinkled leaves and has great heat tolerance. 88 days.

3. RED METEOR is a red cabbage with a large, firm head. It is a good choice for both spring and fall. 75 days.

Carrot
Daucus carota sativus

Whether you eat them raw, sautéed, or cooked, this easy-to-grow root crop has a distinct, sweet flavor that will make you want to plant an extra row next year.

Planting & Growing

Plant in full sun and moist, well-drained soil. Deep, loose soil is a must. Roots can become twisted or forked in heavy or stony soil. Sow seeds in the garden two to four weeks before the last frost date, or in warm climates, in late summer and autumn for winter or spring crops. Carrots taste best when grown at temperatures between 60°F and 70°F. Sow seeds ¼ inch deep, ½ inch apart, in rows 12 to 24 inches apart.

Carrots are slow to germinate. They often germinate sporadically over a one- to three-week period. To speed germination, water lightly daily if the soil is dry. Thinning seedlings is critical to producing long, uniform carrots. Thin to 1- to 4-inch spacing (depending on the variety and size of root desired) before the plants are 2 inches tall.

Carrots are not drought-tolerant. Seeds need constant moisture while germinating. After the seedlings appear, water deeply every few days as needed. Carrots don't compete well with weeds, so hand-weed, especially early in the season. After weeding, apply an organic mulch such as straw around rows. As the carrots mature, cut back on water or the roots may crack.

Harvesting

Begin pulling carrots as soon as they're at full color. Small roots tend to be juicier and more tender. If the tops break off when you pull them, use a garden fork to gently pry the roots loose. In northern areas, wait until after a heavy frost before digging the rest of the carrots; the cold will increase their sweetness.

Carrots can be overwintered in the ground. In fall, cut the foliage to about 1 inch tall and mulch the plants with a 6- to 8-inch-thick layer of straw. Carrots keep for several months in the refrigerator.

VARIETIES

1. ROYAL CHANTENAY has strong tops, making for easy pulling. Great for juice or storage, this variety is bright orange. 5–6 inches long. 70 days.

2. PURPLE HAZE has purple skin, an orange core, and sweet, tender flesh. Its color fades when cooked. 10–12 inches long. 70 days.

3. DANVERS HALF LONG is a very easy-to-grow variety with sweet flavor and tender flesh. It produces notably uniform roots. It's a good choice for all soils. 6–8 inches long. 78 days.

4. BOLERO HYBRID is a disease-resistant Nantes variety that is great for growing in fall and stores exceptionally well. 7–8 inches long. 75 days.

5. THUMBELINA is a small, almost round baby carrot about the size of a silver dollar. It's a good variety for baking. 2 inches long. 65 days.

Cauliflower

Brassica oleracea Botrytis group

Growing cauliflower requires a little planning and some luck. Unlike its easy-to-grow cousin broccoli, cauliflower has exacting growing requirements. It thrives in moist soil and consistently cool weather.

Planting & Growing

Plant in full sun and well-drained, fertile soil. Before planting, mix a 2-inch-thick layer of compost into the soil. To help reduce diseases, do not plant cauliflower or other cole crops, such as cabbage and broccoli, in the same location more than once every three years.

Start cauliflower from transplants in early spring or fall. Cauliflower is sensitive to cold temperatures. In spring, set out transplants no earlier than two to three weeks before the last frost. Start cauliflower early enough so that it matures before the heat of summer but not so early that it is injured by cold. Plant fall crops 90 days before your first fall frost date. Cauliflower needs plenty of room to grow. Space plants 18 to 24 inches apart in rows 36 inches apart. Fertilize with a complete fertilizer such as 5-5-5 at planting time, and water frequently to keep soil consistently moist.

Cauliflower produces the best heads when it grows vigorously from seedling stage until harvest. After fertilizing at planting, fertilize again one month later with a high-nitrogen fertilizer such as 15-5-5. When the head begins to form (the plant shows 2 to 3 inches of white curd at the growing point), it is ready to blanch. Blanching ensures a bright white head and a mild flavor. To blanch, wrap the long outer leaves over the head and hold them together with twine, clothespins, or rubber bands. Color varieties don't need blanching.

Harvesting

Pick a head when it is 6 to 8 inches in diameter, about 10 days after blanching. Harvest before the curds separate and develop a ricelike appearance. Use a sharp knife to cut the head below the inner leaves. Store cauliflower in the refrigerator.

YOU
— SHOULD KNOW —
Available in purple, chartreuse, and orange in addition to the typical white, cauliflower is an eye-catching addition to the table and the garden.

VARIETIES

1. SNOW CROWN HYBRID is a large white variety that is heat- and cold-tolerant and matures quickly. 60 days.

2. GRAFFITI is a purple variety that turns smoky purple when cooked. 80 days.

3. CHEDDAR HYBRID produces orange heads that remain orange after cooking. 68 days.

Celery

Apium graveolens dulce

Celery is the plant to grow if you're looking for a challenge. It's difficult to start from seed, requires very specific temperatures for good growth, and demands consistently moist soil.

Planting & Growing

Plant in full sun and moist, well-drained soil. Celery will tolerate slightly wet soils. Enrich the planting area by incorporating a 2-inch-thick layer of compost before planting. Celery grows best in areas with moderate summer and winter temperatures.

Start celery from seeds indoors 10 to 12 weeks before your last spring frost date. Soak seeds overnight to speed germination.

Sow several seeds per pot and cover them lightly with soil, because celery seeds require light to germinate. After the last chance of frost has passed, transplant seedlings into the garden, spacing them 12 inches apart in rows 18 inches apart. Do not plant outside too early; 10 or more days with temperatures below 55°F will cause celery plants to bolt.

Keep the soil evenly moist by applying 1 inch or more of water per week. Lack of water will produce bitter stalks. Cover the soil with a 2- to 4-inch-thick layer of organic mulch to conserve moisture and suppress weeds around the shallow-root plants. Fertilize celery monthly with a balanced fertilizer such as 5-5-5.

Blanching the stalks gives them a mild flavor. Wrap the mature stems with any convenient light-blocking cylinder. Then mound 6 inches of soil around the base of the plant. Stalks are usually ready for harvest two to three weeks later. Be sure the cylinder does not block water from reaching the roots; consistent moisture is the key to good flavor.

Harvesting

Start harvesting individual stalks when they reach about 10 inches tall, cutting them at the base of the plant with a sharp knife. You can also harvest the entire plant at one time. Store celery in a refrigerator for up to two weeks.

VARIETIES

1. GIANT RED RESELECTION has good red color and hardiness. 120 days.

2. VENTURA is a widely grown variety that's disease-resistant and adaptable. 100 days.

CONQUISTADOR is an early-maturing variety that grows well under drought and heat stress. 80 days.

GOLDEN SELF-BLANCHING is a unique pale-yellow variety with a mild flavor. 110 days.

Chard, Swiss chard

Beta vulgaris cicla

Popular in the landscape and on the table, red-, yellow-, white-, or orange-stalk chard is packed with color, texture, and vitamin A. The leaves and stalks are edible and tasty.

Planting & Growing

Plant Swiss chard in full sun and moist, well-drained soil. Chard tolerates some shade, especially in summer. It grows best in fertile soil. Incorporate a 2-inch-thick layer of compost into the soil before planting. Chard's strong, upright stalks are perfect for growing in container gardens. Combine chard with additional greens for a patioside salad garden. Because chard is so colorful and beautiful, it is often used in ornamental containers combined with flowers. Edible landscaping is a hot trend, and chard is often used in landscape plantings alongside traditional trees, shrubs, and perennials.

Start chard from seeds or transplants planted directly in the garden after the danger of frost has passed. Soak seeds overnight to hasten germination. Sow seeds ½ inch deep and 2 inches apart in rows 24 inches apart. Thin seedlings to 12 inches apart after they develop four leaves.

Keep the soil evenly moist and weed-free by mulching with an organic material such as straw or grass clippings. Chard produces best when given ample nutrients. Sidedress plants with a 2-inch-thick layer of compost one month after planting, or fertilize with a liquid high-nitrogen fertilizer.

As plants age, the older leaves become tough. In midsummer, after harvesting several stems, cut plants back to 3 to 5 inches tall to encourage a flush of new, tender growth.

Harvesting

Chard can be harvested throughout the summer. Start picking outer leaves when plants are about 5 inches tall. Removing the outer leaves encourages the development of tender inner leaves. Cut the whole plant at ground level before a hard freeze.

Store unwashed leaves and stalks in plastic bags in the refrigerator crisper for just two to three days.

YOU _ SHOULD KNOW _
Chard can be used in place of spinach in any recipe, but it must be cooked a bit longer. Unlike spinach, chard does not bolt in hot weather, making it an excellent summer green.

VARIETIES

1. BRIGHT LIGHTS produces stem and leaf veins of many colors, including gold, pink, orange, purple, red, and white, with slightly ruffled, mild-tasting leaves. It's slightly less frost-tolerant than other chard varieties. 55 days.

2. BRIGHT YELLOW bears yellow stems and veins on deep green leaves. 57 days.

3. RHUBARB produces dark green, red-veined leaves on deep red stems. 59 days.

Collards

Brassica oleracea Acephala group

Collards are cabbages that don't form heads. Instead they produce clusters of stalks and leaves that are loaded with vitamins A and C. Plants grow best in warm climates, but they are frost-tolerant.

Planting & Growing

Plant collards in full sun and moist, well-drained soil. Collards tolerate some shade in summer. They grow best in fertile soil. Mix a 2-inch-thick layer of compost into the soil before planting. To help reduce diseases, do not plant collards or other cabbage-family crops, such as cabbage, broccoli, and cauliflower, in the same location more than once every three years.

For a summer crop, sow seeds in the garden four weeks before the last frost date. For a fall crop, sow seeds three months before the first fall frost. Plant seeds ½ inch deep and 1 inch apart, or transplant seedlings 6 to 8 inches apart. Grow collard greens 24 to 36 inches apart.

Although collards tolerate drought, they grow best in moist soil, so be sure they receive at least 1 inch of water per week. Mulch with an organic material such as straw or grass clippings to conserve soil moisture, keep the soil cool, and prevent weed growth.

Harvesting

Pick leaves as needed, harvesting outer leaves of the plant first. The top bud is a delicacy, but don't pick it if you want the plant to continue making leaves. You can also harvest the whole plant at once, 50 to 70 days after seeding.

As with other cole crops, collards' flavor improves with frost in fall. Many varieties are so cold-hardy that harvest can continue through snow in early winter.

Collards' tolerance to cold makes them store better than most other greens. Wrap unwashed leaves in moist paper towels and place in a sealed plastic bag for as long as one week.

VARIETIES

1. CHAMPION is a popular, compact Vates-type variety that's slow to bolt. 60 days.

2. FLASH HYBRID is known for high yields of smooth leaves and is also slow to bolt. 78 days.

3. GEORGIA produces sweet ruffled leaves over a long growing season. 60 days.

Corn

Zea mays

Fresh corn is the best corn, and by growing a few rows of sweet corn outside your back door, you'll have the best corn on the block. Sow successive crops every two weeks through early July.

Planting & Growing

There are three main types of sweet corn based on their genetic background, plus specialty corns such as popcorn and decorative corn:

Standard sweet corn hybrids (Su varieties) are best suited for being picked, husked, and eaten within a very short time.

Sugary enhanced hybrids (Se varieties) contain significantly more sugar than Su varieties while maintaining their superior taste and texture that is synonymous with great sweet corn. Se varieties hold their taste longer than Su varieties and are the gourmet corns of choice for gardeners.

Supersweet hybrids (Sh2 varieties) are exceptionally sweet, but they tend to have a tough-skin texture that is not readily apparent when eaten fresh but becomes more noticeable in frozen or canned corn.

Specialty corn includes varieties grown for popping, those grown for their colorful ears used in fall decorations, and baby corn, which is used in Asian cuisine.

Plant in full sun and moist, well-drained soil. Corn thrives in fertile ground. Incorporate a 2-inch-thick layer of compost into the soil before planting in spring.

Sow corn seeds directly in the garden after the last average frost date. Corn requires warm soil for germination; do not plant it until the soil is at least 55°F. Plant seeds 1 inch deep and 4 to 6 inches apart in rows that are 30 to 36 inches apart. To ensure good pollination, plant in blocks of at least four short rows, as opposed to fewer, longer rows.

YOU
_ SHOULD KNOW _
For a new flavor, instead of smothering an ear of corn with butter, squeeze on fresh lemon or lime juice, or brush it with olive oil and sprinkle with your favorite dried herb blend.

STANDARD HYBRIDS (SU) AND HEIRLOOM VARIETIES

1. SUGAR AND GOLD has bicolor kernels and is excellent for fresh eating or freezing. Easy to grow, this hybrid does especially well in cooler-season areas. 8-inch ears. 75 days.

2. SILVER QUEEN HYBRID has white kernels and is considered one of the best-tasting corn varieties. 7–8-inch ears. 92 days.

GOLDEN BANTAM is an heirloom with yellow kernels. It is a good cultivar for small gardens. 5–7-inch ears. 85 days.

Cross-pollination can be a problem with corn, especially supersweet varieties that cross with standard varieties and become starchy. Avoid problems either by planting varieties that mature at different times or by planting supersweet varieties at least 250 feet away from other types of corn. For a sequential harvest, plant another block of corn two weeks after the first planting. Choose a midseason variety if possible.

Continue planting blocks of corn until early July. If you grow corn in a heavy clay soil in a cool area, presprout seeds to hasten germination. Soak them overnight in warm water, drain, and place them in a partially open clear plastic bag in a warm location. Rinse the seeds daily. In four to five days, the corn will start to sprout. Carefully plant the sprouted seeds in a 4-inch-deep furrow; cover them with 1 inch of soil. Gradually fill in the furrow as the seedlings grow.

Weed carefully around shallow-root corn. Keep corn blocks weeded by hilling the soil around the base of each plant when it is 8 inches tall. Hilling not only kills weeds, but it also helps hold the corn plants upright during windstorms.

Corn is a heavy feeder. Fertilize plants with a high-nitrogen fertilizer when they are knee-high and again when the silks form.

Keep the soil evenly moist by applying 1 to 2 inches of water per week. To prevent diseases, water in the morning so the leaves dry before evening. Water to a depth of at least 6 inches; light sprinklings only encourage shallow-root plants that are more likely to blow over. Thin and curled corn leaves are signs of water stress. The most critical periods for watering are during pollination and ear filling.

If suckers or sprouts form at the base of a plant, leave them. Removing suckers won't increase ear size or quality.

Harvesting

Most corn varieties yield one or two good-size ears per stalk, and some heirlooms produce two or three per stalk. Sweet corn is ready to harvest roughly 20 days after the first silks appear, 60 to 95 days after planting.

SUGARY ENHANCED (SE) VARIETIES

1. PEACHES AND CREAM is a popular bicolor-kernel variety that has great flavor and stores well. It is a vigorous grower. 8-inch ears. 83 days.

2. BODACIOUS is a yellow-kernel variety with excellent flavor. It stores well and is disease- resistant. 8-inch ears. 75 days.

DIVINITY has snow-white kernels and a sweet flavor. 8-inch ears. 78 days.

Perfect harvest time is referred to as the "milk stage." Kernels are smooth and plump but not mature and tough. Puncture a kernel with your thumbnail and a milky sap will squirt out. Sweet corn remains in the milk stage for less than one week. As harvest time approaches, check kernels frequently so they do not become too mature

Other signs that the corn is ready for harvest are drying and browning of the silks, fullness of the tip kernels, and firmness of the unhusked ear. A nighttime raid by raccoons almost always indicates the corn is ripe.

Harvest by pulling the ear downward sharply and twisting to break the shank or stem below the ear without breaking the parent stalk. If a plant produces more than one ear, often both ears are ready for harvest at the same time.

Unhusked corn can be stored in the refrigerator for about one week. Freezing is the best preservation method.

Baby corn, popular in many Asian dishes, is easy to grow at home. Grow it much like sweet corn, except harvest the ears one or two days after silks emerge, when the cobs are only 2 to 4 inches long.

Harvest popcorn and ornamental corn once the stalks and husks are brown and dry. In rainy regions, cut the stalks when the corn is mature, and hang them to dry in a well-ventilated place away from rain and animals.

PROTECTING YOUR CROP

BHG TEST GARDEN TIP

Birds are notorious corn stealers. They pull up young corn sprouts to eat the seeds. They also sit on the maturing ears and peck away at the tender kernels. To protect your corn crop from marauding bands of birds, cover young seedlings with a floating row cover to prevent damage. Cover a small block planting with bird netting to prevent birds from eating the ears. Raccoons, too, have an appetite for corn. An electric fence can keep them away. In small plantings, consider covering individual ears with paper bags after pollination to thwart raccoons.

SUPERSWEET (SH2) HYBRIDS AND SPECIALTY VARIETIES

1. ILLINI XTRA SWEET is a variety with yellow kernels that freezes well. The plant grows 8 feet tall. 8-inch ears. 85 days.

2. HOW SWEET IT IS is a cold-sensitive variety with white kernels. It holds its quality well on the stalk and after harvest. 8-inch ears. 85 days.

3. HONEY 'N PEARL has tender bicolor kernels. It matures about 10 days before other varieties. 9-inch ears. 76 days.

4. MIRAI HYBRID is a sweet but not too sugary variety that stores well for up to six weeks in the refrigerator. 7–8-inch ears. 71 days.

5. BONUS is a baby corn. 2–4-inch ears. 32 days.

Cucumber
Cucumis sativus

Easy to grow and productive, a couple of cucumber plants will easily produce enough fruit for a family of four—you might even have some extra bounty to share with friends and neighbors.

Planting & Growing

Plant in full sun and moist, well-drained soil. Cucumbers require fertile ground. Add nutrients before planting by incorporating a 2- to 3-inch-thick layer of compost into the soil. Cucumbers are best started from seeds planted directly into the garden. Seeds require warm soil to germinate. Don't rush to plant cucumbers too early; wait until after the chance of frost has passed. For an earlier crop, start seeds indoors.

Sow seeds ½ inch deep and 2 inches apart in rows 4 feet apart. Thin plants to 12 inches apart. Or sow four to six seeds per hill and thin to three plants per hill after the true leaves emerge. In cool areas, protect seedlings with a floating row cover until the weather has warmed. Remove the row covers before the cucumbers flower so bees can pollinate blossoms. Cover cucumber beds with a 2- to 4-inch-thick layer of organic mulch to suppress weeds and conserve soil moisture. Cucumbers need a steady supply of water. Dry conditions cause bitter flavor. Provide at least 1 inch of water per week. Grow trailing cucumbers—which can trail up to 5 feet—onto a trellis.

Harvesting

Once cucumber fruits form, they grow quickly, especially during periods of warm, humid weather. Check plants every few days to keep up with the harvest. The more you harvest, the more the plants produce. Start harvesting slicing, burpless, and Asian cucumbers when the fruits are 6 to 9 inches long. Harvest pickling cucumbers when the fruits are less than 2 inches in diameter and 2 to 4 inches long. Store cucumbers in the refrigerator.

VARIETIES

1. COUNTY FAIR is an excellent pickling cucumber with notable bacterial wilt resistance. It matures quickly. 3 inches. 50 days.

2. MARKETMORE 76 is a popular slicer that produces uniform fruit. Plants have good disease resistance. 8–9 inches. 63 days.

3. STRAIGHT 8 is a slicer grown for its evenly dark green fruit and excellent flavor throughout the growing season. 8 inches. 58 days.

4. TASTY JADE is an Asian cucumber that produces high yields on vigorous vines. 12 inches. 54 days.

5. SWEET SUCCESS is a burpless cucumber that is disease-resistant. 14 inches. 54 days.

SALAD BUSH is a bush cultivar that is good for growing in containers. 8 inches. 57 days.

Eggplant
Solanum melongena

Glossy purple, white, orange, green, or bicolor fruits and bold foliage make eggplant a pretty plant for the edible landscape. Eggplant thrives in warm-summer areas.

Planting & Growing

Plant in full sun and well-drained, fertile soil. Eggplant is a heavy feeder. Boost the nutrient content of soil before planting by mixing in a 2- to 4-inch-thick layer of compost. Reduce diseases by not planting eggplant or any other tomato-family crops, such as peppers and potatoes, in the same ground for three years.

Eggplant is easiest to grow from purchased transplants. Wait until the soil has adequately warmed—about two weeks after the last average frost date—to set plants out in the garden. Cool conditions can weaken plants; frost will kill them. Space plants 18 to 24 inches apart in rows that are 30 to 36 inches apart. Apply a starter fertilizer at planting. In cool areas, protect young transplants with a floating row cover if necessary. Keep the area around plants weed-free by spreading a 2-inch-thick layer of organic mulch. Provide plants with 1 to 2 inches of water per week. Fertilize them monthly with a balanced fertilizer such as 5-5-5. Stake individual plants or use small tomato cages to keep the plants upright and long fruits straight and off the ground.

Harvesting

Pick eggplant 60 to 90 days after transplanting outside. Ripe fruits are shiny and firm to the touch. An eggplant is ripe if the skin bounces back when you press it with your finger. If it is still hard, the eggplant is not ripe. If your finger indents the skin, the fruit is overripe and should be composted. The more you pick, the more fruits will continue to develop. Use a knife or shears to cut the fruit from the plant stem. Eggplant bruises easily; handle with care. It does not store well and should be eaten soon after harvest.

YOU
— SHOULD KNOW —
There are three types of eggplants: large oval fruits grow 6 to 10 inches long; cylindrical fruits grow 6 to 12 inches long; and round varieties produce small fruits 2 to 4 inches in diameter.

VARIETIES

1. BLACK BEAUTY is a favorite producing large, oval fruit with purple-black skin. Ideal for cooking. 6–7 inches. 80 days.

2. DUSKY is a large, oval-fruit cultivar that matures early. It is a compact plant and good for containers. 6–7 inches. 60 days.

3. PURPLE BLUSH is another large, oval cultivar. The very sweet fruit has white skin tinged with purple. 6 inches. 62 days.

4. CRESCENT MOON is a very productive cylindrical cultivar with creamy white skin. 6–7 inches. 62 days.

5. LITTLE FINGERS produces showy, purple, cylindrical fruits. 6–8 inches. 68 days.

6. EASTER EGG is a favorite ornamental edible with egg-shape white fruit. 2 inches. 52 days.

7. TWINKLE yields many small, round purple-and-white fruits. A great choice for small gardens or containers. 4–5 inches. 60 days.

Garlic
Allium sativum

Garlic is exceptionally prolific. One pound of cloves can produce 7 to 10 pounds of garlic the following year. The trick to growing garlic is remembering to plant it in fall.

Planting & Growing

Plant in full sun and well-drained soil. Garlic thrives in slightly dry sites. Incorporate a 2-inch-thick layer of compost into the soil. Plant garlic around the first frost date in fall. In mild-winter areas, you can plant until January. Purchase garlic bulbs or sets from a nursery or mail-order source. Do not plant garlic purchased at the grocery store; it is often not hardy and has been treated to prevent sprouting.

Garlic grows best during cool weather and stops growing at temperatures above 90°F. You can also plant garlic in the early spring, but plants will yield smaller bulbs. Plant by setting individual cloves, pointy side up, 6 inches apart and 2 to 3 inches deep in rows 12 to 24 inches apart. Plant elephant garlic 8 inches apart and 6 inches deep.

Water garlic well in the fall to promote root growth. In cold-winter areas, mulch after a few hard freezes with a 4- to 6-inch-thick layer of straw to prevent the bulbs from heaving out of the ground. Garlic competes poorly with weeds; hand-weed regularly to encourage the plant to produce large bulbs.

Harvesting

When about half of the garlic leaves begin to yellow and wilt, stop watering and knock over the tops. Let the garlic cure for one week in the garden. Harvest the bulbs, knock off any extra soil, and hang the garlic to dry in a cool, shady location with good air circulation. After the tops are dry, trim them off to ½ inch above the bulb and trim the roots at the base of the bulb. Store the garlic in mesh bags in a cool room.

VARIETIES

1. INCHELIUM RED is a softneck that produces hard-to-peel cloves that are white with purple skin. However, it's one of the best softneck varieties for cold climates.

2. PERSIAN STAR is a hardneck that produces 8 to 10 purple-skin cloves per bulb. It's a good warm-climate variety.

3. RUSSIAN RED is a hardneck that has purple stripes, six to nine large cloves per bulb, and good winter hardiness.

Kale

Brassica oleracea Acephala group

Incredibly popular with dietitians, chefs, and foodies, kale is one of the most nutrient-dense vegetables available. Colorful leaves sprout in a variety of shapes and colors.

Planting & Growing

Plant in full sun and moist, well-drained soil. Kale tolerates partial shade, especially during the heat of summer. It grows best in soil that is high in organic matter. Incorporate a 2-inch-thick layer of compost in the growing location before planting.

To help reduce diseases, do not plant kale or other cabbage-family crops, such as cabbage, broccoli, and cauliflower, in the same location more than once every three years.

Plant seeds or transplants four weeks before your last frost date in spring for a summer harvest, and again six weeks before your first frost date in fall for autumn and early-winter harvest. In warm climates, plant kale in winter for an early-spring harvest.

Sow seeds ½ inch deep and 1 inch apart. Thin to 18 inches apart. Plant transplants 18 inches apart in rows 24 to 36 inches apart. When seedlings are 4 inches tall, fertilize with a liquid high-nitrogen plant food. Mulch with a 2- to 3-inch-thick layer of organic material, such as straw, to conserve moisture, keep the soil cool, and prevent weed growth.

Harvesting

Pick baby greens 20 to 30 days after seeding and mature leaves 50 to 75 days after seeding. Wait to harvest leaves until after frost or cold weather has turned the leaves sweeter.

To keep a plant producing, pick the big outer leaves and let the center continue to grow. The tender, young center leaves are fine in salads. The larger, older leaves are chewier and best steamed, sautéed, or cooked like cabbage.

Store fresh greens for up to one week in the refrigerator.

YOU
– SHOULD KNOW –
Kale is a great plant for containers. Combine it with edible flowers for a colorful edible container garden, or simply mix it with your favorite annuals.

VARIETIES

1. TOSCANO is a kale with long, thin, puckered dark green leaves that tolerate heat and cold. 65 days.

2. REDBOR HYBRID features highly attractive frilly burgundy-red leaves that darken in cold weather. 55 days.

3. RED RUSSIAN has purple stems and purple-veined, flat leaves that are more tender than those of other frilly kale varieties. 50 days.

Kohlrabi

Brassica oleracea Gongylodes group

With an appearance similar to a creature out of a Dr. Seuss book, kohlrabi is a unique member of the cabbage family. Like broccoli and cauliflower, it thrives in cool weather.

Planting & Growing

Plant in full sun and moist, well-drained soil. Kohlrabi thrives in soil that is high in organic matter. Incorporate a 2-inch-thick layer of compost into the garden site before planting. To avoid diseases, rotate crops; do not plant a cabbage-family crop in the same ground for three years.

Direct-sow seeds four to six weeks before your last average frost date. Or set out transplants two to three weeks before your last average frost date. Sow again for a fall crop about 10 weeks before your first fall frost date. Plant seeds ½ inch deep and 1 inch apart in rows 18 inches apart. Transplant seedlings and thin direct-sown seeds to 8 inches apart. Temperatures below 45°F will force the plant to bolt. Conversely, hot weather causes the stems to become tough and woody.

Three weeks after transplanting kohlrabi, sidedress it with a balanced fertilizer such as 5-5-5. Keep the soil moist by watering as needed, providing at least 1 inch per week. Hand-weed carefully around plants to avoid disturbing the shallow roots. Mulch with a 2-inch-thick layer of organic material, such as straw or grass clippings, to conserve soil moisture, keep the soil cool, and prevent weed growth.

Harvesting

For best quality, begin harvesting 45 to 65 days after transplanting, when the stems are 1 inch in diameter. Continue to harvest until stems reach 3 inches in diameter. On most varieties, any stems larger than 3 inches will be tough and woody.

Kohlrabi lasts for three weeks or longer in a refrigerator crisper drawer. The stems also freeze well when peeled, diced, and blanched. Young leaves may be steamed and eaten like greens.

VARIETIES

1. KOLIBRI is a purple-skin variety with fiberless white flesh. 50 days.

2. EARLY WHITE VIENNA has smooth light green skin and mild-flavor, tender white flesh. 55 days.

3. KOSSACK HYBRID produces an 8- to 10-inch-diameter stem with green skin and white flesh; it isn't woody despite its size. 75 days.

Leek

Allium porrum

Considered a gourmet vegetable by many people, leek is very easy to grow. This cool-season vegetable requires a long growing season. Give plants an early start, rich soil, and ample moisture.

Planting & Growing

Plant in full sun or part shade and moist, well-drained, fertile soil. Good drainage is essential in growing leeks. In clay or heavy soils, plant them in a raised bed. Leeks thrive in soil that is enriched with organic matter. Incorporate a 2-inch-thick layer of compost into the garden before planting.

Leeks have striking blue-green foliage that is a bold addition to the landscape. Plant a few rows of this showy vegetable alongside perennials, shrubs, and other traditional landscape plants.

Direct-sow leeks in the garden four weeks before your last frost date. They grow to a larger size if started as seedlings indoors. Start transplants eight weeks before the last frost date in your area. Set out transplants on or just after the last frost date. Direct-sow seeds ½ inch deep and 1 inch apart in rows 18 inches apart. Thin seedlings to 6 inches apart. Set transplants about 6 inches apart and 4 inches deep in 8-inch-deep trenches spaced 18 inches apart.

To blanch stems, slowly fill in the trenches as the plants grow, or mound about 6 inches of soil around the stems. Keep soil evenly moist by applying 1 inch of water weekly or as needed. Hand-weed frequently to keep the soil around the growing leeks free of weeds.

Harvesting

Leeks take 90 to 120 days to mature, and they taste sweeter after a frost. Harvest when the stem is at least ½ inch in diameter. The best leeks will have a white stem or shank at least 3 inches long. Although leek leaves are edible, trim the tops to a manageable size for cooking.

In mild climates, overwinter leeks and harvest in early spring. In cold areas, mulch leeks with a 4- to 6-inch thick layer of straw to protect the plants when overwintering them in the garden. Keep leeks in a refrigerator for up to one week.

YOU
— SHOULD KNOW —
Choose leeks when you are looking for a sweet onion flavor in salads, soups, and stir-fries. In areas with mild winters, mulch leeks and enjoy garden-fresh flavor in the depths of winter.

VARIETIES

1. GIANT MUSSELBURGH is a Scottish heirloom that produces 2- to 3-inch-thick stems and is very cold-tolerant. 105 days.

2. LANCELOT HYBRID is a cold-tolerant variety with bold blue-green leaves. 100 days.

3. KING RICHARD is a tall, thin variety with medium-size green leaves. 75 days. This fast-growing variety can be harvested early for baby leeks.

YOU
SHOULD KNOW

There are four types of lettuce: looseleaf (doesn't form heads), crisphead (forms tight heads), butterhead (forms small, soft heads), and romaine (forms upright heads).

VARIETIES

1. SALAD BOWL is a looseleaf lettuce with a pleasing mix of red- and green-leaf varieties. It's good in hot areas. Green and red. 45 days.

2. BLACK SEEDED SIMPSON is an easy-to-grow looseleaf variety with large, crinkly leaves. Light green. 46 days.

3. ROYAL OAK LEAF is a looseleaf variety with a unique leaf shape. It has good heat tolerance. Dark green. 50 days.

4. RED SAILS is a looseleaf lettuce with eye-catching red-fringed leaves. It stays mild without bitterness and is good for warm regions. Burgundy red. 55 days.

5. LITTLE GEM is a very early-maturing crisphead. Small 4-inch heads. Green. 55 days.

6. BUTTERCRUNCH has a yellow blanched heart in the center of tightly bunched leaves. This butterhead has a crisp and sweet flavor. Dark green. 46 days.

7. PARRIS ISLAND COS is an old-time favorite romaine with a white blanched heart. It is disease-resistant and slow to bolt. Green. 68 days.

Lettuce
Lactuca sativa

Lettuce usually leads the charge from garden to table. This fast-growing crop can be planted as soon as the soil can be scuffled with a hoe in early spring. It thrives in cool weather and is easy to grow.

Planting & Growing

Plant in full sun or part shade and moist, well-drained soil. Lettuce yields best in full sun during cool weather, but it also does especially well in part shade when temperatures rise above 75°F. It's easy to grow in a container.

Sow looseleaf, butterhead, and romaine types in early spring as soon as you can work the soil. Sow small beds every three weeks until late spring. Start sowing again in late summer for a fall or winter harvest. Lettuce can become bitter and bolt in summer heat. Sow seeds ¼ inch deep and 1 inch apart in rows about 18 inches apart.

Start crisphead lettuce varieties indoors four to six weeks before the last frost date in your area to transplant three to four weeks later. After three or four leaves form, thin looseleaf varieties to 4 to 6 inches apart, butterhead and romaine types to 6 to 10 inches apart, and crisphead to 10 to 12 inches apart in the row.

Lettuce has a shallow root system. Pull weeds by hand or hoe lightly to avoid damaging roots. Keep the soil consistently moist but not waterlogged. Mulch the rows with a 2- to 3-inch-thick layer of organic mulch to keep the soil moist, cool, and weed-free.

Harvesting

Pick the outer leaves of butterhead, looseleaf, and romaine varieties when the leaves are 2 inches long, 40 to 50 days after seeding. When the leaves reach 4 to 6 inches long, cut the whole plant to within 1 inch of the ground with a sharp knife. If lettuce is harvested in spring, new leaves will emerge later before the hot weather. If harvesting lettuce in late spring or fall, pull up the whole plant. Pick crisphead lettuce when the center is firm, 60 to 80 days after seeding. Store lettuce in a plastic bag in the refrigerator for a week.

Melon

Cucumis melo

Sweet garden treasures, heat-loving melons hide under rambling vines and leafy foliage. Melon vines require much garden space for good production and are not suited to small gardens.

Planting & Growing

Plant in full sun and well-drained soil. Melons grow best in soil high in organic matter. Add a 2-inch-thick layer of compost into the soil before planting. Melons also need heat to germinate. Wait until two weeks after your last frost date to sow seeds. Or start seeds indoors four weeks before your last frost date. Melon seedlings are sensitive to root disturbance, so plant seeds in individual peat pots that can be planted in the garden without disturbing the roots. In the garden, sow seeds in hills 4 to 6 feet apart, with six seeds per hill. Set transplants 12 to 18 inches apart in rows 36 inches apart.

Melons need ample space, nutrients, and water to grow. Thin seeded plants to three seedlings per hill after the first set of true leaves appears. Keep plants well-watered: at least 1 inch per week and more during hot, dry, windy periods. The most critical watering periods are when the vines are flowering and fruiting. Spread a 2-inch-layer of mulch around plants to conserve soil moisture. Prevent rot and insect damage on ripening fruits by placing melons on cardboard, upside-down pots, or pieces of wood. Hasten ripening of fruits by removing vine tips and new flowers when nights grow cool.

Harvesting

Harvest muskmelon when the vine easily separates, or slips, from the melon's stem. This "slip stage" signifies the time when the fruit has absorbed the maximum amount of sugar. The rind, too, will darken to a tan or yellow when the fruit is fully ripe. Harvest honeydew, casaba, and crenshaw melons when the green rind turns pale yellow and the blossom end of the fruit is slightly soft. Harvest them a few days before full maturity to continue ripening off the vine at room temperature. Store melons in the refrigerator.

> **YOU SHOULD KNOW**
> There are many types of melons: muskmelons (also called cantaloupes), charentais, winter melons (which include honeydews), crenshaw, and casaba.

VARIETIES

1. HALE'S BEST is an heirloom muskmelon with sweet, fragrant salmon-color flesh. It is very productive. 3–4 pounds. 80 days.

2. SUPERSTAR lives up to its name by producing many large muskmelons with orange flesh. 6–8 pounds. 86 days.

3. PASSPORT is a specialty tropical melon with mint-green flesh and a pleasing tropical fruit flavor. 5–6 pounds. 73 days.

4. CHARENTAIS is a French heirloom with sweet orange flesh and a bold melon fragrance when it is ripe. 2–3 pounds. 80 days.

5. EARLY CRENSHAW produces large, oblong fruits with pink, creamy flesh. 14 pounds. 90 days.

6. VENUS is a honeydew with a golden rind and juicy, fragrant white flesh. 3–4 pounds. 88 days.

7. SUPER DEW is a very productive honeydew melon. It has fragrant white flesh with green edges. 6 pounds. 80 days.

Mesclun mix

The word *mesclun* is French and originally referred to a mixture of tender salad greens that were wild-harvested in early spring. Today mesclun is cultivated in gardens and containers.

Planting & Growing

Plant in full sun or part shade and moist, well-drained soil. Mesclun mixes thrive in soil that is high in organic matter. Mix a 2-inch-thick layer of compost into the garden before planting.

Mesclun, like lettuce, is easy to grow in a container. Plant it with pansies, an edible early spring flower, for a cheerful burst of color.

Sow seeds in the garden two to four weeks before the last frost date and every two to three weeks in spring until early summer. Start sowing again in late summer for a fall harvest. In mild climates, sow seeds in fall for a winter harvest. Sow seeds ¼ inch deep and ½ inch apart in 24- to 36-inch-wide rows. Cover the seeds with fine soil, potting soil, or sand.

The exact greens used to create a mesclun mix lend it unique flavor. There are mixes that include mustard greens and have a spicy tang. Others include greens that are a hallmark of Asian cuisine or Italian cooking. If you have space, grow a few rows of mesclun and enjoy the many flavors of leaf lettuce.

Keep the planting moist until the seeds germinate. In cool areas cover the bed with a floating row cover to warm the soil in spring, prevent insects from attacking, and keep the bed moist. Hand-weed as needed, though a thickly sown planting rarely requires weeding.

Harvesting

Begin harvesting baby greens 14 to 30 days after sowing, when the leaves become 4 to 6 inches long. Handpick individual leaves, or cut whole plants to 1 inch above the ground. If cut in spring, the plant can regrow for a second harvest. After cutting, water well.

Mesclun mix leaves do not store well and should be eaten soon after harvest. Gently wash and dry the leaves, and store them in a plastic bag in the refrigerator crisper for a few days.

VARIETIES

1. ROCKY TOP mix is a colorful mix of 'Rouge d'Hiver', 'Trout Back', 'Red Salad Bowl', 'Rave', and 'Parris Island Green' romaine lettuces. 40 days.

2. SALAD MIX is specially made by combining red mustard greens and arugula. 40 days.

3. PROVENÇAL WINTER MIX is a mildly spicy mix of arugula, chervil, endive, French lettuces, Italian parsley, mache, and radicchio. 32 days.

Okra

Abelmoschus esculentus

This tall-growing vegetable is in the hollyhock and hibiscus family. Like its cousins, it has showy flowers and reaches impressive heights. Plant breeders have also developed shorter plants.

Planting & Growing

Plant okra in full sun and well-drained soil. It is drought-tolerant but will not tolerate constantly moist sites. If your soil is poorly drained, plant okra in raised beds or in a container.

Okra thrives in soil that is high in organic matter. Incorporate a 2-inch-thick layer of compost into the soil before planting. Plant transplants or sow seeds two weeks after all danger of frost has passed and the soil temperature is at least 60°F. In cool-summer areas, start seedlings indoors six to eight weeks before your last frost date.

Prior to sowing seeds, soak them in water for one hour to soften their seedcoats. Okra seedlings don't like to be disturbed, so plant seeds in individual peat pots when growing seedlings indoors to prevent damage to the roots while transplanting.

Plant okra seeds ½ inch deep or place transplants 12 to 24 inches apart in rows 24 inches apart. Water plants deeply every 7 to 10 days, allowing the soil to dry out between waterings. Deep irrigation is particularly important during flowering and pod development.

Harvesting

Pick okra pods when they are 2 to 4 inches long, five or six days after flowering. Use scissors to snip the tough stems from the plant. Harvest frequently, especially during hot weather, because pods become tough quickly. If you overlook some pods when harvesting and they become large and tough, pick them and toss them in the compost pile. These old, mature pods sap nutrients from the plant that could go into making new, young pods.

Store pods in the refrigerator for five to seven days, or blanch and freeze them for longer storage.

YOU
_ SHOULD KNOW _
Okra is a powerhouse of valuable nutrients and fiber. Its flavor is similar to that of eggplant. An ingredient in gumbo, okra also goes with tomatoes, onions, corn, and shellfish.

VARIETIES

1. ANNIE OAKLEY II is a good variety for northern regions, producing pods on 3- to 4-foot-tall plants. 55 days.

2. BURGUNDY has colorful red stems and pods on 7-foot-tall plants; the pods turn deep purple when cooked. 75 days.

3. LITTLE LUCY grows only 24 inches tall and produces 4-inch-long burgundy pods. It's a great cultivar for containers. 55 days.

Onion
Allium cepa

A key to success with onions is choosing the right variety for your region. They produce bulbs according to the number of hours of daylight they receive.

Planting & Growing

Plant in full sun and moist, well-drained soil. Onions thrive in fertile soil. Mix a 2-inch-thick layer of compost into the soil before planting. Onions don't grow well in waterlogged soil. Plant in raised beds or containers if your soil is excessively moist.

Start onions from seeds, transplants, or sets. Sets and transplants are easiest. Choose sets if you want green onions. Sets also produce good dry onions for slicing and storage. Transplants regularly produce large onions for slicing. Use seeds to grow scallions. Plant onions as soon as the soil can be tilled in spring in the North or early fall in the Deep South. Plant sets or transplants 4 to 6 inches apart. Place the onion sets about 2 inches deep in the soil so the pointed end is just showing aboveground. Sow seeds ½ inch deep and 3 inches apart. If you plan to harvest the tops for scallions, space the seeds 2 inches apart and thin the seedlings.

About 1 inch of water per week is needed, especially when bulbs begin to increase in size. Keep onion plants moist and weed-free by mulching between the onion beds. Remove flower stems if they form. Side-dress plants with fertilizer every three to four weeks.

Harvesting

Pick scallions when they are 6 to 8 inches tall, usually eight weeks after planting. Harvest green onions anytime after the bulb forms. Storage onions take three to five months to mature in the North; in mild climates, fall-planted onions mature in early summer. Once the tops start yellowing, stop watering. When half of the stems have collapsed, bend the rest down. After one more week, you can pull up the bulbs. Lay them in a warm, dry place. When the skin is dry and papery, cut off the foliage.

VARIETIES

1. GIANT RED HAMBURGER is a short-day onion with sweet white flesh. It matures earlier than many other large onions. Dark red. 95 days.

2. AMBITION is a shallot that can be grown in all regions. It has reddish-copper skin and white flesh. Grow it from seed. Red. 100 days.

3. SUPER STAR is adapted to growing in all regions and regularly produces 1-pound bulbs with a mild, sweet taste. White. 109 days.

4. CANDY has a welcome mild flavor and can be grown anywhere. It grows very large in the South. This onion stores fairly well. Yellow. 110 days.

5. REDWING is a long-day onion with pungent red flesh. It stores very well. Red. 110 days.

6. COPRA has firm, sweet flesh and is an early-maturing, long-day storage onion. Yellow. 104 days.

7. WALLA WALLA is a classic long-day onion with a sweet, juicy flavor. In mild-winter areas, plant it in fall. Yellow. 125 days.

Parsnip
Pastinaca sativa

Parsnip is one of the hardiest vegetables. In fact, the root does not develop its sweet flavor until after soil temperatures hover around freezing for two to four weeks in fall. It's a good keeper, too.

Planting & Growing

Plant in full sun and well-drained soil. Parsnip tolerates some shade but yields better in full sun. Loose, rock-free soil is essential for growing this root vegetable. It does not grow well in clay. If your soil is clay or poorly drained, grow parsnip in raised beds that are at least 12 inches tall and filled with loose, fertile soil.

Parsnip requires a long growing season. Sow seeds directly in the garden about two weeks before your last frost date. Plant seeds ½ inch deep and ½ inch apart in rows 18 inches apart. The seeds take about three weeks to germinate when they receive consistent moisture. Because parsnip is slow to germinate, mark the spot by planting radishes in the same row.

Thin seedlings to 4 inches apart after true leaves emerge. Weed by hand to protect their roots. After the plants are established, mulch between rows with a 2- to 3-inch-thick layer of organic material, such as straw or grass clippings, to keep the soil cool and moist and to prevent further weed growth.

Harvesting

Parsnip tastes best when exposed to two to four weeks of low temperatures, during which the starch in the roots is converted into sugars. In warm areas, you can harvest roots all winter.

In northern areas, mulch the parsnip bed with a 2- to 4-inch-thick layer of straw in late fall to protect the plants from freezing weather. In late winter or early spring, remove the mulch and harvest the roots before they start to grow again. A spading fork is handy for dislodging the large roots. They can be stored in the refrigerator for up to two months.

YOU
_ SHOULD KNOW _
Parsnip's sweet, nutty flavor is especially tasty when the roots are mashed like potatoes, chopped in soups and stews, or sliced and glazed with butter and brown sugar for a side dish.

VARIETIES

1. ANDOVER has long, slender, disease-resistant roots. 120 days.

2. GLADIATOR is a fast-maturing variety with silky smooth white skin and good disease resistance. 105 days.

3. COBHAM IMPROVED MARROW is a disease-resistant variety that stays smooth when grown in heavy soils. 120 days.

Peanut
Arachis hypogaea

Depending on the variety, peanut plants vine or bunch. After the flowers fade, short stems called pegs form; the pegs push their way underground, where shells and nuts develop.

Planting & Growing

Plant in full sun and well-drained soil. Peanuts do not grow well in clay or poorly drained soil. Sow seeds or set out transplants two weeks after your last frost date. Peanuts require warm soil for germination. In cold-winter areas, start seedlings indoors four weeks before your last frost date. Plant seeds 2 inches deep and 4 inches apart in rows 24 inches apart for bunching types and 36 inches apart for vining types.

Thin bush-type seedlings to 6 to 8 inches apart and vining seedlings to 12 to 15 inches apart once true leaves form. Shallowly hoe around peanut plants, mounding the soil to remove weeds and to allow the pegs to easily make their way underground. Once the pegs enter the soil, stop weeding. That's also the time to mulch with a 1- to 2-inch-thick layer of organic material such as straw. After the flowers fade, sidedress the peanuts with a low-nitrogen fertilizer. Keep the beds well-watered, especially when the pegs are forming; deliver at least 1 inch of water a week during dry periods.

Harvesting

Harvest peanut plants after the leaves have yellowed and the plants have begun to dry, usually three to four months after seeding. Pull or carefully dig up individual plants with a spading fork and shake off the loose soil. Mature peanuts will have ridged shells and filled pods. Dry the plants and pods for one week in a warm, well-ventilated location indoors. Separate the pods from the plants and continue to dry the shells for another week. Peanuts stored in the shell in a cool, well-ventilated location can last for months. Shell and roast the peanuts as needed. Roast at 325°F for 20 minutes.

VARIETIES

1. VIRGINIA JUMBO is a vining type that bears two or three large nuts per shell and up to 50 shells per plant. 120 days.

2. EARLY SPANISH is a bush type that matures quickly, producing two or three papery, red-skin nuts per shell. 100 days.

3. TENNESSEE RED VALENCIA is a bush type that makes two to five red-skin nuts per shell. 110 days.

Pea

Pisum sativum

Garden-fresh peas are the ultimate springtime treat. This cool-season crop thrives in cool, moist weather and can be planted in early spring as soon as the soil can be worked.

Planting & Growing

Plant in full sun and well-drained soil. Peas will grow in part shade, but they yield best in full sun. Peas don't grow well in poorly drained soil. If you garden in heavy clay soil, plant peas in raised beds. Add a 2-inch-thick layer of compost into the soil before planting.

Sow peas in early spring as soon as the soil reaches 45°F and can be worked. Sow seeds 1 inch deep and 2 inches apart in rows 8 to 12 inches apart. In hot, dry areas, dig a trench 2 inches wide and 4 inches deep, moisten the soil, and plant the seeds; cover them with 2 inches of soil. Rainwater will collect in the trench, aiding pea germination and early growth. Slowly fill in the trench as the peas grow.

Keep beds weed-free, especially for the first six weeks that peas are growing. Maintain even soil moisture; apply 1 inch of water per week. Mulch plants with a 2-inch-thick layer of organic material.

Harvesting

Harvest snap peas when the pods first start to fatten but aren't completely full. Don't shell them; instead, eat the whole pod. Overmature pods become stringy or fibrous. Snap pea vines continue to produce pods as long as the weather is cool and plants are healthy.

Harvest snow peas when the pods are still flat and the seeds inside are small and undeveloped, usually five to seven days after flowering. If you miss a few pods, let the peas inside mature and harvest them like garden peas. Pick pods every few days, and snow peas will continue to produce. Store snap and snow peas in the pod in the refrigerator.

Pick garden peas when the pods are full and rounded. Pick a few pods every day or two near harvest time to determine when the peas are at the perfect stage for eating. Garden peas are best when they are fully expanded but immature, before they become starchy.

> **YOU**
> — SHOULD KNOW —
> Edible pod peas are eaten whole. Snow peas and snap peas fall into the edible pod group. Garden peas, also called English peas, are grown for their plump, juicy peas inside the pods.

VARIETIES

1. DWARF GREY SUGAR is a 36-inch-tall, vining snow pea with sweet pods. It is a good source of pea shoots. 66 days.

2. ALDERMAN TALL TELEPHONE is a vigorous garden pea that produces 6- to 8-foot-tall vines. This popular heirloom has large pods. 74 days.

3. WANDO has good heat tolerance, making it a good choice for mid- to late-spring plantings. It is an heirloom garden pea with 24- to 36-inch-tall vines. 68 days.

4. ECLIPSE peas are known for keeping their sweet taste long after harvest. This garden pea produces 36-inch-tall vines. 63 days.

5. SUGAR ANN is easy to grow. The 24-inch-tall bush plants support themselves and don't require staking. 52 days.

6. SUGAR SNAP has extra-sweet pods and peas on 6-foot-tall vines. 65 days.

7. SUPER SUGAR SNAP has improved disease resistance and 4- to 5-foot-tall vines. 64 days.

Pepper
Capsicum annuum

Peppers are an essential ingredient in salsa, a key component of many ethnic cuisines, and a vitamin-packed snack. This plant is also eye-catching and easy to grow in a container.

Planting & Growing

Peppers come in many types, providing colorful garden interest as their fruits ripen from green to orange, yellow, red, purple, and brown.

Sweet peppers may be bell-shape, small and round, or shaped like a horn. Bell peppers are the most popular garden variety of sweet peppers. Left to ripen, they turn red, purple, orange, or yellow and contain various amounts of sugar, depending on the variety. Green bell peppers are the most common.

Paler green and yellow elongated sweet pepper varieties often have a more intense flavor. All sweet peppers are crisp and refreshing raw and pleasantly assertive when cooked to tenderness. Because peppers require a long, hot growing season, in cool regions or areas with short growing seasons they may never develop their ripe color.

Chile, or hot, peppers are famous throughout the world, from the spicy cuisines of Mexico, India, Thailand, and Africa, to the subtle flavor they impart on the most delicate dishes. The hot varieties can be picked at any color stage but are hottest if they are allowed to fully ripen.

Chile peppers include Anaheims, anchos, jalapeños, serranos, hot wax, tabasco, cayenne, and habanero peppers that ripen through a wide range of colors including yellow, orange, purple, and even brown. Some chile peppers turn bright red, which is more often an indication of ripeness than hotness. The burning sensation associated with fiery chiles is attributed to chemical compounds in the walls surrounding the seeds. The pepper flesh is usually not as hot as the scorching seeds.

Peppers are ranked on a scale called the Scoville Heat Scale according to their hotness or the amount of a chemical compound

AVOID PEPPER PROBLEMS

To avoid soilborne diseases when planting peppers, rotate crops each year. As a common practice, do not plant a tomato-family relative (tomato, tomatillo, potato, or eggplant) in the same place for three years. This will keep soilborne diseases from affecting your pepper crops. Another problem that can beset peppers is blossom-end rot. This physiological condition causes the base of pepper fruits to rot. To avoid this problem, mulch around plants (even in containers) and keep plants evenly watered and fertilized.

called capsaicin in their fruit and seeds. The scale starts with bell pepper at 0 and goes up to hot peppers, such as habanero, rated at more than 500,000 at the hottest. Some peppers are so hot that handling them can burn your hands.

The measurement is imprecise due to differences in varieties and individual tastes. However, the rating is useful for knowing which types of peppers are hotter than others. Plant in full sun and well-drained soil. At least eight hours of direct sunlight a day are essential for good plant growth and pepper formation. Peppers thrive in soil that is high in organic matter. Prior to planting, mix a 2-inch-thick layer of compost into the planting site.

Peppers are easy to grow in containers. Choose a large, sturdy pot to support the plants, which will become heavy with fruit at harvest. Peppers are easiest to grow from transplants. Set out transplants when the soil temperature is at least 60°F, about two weeks after the average last frost date. Peppers can also be extremely attractive in window boxes. Their bright colors and interesting shapes make them ideal partners for sun-loving annuals.

Peppers are sensitive to frost. If a late frost is predicted, protect peppers by covering them with cloth, an empty pot, or a 5-gallon bucket. Peppers require a long growing season and in most regions must be started from transplants or seeds planted indoors six to eight weeks before the last frost date.

The increasing popularity of unique pepper varieties has made many more available as transplants, nearly eliminating the need to start plants from seeds.

If you decide to start plants from seeds, sow seeds ¼ inch deep and maintain soil temperatures of at least 80°F for best germination. Be sure to place seedlings in a bright, sunny location. Lack of light will produce leggy, unproductive transplants.

YOU
_ SHOULD KNOW _
Roast peppers under a broiler, over an open flame, or on the grill until the skin is black. While the peppers are still hot, place them in a paper bag to allow the steam to loosen the charred skin.

SWEET BELL VARIETIES

1. CALIFORNIA WONDER has thick walls and is good for stuffing. The green bells are produced on leafy plants that protect fruit from sunburn. The fruits ripen green to red. 4 inches. 65 days.

2. CHINESE GIANT is known for its huge fruits. It ripens green to red. 6 inches. 75 days.

3. PURPLE BEAUTY is an heirloom with purple fruits on a short, bushy plant. Purple fruits mature to red. 4 inches. 75 days.

Peppers grow best when temperatures are between 70°F and 80°F. Temperatures below 60°F or above 90°F cause pepper flowers to drop. Protect the plants under a floating row cover to keep them warm or under a shade cloth so they remain cool.

Apply supplemental fertilizer after the first flush of peppers is set. A balanced fertilizer (such as 5-5-5) is a good choice; avoid high-nitrogen fertilizers, which promote lush foliage growth but few flowers and fruits.

The fastest way to deliver fertilizer to pepper plants is with a liquid fertilizer product. Following package directions, mix the fertilizer with water in a watering can. Convenient hose-end canisters of fertilizer make mixing water and nutrients as simple as attaching the canister to your garden hose and watering the plants as you normally do. Look for these products at your local garden center.

Keep plants well-weeded and watered. Apply a 2- to 3-inch-thick layer of organic mulch, such as straw or grass clippings, after the soil has warmed to prevent further weed growth and conserve soil moisture.

Apply at least 1 inch of water per week, being careful not to get the foliage wet when possible. Water early in the day so foliage has time to dry before night. Wet leaves at night will foster diseases. Watering is especially important at bloom time, or blossoms may drop without setting fruit.

Plants with exceptionally large fruits occasionally need staking. Sink a sturdy stake into the ground alongside the plant, and use twine or cloth to gently anchor the plant's main stem to the stake. Continue anchoring the stem to the stake as the plants grow so they don't topple in a midsummer windstorm.

Harvesting

Green bell varieties are usually picked when they are fully grown and mature—3 to 4 inches long, firm, and green. When the fruits are mature, they break easily from the plant. Less damage is done to the plants, however, if the fruits are cut rather than pulled off. That way you won't run the risk of splitting a plant's stems.

SWEET ELONGATED OR ROUND PEPPER VARIETIES

1. CORNO DI TORO is an Italian heirloom with long, curved fruits. It is very productive. 8–10 inches. 68 days.

2. SWEET BANANA starts yellow and matures to red. This sweet, mild-tasting pepper is easy to grow. 4 inches. 68 days.

3. RED SWEET CHERRY has round, sweet, slightly tapered fruits. It is a favorite addition to salads, and the plants grow well in containers. 1–2 inches. 78 days.

Red, yellow, orange, and brown bell pepper fruits can be left on the plant to develop full flavor and ripen to their mature color, or they can be harvested at any color stage. You can leave them on the stems and harvest them as you need them, unlike other vegetables that may lose their flavor.

Harvest hot peppers in the green or red stage. Watch them carefully; they are quicker to turn red than sweet peppers. The longer hot peppers stay on the plant, the hotter they will become. For example, green jalapeños are less hot than those that have been allowed to ripen to redness.

Hot peppers vary in hotness depending on weather and stress. Plants suffering from water or nutrient stress produce fewer but hotter peppers. Cool, cloudy weather makes peppers less hot. Wear gloves when harvesting and handling hot peppers to protect your hands and face from capsaicin, the chemical compound that makes peppers hot.

Continually harvest peppers throughout the summer. All types of peppers will develop fruit up until frost.

HANDLING HOT PEPPERS

When working with fresh chiles, wear rubber gloves or disposable plastic gloves, or cover your hands with small plastic bags. If your bare hands do touch the peppers, wash your hands and nails well with soap and hot water. If you get some of the oils in your eyes, flush them with cool water. Oils from chiles can transfer to knives and cutting surfaces, so wash tools and surfaces with hot, soapy water after use to prevent the oils from transferring to other foods.

HOT PEPPER VARIETIES

1. ANCHO 211 has mildly hot, heart-shape fruits. They are good for stuffing, making chile rellenos, and drying. 4 inches. 80 days.

2. EARLY JALAPEÑO produces thick-walled fruits about 20 days before similar hot peppers. They have a full jalapeño flavor. 2 inches. 60 days.

3. KUNG PAO has very hot, slender fruits that mature to red. 4–5 inches. 85 days.

4. HABANERO produces golden orange, wrinkled fruits that are blisteringly hot at maturity. 1–2 inches. 110 days.

5. BLACK PEARL is a dwarf plant with black leaves, stems, and immature fruits. The fruits turn red at maturity. This plant is good in pots. ¾ inch. 60 days.

Potato

Solanum tuberosum

While the potato most people are familiar with is the white-flesh Irish potato, there are many other varieties of this native South American plant that offer red, blue, yellow, or bicolor flesh.

Planting & Growing

Potatoes offer you a grand palette of options. Plant three or four different varieties and explore different colors, shapes, and flavors. If you don't have a plot of ground in which to grow potatoes, you can grow them in containers. There are several types of potatoes for home gardens.

Early potatoes mature in 65 days.

Midseason potatoes are ready to harvest 75 to 80 days after planting.

Late potato varieties require 90-plus days to reach maturity.

Fingerling potatoes produce long, thin tubers that resemble fingers. They may fall into any of the maturity groupings.

Growing potatoes is easy. Plant in full sun and well-drained soil. Potatoes will rot in poorly drained soil or heavy clay. They grow best in soil that is rich in organic matter. Incorporate a 2-inch-thick layer of compost into the garden prior to planting.

Prevent disease by planting potatoes and tomato-family members, including tomatoes, peppers, and eggplant, in the same ground only once every three years.

Plant potatoes two to four weeks before your last frost date. In warm regions, plant them in the fall or winter. Potatoes are easiest to start from certified disease-free seed potatoes. These small, sprouted pieces of potato readily send out roots and shoots and produce a large crop of spuds. Potatoes form best at soil temperatures between 60°F and 70°F.

Presprouted seed potatoes develop faster than those without sprouts. To form sprouts, set uncut seed potatoes in a sunny place for one to three days before planting. Sprouting happens when the buds swell and expand.

Small seed potatoes—those less than 2 inches across—can be planted directly in the ground, but cut the larger ones into pieces.

HEALTHY ROTATION

BHG TEST GARDEN TIP

Growing a pest- and disease-free potato crop is often as simple as practicing crop rotation. By planting potatoes and their close relatives—tomatoes, peppers, and eggplant—in a new area each year, you'll thwart perennial pests by moving their crop of choice out of the immediate area. Combine crop rotation with growing certified disease-free tubers and cleaning up all the plant debris in fall for a hefty harvest of spuds. These easy methods will help to prevent common potato problems such as potato scab, blight, and other diseases.

Use a sharp knife to cut 1-inch fleshy chunks, each with two or more eyes. Dry the pieces overnight to form a callus layer on the cut ends and to help protect them from rot.

Plant pieces, as well as whole seed potatoes, eyes up in trenches dug 4 inches deep in heavy soil and 6 inches deep in light soil. Space the tubers 12 to 15 inches apart in rows 24 inches apart. Cover potatoes with 2 to 4 inches of soil.

Keep the soil evenly moist until sprouts emerge, usually about one week after planting. When sprouts are 6 to 8 inches tall, hill the soil around them, creating a mounded ridge. Hill the potato rows again two to three weeks later.

Hilling creates an area of loose soil where tubers can easily form and shades the potato tubers from the sun.

Harvesting

Harvest small, 1- to 2-inch-diameter new potatoes six to eight weeks after planting, usually when the plants are flowering. Use a small digging fork to loosen the soil and lift the small tubers by hand, then replace the soil. Be careful not to stab the fork into the potatoes, thereby damaging them.

You can enjoy potatoes all summer. Dig up a few potatoes from each plant, but don't harvest all of them at once. Once the potato plant tops start dying back, harvest them all. Dig and lift the entire plant with a garden fork and pull off the tubers.

Sort tubers after harvest. Separate the damaged tubers into a pile for eating first. Tubers that have been nicked or punctured during harvest can be eaten immediately but won't be good for long-term storage. Gently remove the loose soil from around the tubers.

Cure harvested potatoes unwashed in a dark, humid place at 65°F to 70°F for two weeks. Then move the potatoes to a cool, dark, humid cellar, shed, or garage to store at 40°F to 50°F for up to nine months, depending on the potato variety. Don't allow the potatoes to freeze while in storage.

YOU
_ SHOULD KNOW _
Potatoes form below the soil surface, but they are not roots. They are specialized underground storage stems called tubers.

VARIETIES

1. DARK RED NORLAND produces oblong tubers with red skin and white flesh. Tasty harvested as new potatoes, the variety is resistant to scab and foliar diseases. Early.

2. YUKON GOLD has yellow skin and moist yellow flesh; the plant is drought-tolerant and very productive. Early.

3. RED CLOUD has crimson skin and dry white flesh. It stores well. Midseason.

4. CARIBE is grown for its blue-purple skin and pure-white flesh. This variety is good harvested as a new potato. Early.

5. ALL BLUE is an heirloom with unique blue skin and moist purple flesh. It is excellent for purple mashed potatoes. Late.

6. RUSSIAN BANANA is a fingerling type with a banana shape and yellow skin and flesh. The tuber's waxy texture makes it a good boiling potato. Late.

7. BUTTE is a classic Idaho baking potato with russet skin and white flesh. Butte has 20 percent more protein and 58 percent more vitamin C than other varieties. Late.

VARIETIES

1. HOWDEN is a classic big pumpkin with defined ribs that is good for carving. Two or three fruits, each 20–30 pounds. Deep orange. 115 days.

2. BABY BEAR is a mini pumpkin with flesh good enough for pies. The seeds are good for roasting. 8 to 10 fruits, each 1–2 pounds. Deep orange. 105 days.

3. BABY BOO is a decorative mini pumpkin that is 2–3 inches in diameter. Harvest before the skin turns yellow. 8 to 10 fruits. White. 90 days.

4. DILL'S ATLANTIC GIANT produces the largest pumpkins, some more than 1,000 pounds. It requires a lot of space. Pink-orange. 120 days.

5. LONG ISLAND CHEESE is a flattened, ribbed pumpkin that resembles a cheese wheel. It has deep-orange flesh and is good for pies. Two fruits, each 6–10 pounds. Tan. 108 days.

6. LUMINA is creamy white with smooth skin and orange flesh. Three or four fruits, each 10 pounds. White. 85 days.

7. SMALL SUGAR is an heirloom favored for pies and canning. Three or four fruits, each 5–8 pounds. Orange. 100 days.

Pumpkin
Cucurbita species

From tiny white pumpkins to massive jack-o'-lanterns, pumpkins come in all shapes, sizes, and flavors. If you grow pumpkins for cooking and baking, be sure to choose a variety bred for flavor.

Planting & Growing

Plant in full sun and well-drained soil. Good drainage is important. Plants languish in poorly drained soil, and fruits are more likely to rot when they rest in wet or boggy soil. Pumpkins grow best in soil high in organic matter. Incorporate a 2-inch-thick layer of compost into the soil prior to planting.

Sow seeds in the garden when the daytime air temperature consistently reaches 70°F. In cool-summer areas, start seeds indoors four weeks before your last frost date, and transplant the seedlings after the danger of frost has passed. Starting seeds indoors ensures that winter squash has adequate time to mature in cool-summer areas. Sow seeds 2 to 4 feet apart in rows 5 to 8 feet apart. Or plant five to seven seeds in hills spaced 4 feet apart, thinning to three plants per hill after true leaves form.

Apply 1 to 2 inches of water per week, increasing frequency during dry periods. Mulch plants with an organic mulch, such as straw or grass clippings, after the soil has warmed. Once pumpkin vines start running, fertilize plants with a high-nitrogen fertilizer. In cool-summer areas, pinch off blossoms and small fruits that form late in the season. These won't have time to mature before frost and will take energy away from the existing maturing fruits.

Harvesting

Leave pumpkins on the vine until they reach a mature size and turn the appropriate skin color for their variety. The rind will feel hard when you press it with your thumbnail. Harvest fruits before a hard frost. Use a clean, sharp knife to cut the stems 2 inches above the fruits. Place pumpkins in an 80°F to 85°F, humid room for two weeks to cure. Store them in a dark location at 50°F to 55°F. Most pumpkins can be stored for two to three months.

Radish

Raphanus sativus

Ready to harvest 25 to 30 days after planting, radishes are a fun crop to grow in early spring. They require just a few inches of space and are perfect for small-space gardens and container plantings.

Planting & Growing

There are several types of radishes for home gardens:

Spring radishes mature quickly and grow best during cool conditions.

Round red radishes with crunchy texture and hot, spicy flavor are most familiar.

French radishes, cylindrical types that mature earlier than round radishes, have white skin and red skin tipped in white.

Winter radishes grow into large round or elongated roots. Slower to develop than spring radishes, they remain crisp longer, are more pungent, and can hold in the ground longer.

For best yields, plant in full sun and well-drained soil. Radishes will tolerate some shade. Incorporate a 2-inch-thick layer of compost into the soil before planting. Rake the soil smooth, removing any rocks or debris, to promote good radish formation. Sow seeds in the garden three to four weeks before the last average frost in spring and six weeks before the first frost in fall. Make successive sowings every week or two in spring to extend the harvest. Winter radishes can be sown in midsummer for fall harvest.

Sow seeds ½ inch deep and 1 inch apart in rows 10 inches apart. Interplant carrots, beans, and cucumbers with radishes to maximize your planting space. Thin small-root regular spring radishes to 2 inches apart when they are 1 inch tall.

Harvesting

Harvest spring radishes as soon as the roots are large enough to eat. Radishes left in the ground too long can crack, become woody, develop a seed stalk, and have a hot flavor. Harvest winter radishes when they reach full size. Store both types of radishes in the refrigerator.

YOU
_ SHOULD KNOW _
Radish foliage is edible and lends a slight peppery flavor to salads. Save thinned seedlings and the tops of mature radishes to spice up a bowl of greens.

VARIETIES

1. CHERRY BELL is an exceptionally fast-growing spring variety that produces round, red radishes. 22 days.

2. FRENCH BREAKFAST is a spring radish that has oblong red roots with white tips; it tolerates warm temperatures well. 23 days.

3. APRIL CROSS is a 12- to 16-inch-long white winter radish that is best planted in fall for spring to early summer harvest. 55 days.

Rhubarb
Rheum rhabarbarum

Exceptionally hardy, rhubarb is a bold, long-lasting plant in the edible landscape. Its large leaves remain dark green through mid- to late summer. Rhubarb is ideal for pies, tarts, and jams.

Planting & Growing

Plant rhubarb in full sun and moist, well-drained soil. Be sure to plant it where it will not be disturbed because it can be productive for many years. A perennial bed or shrub bed makes a fine planting place for rhubarb.

Plant crowns in early spring as soon as the ground can be worked. Plant so the central bud is 2 inches below the soil line. Space the crowns 6 feet apart.

Spread a 2-inch-thick layer of compost around new plants when the air temperature rises above 80°F. Keep the soil evenly moist and weed-free. Cut off any flower stalks that develop down to the base of the plant. Rhubarb thrives with adequate soil nutrients. Apply a complete plant fertilizer annually in spring. After harvest, spread a 2-inch-layer of compost around plants.

When the leafstalks become thin (usually after six to eight years), dig and divide the plant in spring or fall. Divide the crown so the new plant has some buds and a generous amount of roots, then replant. Keep divided plants well-watered the first year.

Harvesting

Rhubarb leafstalks develop the best color and flavor when harvested during cool weather. Leave first-year plants unharvested. During the second year, harvest with a sharp knife or break stalks off by holding them close to the base and pulling down and to one side. Remove the leaves. Harvest for one week. In the third year, harvest all stalks larger than 1 inch wide for eight weeks.

Compost the leaves; although the leafstalks are completely edible, rhubarb leaves contain oxalic acid and are poisonous.

Store unwashed leafstalks in a plastic bag in the refrigerator for up to two weeks.

VARIETIES

1. VALENTINE has deep red stalks; it grows faster than other red varieties and can be harvested sooner.

2. MACDONALD is a high-yielding variety with green stems that have red overtones; it grows well in heavy clay soils.

3. CANADA RED is a popular variety with long, thick stalks that are extra sweet.

Rutabaga, Swede turnip

Brassica napus

A cross between a cabbage and a turnip, rutabaga produces large roots and bitter leaves. The roots, with white or yellow flesh, have a sweet, nutty flavor when they mature in cool weather.

Planting & Growing

Plant in full sun or part shade and loose, well-drained soil. Rutabagas don't require rich soil and will readily adapt to a variety of growing conditions, including containers. Choose a pot that is at least 12 inches deep. Before planting, remove rocks and debris from the soil to promote smooth, round rutabagas.

Sow seeds in the garden four weeks before the last frost date in spring for an early summer crop or 90 to 100 days before the first fall frost for an autumn crop. In warm-summer areas, rutabaga produces larger roots and tastes sweeter when sown in midsummer for harvest in fall. Sow seeds ½ inch deep and 2 inches apart in rows about 24 inches apart.

Thin seedlings to 8 inches apart once true leaves form. Hand-weed the bed. Mulch with a 2- to 3-inch-thick layer of organic material such as straw after weeding to maintain soil moisture and to keep the soil cool. Provide plants with 1 to 2 inches of water per week, especially during periods of hot, dry weather.

Harvesting

Pull rutabaga roots when they are 3 to 5 inches in diameter, about 90 days after seeding. Fall-grown roots taste sweeter if exposed to a few frosts before harvest. Because rutabaga can withstand frost, pick only what you need that day and leave the rest in the garden.

To store rutabaga, trim off the foliage with a sharp knife to within 1 inch of the crown. The roots can be stored for two to four months at 35°F and high humidity. You can also store rutabaga in the garden during winter by mulching the bed with a 6- to 8-inch-thick layer of straw in fall.

YOU
— SHOULD KNOW —
Rutabagas are used much like potatoes in cooking. Peel and dice the roots and add them to soups and stews; mash or steam them for a side dish.

VARIETIES

1. PURPLE TOP features huge yellow roots with fine-grain flesh that turns orange when cooked. 90 days.

2. MARIAN, which has pale purple shoulders, keeps well and is disease-resistant. 90 days.

3. LAURENTIAN roots have dark purple shoulders with pale yellow skin below and sweet, mild flesh. 95 days.

Spinach
Spinacia oleracea

Scrumptious in a fresh salad and lovely in the garden, spinach is a plant for the edible landscape. Plant spinach through a perennial border, or use it as a tiny, tidy hedge around a plot of early-season vegetables. Plant a late-summer crop for harvest in fall.

Planting & Growing

Try several different types of spinach in your garden:

Smooth-leaf spinach produces relatively flat leaves that are easy to wash and clean after harvesting.

Crinkle-leaf or savoy spinach has highly textured leaves with more body than smooth-leaf types.

Plant in full sun or part shade and moist, well-drained soil. Spinach grows well in containers. It grows best in soil that has generous amounts of organic matter. Mix a 2-inch-thick layer of compost into the soil before planting.

Begin sowing seeds in the garden four to six weeks before your last spring frost date. Spinach seeds can germinate in soils as cool as 35°F. If the soil was prepared in fall, seeds can be scattered over frozen ground or snow cover in late winter, and they will germinate as the soil thaws. In warm areas, plant seeds in fall to harvest during winter. To speed germination, soak seeds in warm water overnight. Sow seeds ¼ inch deep and 1 inch apart in rows 12 inches apart, or scatter seeds in a raised bed. If you are planting a fall crop, chill the seeds in the refrigerator for one to two weeks before planting.

Thin seedlings to 6 inches apart when they're 3 inches tall. Maintain cool, moist soil by watering regularly and mulching with a 2- to 3-inch-thick layer of an organic material such as straw. It's best to water in the morning so the leaves can dry before evening.

Harvesting

Begin harvesting individual leaves 20 to 30 days after sowing, when there are five or six leaves on the plant. Harvest whole plants in 35 to 50 days. Harvest leaves until hot weather causes seed stalks to form. Store spinach leaves in a plastic bag in the refrigerator.

VARIETIES

1. BLOOMSDALE LONG STANDING is a classic crinkle-leaf variety that's quick-growing and slow to bolt. 42 days.

2. OLYMPIA is a smooth-leaf variety that is slow to bolt, disease-resistant, and productive. 45 days.

3. ORIENTAL GIANT produces large, smooth 12- to 15-inch-long leaves and yields up to three times more foliage than other varieties. 40 days.

Squash
Cucurbita species

Squash plants are some of the most productive vegetables in the garden. They produce several pounds of fruit and edible flowers. There are options for small-space gardens and containers.

Planting & Growing

Plant in full sun and well-drained soil. Good drainage is very important when growing squash. Not only do plants languish in poorly drained soil, but fruits are more likely to rot when they rest on wet or boggy ground. Squash grows best in soil that is high in organic matter. Add a 2-inch-thick layer of compost into the soil.

Sow seeds in the garden when the daytime air temperature consistently reaches 70°F. In cool-summer areas, start seeds indoors four weeks before your last frost date and transplant the seedlings after the danger of frost has passed.

Plant seeds of bush varieties of summer and winter squash 1 to 2 inches deep and 2 to 3 feet apart in rows spaced 3 to 5 feet apart. For vining varieties, sow seeds 2 to 4 feet apart in rows 5 to 8 feet apart. Or plant five to seven seeds in hills spaced 4 feet apart, thinning to the three strongest plants per hill after true leaves form. Squash requires a constant supply of moisture. Apply 1 to 2 inches of water per week; increase the frequency during dry periods. Once squash vines start running, fertilize plants with a high-nitrogen fertilizer.

Harvesting

Zucchini, crooknecks, and straightnecks taste best when picked small, about 6 inches long. Pattypan, or scallop, squash is best harvested when the fruit is 3 inches across. Store the squash for up to two weeks in the refrigerator. Leave winter squash on the vine until they reach a mature size and turn the appropriate skin color for that variety. The rind will feel hard when you press it with your thumbnail. Harvest fruits before a hard frost. Place winter squash in an 80°F to 85°F, humid room for two weeks to cure. Store them in a dark location at 50°F to 55°F. Most winter squash can be stored for two to three months under these conditions.

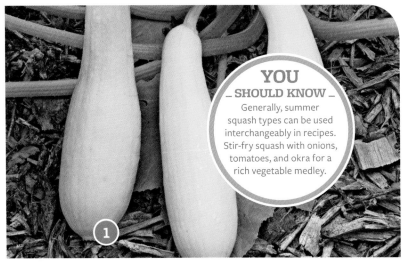

YOU _SHOULD KNOW_
Generally, summer squash types can be used interchangeably in recipes. Stir-fry squash with onions, tomatoes, and okra for a rich vegetable medley.

SUMMER SQUASH VARIETIES

1. **YELLOW STRAIGHTNECK** is a bush straightneck type. Creamy yellow. 50 days.

2. **BLACK BEAUTY** is a zucchini type with excellent smooth, straight fruits. Dark green. 60 days.

3. **SUNBURST** produces pattypan-type fruit that is very tender. The vigorous plant is easy to grow and productive. Deep yellow. 52 days.

4. **EARLY SUMMER CROOKNECK** is a striking heirloom with bumpy skin. It produces many fruits over a long season. Yellow. 53 days.

WINTER SQUASH VARIETIES

5. **RED KURI** is a hubbard type with a teardrop shape. Two or three fruits, each 4–7 pounds. Red orange. 92 days.

6. **SWEET DUMPLING** is a delicata type with teacup-shape fruits with sweet orange flesh. 8–10 fruits, each 4 inches wide. Ivory with dark green stripes. 100 days.

7. **WALTHAM** is a cylindrical, 9-inch-diameter butternut type with sweet orange flesh. Four or five fruits, each 4–5 pounds. Tan. 105 days.

Sweet potato
Ipomoea batatas

Easy-to-grow sweet potatoes require a long, frost-free growing season to mature large roots. The plant's thick storage roots are high in vitamin A and can be stored into the winter.

Planting & Growing

Plant in full sun and well-drained soil. Grow plants in a raised bed if soil drainage is poor. Sweet potatoes are normally started from small plants called slips that are planted in the garden two weeks after the last average frost date. Create a 6- to 12-inch-high raised bed, and amend the soil with a 2- to 3-inch-thick layer of compost. Plant certified disease-free sweet potato slips 12 to 18 inches apart in rows 4 feet apart for vining plants and 30 inches for bush types.

In cool-summer areas, lay black plastic over the raised bed two weeks before planting time to warm the soil, and plant the slips into holes poked in the plastic at the appropriate spacing.

Keep the area around plants weed-free until the vines begin to run and can crowd out competing plants. Then mulch around plants with a 2- to 3-inch-thick layer of organic material. Keep the slips well-watered for the first few weeks and consistently moist until the last month of growth. Reduce watering three to four weeks before harvesting to avoid root rot.

Harvesting

Most sweet potato varieties can be harvested beginning 90 days after planting. Harvest after the vines are lightly frosted and the leaves show a little yellowing. Plants left in the ground too long will either rot from the cold soil temperatures or, in warmer areas, continue to grow larger roots. With a garden fork, carefully dig up the vines and separate the sweet potato roots.

Cure for one to two weeks in a room with high humidity and a temperature of 80°F to 90°F. Store cured roots wrapped in newspaper in a dry location at 55°F to 60°F. Allow roots to sit a few weeks before you begin eating them. Starches begin converting to sugar in storage; it takes six to eight weeks for sweet potatoes to develop sweetness.

VARIETIES

1. CENTENNIAL is a fast-maturing vining type with red skin and orange flesh. This variety is good for Northern gardens. 90 days.

2. GEORGIA JET is a productive vining variety with red skin and orange flesh. 100 days.

3. VARDAMAN is a bush variety with golden skin and deep orange flesh. 95 days.

Tomatillo, husk tomato

Physalis ixocarpa

A relative of tomato, tomatillo is a Central America native that has been used in cooking for thousands of years. It is a key ingredient in stews, moles, and salsas.

Planting & Growing

Plant in full sun and moist, well-drained soil. Tomatillos grow best in nutrient-rich soil. Amend the planting area with a 2-inch-thick layer of compost prior to planting. Tomatillos do well in containers. Grow this top-heavy plant in a large, sturdy container.

Set transplants in the garden after the last average frost date. Promote a sturdy plant by pinching off the lowest leaves and burying the stem of the transplant so only the top leaves are aboveground. Roots will emerge along the buried stem. Space transplants 36 inches apart. Tomatillos can also be started from seeds planted eight weeks before the last average frost date.

Keep the soil well-weeded and moist. Mulch with a 2- to 4-inch-thick layer of organic mulch, such as straw, after the soil has warmed to suppress weeds and maintain soil moisture. Mature plants are drought-tolerant.

Fertilize plants with a complete low-nitrogen fertilizer such as 5-10-10 at planting. Use the same fertilizer to sidedress plants once the fruits form, and then fertilize monthly. Tomatillo plants benefit from trellising. They naturally sprawl across the soil. Use a tomato cage or stake to keep the branches and fruits off the ground.

Harvesting

For the best flavor, harvest tomatillos when the papery husk changes from green to tan while the fruit is still green. Use a sharp knife to harvest the fruits. In cool-summer areas, remove the whole plant if frost is forecast, suspending it upside down in a sheltered place to mature the remaining fruits.

Store harvested tomatillos in their husks for up to two weeks in the refrigerator.

YOU SHOULD KNOW

Tomatillo's sweet, tart, and somewhat citrusy flavor is often used to counteract the hottest of chile peppers in many dishes.

VARIETIES

1. TOMA VERDE is an early variety with green fruits that turn yellow at maturity. 60 days.

2. PURPLE, which stores well, features purple skins and very sweet purple-tinged flesh that makes unique-color salsa. 65 days.

3. DE MILPA is an heirloom with small green fruits blushed with purple. 70 days.

Tomato
Lycopersicon esculentum

Whether you enjoy them sliced, stuffed, grilled, dried, juiced, or simply fresh off the vine, the flavor of homegrown tomatoes can't be beat. Tomatoes are the most popular garden vegetable.

Planting & Growing

Tomato plants vary in their growth habit by category:

Determinate tomatoes are small, compact plants. They grow to a certain height, stop, then flower and set all their fruit at once. Since all their fruit ripens within a week or two, determinate varieties are good for preserving.

Indeterminate varieties grow, flower, and set fruit until they are killed by frost. Harvest from an indeterminate variety usually extends over a two- to three-month period, and the yield is generally greater than in determinate varieties.

So what type should you choose? If you are growing tomatoes for immediate enjoyment, choose an indeterminate variety, such as 'Early Girl' and many of the heirlooms, for a long, delicious harvest. If you plan to make and can salsa, plant a few determinate plants, such as 'Celebrity', to ensure you have tomatoes ripe at one time.

While growth-habit designations are useful, a more helpful classification system for this favorite summer fruit is based on taste, fruit size, and growth. The following pages include groups of tomatoes prized for these endearing factors. Heirloom tomatoes offer unique taste, shape, and texture and vary widely from the standard red-orb tomato that was popular for many years. Heirlooms often perish quickly after harvest, but when eaten at perfect ripeness, their flavor trumps that of nearly any other tomato variety.

Thanks to their recently rediscovered delicious taste and lovely shapes and colors, heirloom tomatoes are becoming easier to find. Mass merchants often carry a limited line of heirloom species. Local garden centers are also a good place to look for heirlooms. If you don't see what you are looking for, don't hesitate to ask the staff to grow some heirlooms next season.

Slicers are a group of tomatoes with medium to large fruits that are often sliced horizontally for topping burgers and sandwiches.

HEIRLOOM VARIETIES

1. BRANDYWINE is a popular, pink-skin tomato with soft flesh and full flavor. It has yellow and red versions. 12–16 ounces. 80 days.

2. CHEROKEE PURPLE is a Tennessee heirloom with flavorful, soft-texture, rose-purple skin and red flesh. Highly perishable. 10–12 ounces. 72 days.

3. YELLOW PEAR bears small pear-shape fruits with a sweet flavor. 1–2 ounces. 78 days.

Often red, but also available in yellow and green varieties, slicers tend to be disease-resistant and easy to grow. Some of the most popular backyard tomatoes, including 'Better Boy' and 'Celebrity', are in the slicer group.

Small-fruit tomatoes, also called grape and cherry tomatoes, make perfect snacks. These bite-size tomatoes are packed with flavor and sweet tomato juice. Available in shades of red and yellow, small-fruit tomatoes are often very prolific. One plant can produce several pounds of fruit from midsummer until frost.

Paste tomatoes are typically used for canning whole or making ketchup, paste, and sauces. Their solid, meaty, low-moisture flesh simplifies preserving. Paste-type plants are usually short and set many fruits that ripen all at once. Container tomatoes are short, stocky plants that are easy to grow in hanging baskets and pots. These productive plants often produce small to medium-size fruit, and some varieties require staking to remain upright when loaded with fruit late in the season.

Plant in full sun and well-drained soil. Tomatoes need at least eight hours of direct sunlight a day to produce fruit. Plants need consistent moisture, but they do not tolerate waterlogged soil. If your soil is slow to drain, plant tomatoes in a container or raised bed.

Soil rich in organic matter produces the best tomatoes. Mix a 2-inch-thick layer of compost into your planting site in early spring.

Avoid diseases by not planting tomatoes or other members of the tomato family (eggplant, pepper, potato, and tomatillo) in the same location more than once every three years. Do not plant tomatoes near walnut trees. Tomatoes are particularly susceptible to juglone—a chemical compound found in walnuts.

Plant transplants in the garden after the last average frost date. Although seeds can be directly sown in the garden and plants grown to maturity in warm areas, most gardeners buy transplants or start seeds indoors six to eight weeks before their average last frost date.

When shopping for tomato plants at your local nursery, look for short, stocky plants with dark green foliage. Avoid tall, lanky plants, as they have been growing in their container too long and will take longer to establish in the garden.

Plant small bush varieties 24 inches apart and larger varieties,

SLICER VARIETIES

1. SOLDACKI is a Polish heirloom variety with intense flavor. It has dark pink flesh and produces massive fruits. 24–32 ounces. 80 days.

2. CELEBRITY is a productive and widely adapted cultivar with meaty, red fruits that ripen uniformly. It is good for canning and preserving. A bush form is available. 8–12 ounces. 72 days.

3. BIG BEEF has large yields of uniform red fruit. It produces until frost and has great disease resistance. 10–12 ounces. 73 days.

SMALL-FRUIT VARIETIES

4. SUPER SWEET 100 is an improved version of the classic cherry variety. This vigorous plant has large yields. 1 ounce. 65 days.

5. GOLD NUGGET produces seedless golden fruits on a compact plant. It is a good choice for containers. 1–2 ounces. 60 days.

6. BLACK CHERRY is an heirloom with large cherry-size fruits. It has striking black-red skin and flesh and a complex flavor. 2–3 ounces. 65 days.

especially sprawling indeterminate plants, 36 to 48 inches apart in rows 36 inches apart.

Tomato transplants should be planted deeper than other vegetables. While most plants are transplanted so the top of the soil in their container is level with surrounding garden soil, tomatoes, and their relatives tomatillos, are unique. They can form roots along their stems. The extra roots help anchor the plant and provide more opportunity for water and nutrient uptake, which is especially helpful when starting with tall, leggy transplants.

Prune off the transplant's bottom leaves and set the root ball in a planting hole deep enough so that only the top cluster of leaves is showing aboveground. If the transplant is exceptionally tall, try laying the stem horizontally along a 4- to 6-inch-deep trench in the soil. Turn the uppermost portion of the stem vertically so the top cluster of leaves pokes out of the soil.

After planting, stake or cage all tomatoes with the exception of small bush or patio varieties, which can often support themselves. Waiting a few weeks after planting to install stakes or cages can injure the plant's roots. Cages and stakes keep tomatoes off the ground, helping to prevent fruit rot and numerous diseases.

Tomato cages are typically made of heavy-gauge wire and stand 5 to 6 feet tall. Purchase tomato cages at a garden center or fashion your own out of heavy wire fencing. Firmly anchor the cages to the ground with stakes to keep the plants from blowing over and uprooting themselves during storms. They should have openings wide enough for your hand to reach inside to harvest.

Stakes are another way to help tomatoes stand tall. They need to be at least 8 feet high and 1 inch wide. Pound the stake at least 12 inches into the ground and 4 inches from the plant. Attach the stem to the stake with garden twine, self-adhesive fabric, or strips of cloth.

If desired, fertilize plants monthly with a balanced plant food such as 5-5-5 when the first tomatoes are about the size of golf balls.

After the soil has warmed, mulch plants with a 2- to 3-inch-thick layer of organic mulch, such as straw or finely shredded wood chips, to prevent weeds and to maintain soil moisture. Mulch is also

PASTE VARIETIES

1. AMISH PASTE is an heirloom paste variety with juicy, meaty fruits prized for their intense flavor. 5–7 ounces. 85 days.

2. ITALIAN HEIRLOOM is a popular canning tomato that is easy to peel and has few seeds. Unlike other paste tomatoes, it does not have a plumlike shape. The meaty fruit is large and round. 10–12 ounces. 75 days.

3. ROMA is a standard paste tomato with meaty fruit. It is widely adapted and easy to grow. 2–3 ounces. 78 days.

valuable for preventing soil and soilborne diseases from splashing onto leaves when it rains. At the end of the season, enrich the soil by tilling in the mulch. It will decompose and add valuable nutrients for next season.

Tomatoes grow best when they have consistent moisture. If it rains less than 1 inch per week, supplement by watering. To prevent diseases, avoid wetting the foliage. Use a watering can or wand to deliver water directly to the root zones, or use a drip irrigation system.

Harvesting

Pick fruits when they are firm, full-size, and fully colored. Tomatoes mature and ripen best at temperatures close to 75°F. When the temperature rises about 90°F, the fruits soften and develop poor color. Tomatoes will ripen when picked at their green mature size.

Before a killing frost, harvest all but the greenest fruits and bring them indoors to a 60°F to 65°F room, and wrap them individually in a sheet of newspaper. Check the fruits once a week for ripeness, and remove any tomatoes that are decayed or not showing signs of ripening. Also, whole plants can be uprooted and hung in a warm, sheltered location, where the fruits can continue to ripen.

Once picked, ripe fruits can be stored for up to two weeks at 55°F. They can also be stored in the refrigerator but will not taste as good as those stored at cool room temperature.

Freeze or can tomatoes in summer and lend your wintertime meals garden-fresh taste. Canning tomatoes involves sterilized jars, a hot-water bath, many pounds of tomatoes, and a few hours of your time. Freezing, on the other hand, is a relatively quick and easy process and is an efficient way to preserve four or 40 tomatoes.

Whether you choose to freeze or can tomatoes, the skins are generally removed prior to preservation. To easily peel a fresh tomato, dip the fruit in near-boiling water for about 1 minute, depending upon the skin thickness. Remove the tomato from the water and allow it to cool slightly. The skin should easily peel away.

CONTAINER VARIETIES

1. **PATIO** produces medium-size red fruits on a 2-foot-tall plant. This variety has excellent flavor. 3–4 ounces. 72 days.

2. **BUSH EARLY GIRL** is a compact, 2-foot-tall version of the popular 'Early Girl' with the same size fruit and excellent productivity. 6–7 ounces. 54 days.

3. **TINY TIM** grows just 18 inches tall. It produces grape-size red tomatoes that are excellent for salads. 1 ounce. 60 days.

Turnip
Brassica rapa Rapifera group

Large, round turnip roots are smooth on the outside and meaty on the inside. Flavor is best when turnips mature in cool weather, so plant the crop in early spring or late summer.

Planting & Growing

Plant in full sun or part shade and well-drained soil. Turnips grow best in fertile soil. Mix a 2-inch-thick layer of compost into the garden bed before planting. Loose, rock-free soil produces the best turnips. Sow turnip seeds in the garden four weeks before the last frost date in spring for an early summer crop, and 60 to 70 days before the first frost in fall for an autumn crop. For the best flavor, plant turnips in midsummer for a fall crop. The roots will sweeten in the cool weather.

Plant seeds ½ inch deep and 2 inches apart for large roots and 1 inch apart for small roots in rows 12 inches apart. Thin turnip seedlings to 3 to 4 inches apart when they are 4 inches tall. The thinnings can be eaten as greens.

Keep the soil evenly moist, applying at least 1 inch of water a week. Cultivate lightly when the roots are young, and apply a 2- to 3-inch-thick layer of organic mulch, such as straw, around the roots to maintain soil moisture, keep the soil cool, and deter weeds.

Harvesting

If you plant turnips for greens, harvest the tops as needed when they are 4 to 6 inches tall. Leave the growth point in the center when you're picking individual leaves, and the plants will continue to produce greens and roots. Harvest sweet young turnip roots for salads when they are 2 inches in diameter. Allow some roots to mature to 3 to 4 inches in diameter for cooking and winter storage. Turnip roots taste sweeter when exposed to a light frost.

To store turnip roots, trim off the foliage to within 1 inch of the crown. The roots can be stored for two to four months at 35ºF and in high humidity. You can also store turnips in the garden until the ground freezes by mulching with a 6- to 8-inch-thick layer of straw.

VARIETIES

1. SHOGOIN has tender, mild greens and tasty young roots. 42 days.

2. PURPLE TOP WHITE GLOBE is a 3- to 4-inch round root that's white below the soil line and purple above it. It has tender, crisp white flesh. 50 days.

3. SCARLET QUEEN RED STEM produces slightly fattened, red-skin roots with mild white flesh. Its red stems are attractive in salads, and it also has a green-stem variety. 43 days.

Watermelon

Citrullus lanatus

Watermelon is one of summer's sweetest treats. A long, warm growing season especially favors this crop, but gardeners in northern areas can grow melons when they choose early varieties.

Planting & Growing

Plant in full sun and well-drained soil. Watermelons grow best in highly fertile soil. Incorporate a 2-inch-thick layer of compost in the soil before planting.

If your growing season is long and hot, sow seeds directly in the garden two weeks after your last average frost date in spring when the soil temperature is at least 70°F. Sow seeds in hills 6 feet apart, with six seeds per hill. Sow seeds ½ inch deep. In a cool-weather climate, start seeds indoors in peat pots four to six weeks before the last average frost. Set outside two weeks after the last frost, planting three plants per hill.

Thin direct-seeded plants to three plants per hill after the first set of true leaves forms. When the vines are 12 to 24 inches long, thin again and keep only one or two of the most vigorous vines per hill. Keep plants well-watered, applying at least 1 inch per week and more water during hot, dry, windy periods. The most critical watering periods are when the vines are flowering and fruiting. Hand-weed until the leaves are big enough to shade out weeds.

Keep ripening fruits off the ground by setting them on cardboard, upside-down pots, or pieces of wood. You can hasten ripening by removing vine tips and new flowers when nights grow cool.

Harvesting

Watermelons should be harvested when they are perfectly ripe because they will not ripen off the vine. Use a combination of the following indicators to pick the perfect melon. First, the light green, curly tendrils on the stem near the watermelon usually turn brown and dry when it is ripe. Also, the surface color of the fruit becomes dull. The rind hardens, resists penetration by the thumbnail, and is rough to the touch.

YOU _ SHOULD KNOW _
Because seedless melons do not funnel energy into producing mature seeds, they tend to be sweeter than normal seeded types.

VARIETIES

1. CRIMSON SWEET is an oval melon with sweet red flesh. 15–25 pounds. 85 days.

2. MOON AND STARS is an heirloom with very sweet red flesh and green skin with a yellow moon and stars. 25 pounds. 100 days.

3. YELLOW DOLL has yellow flesh and short vines. Its small fruit is easy to store in the refrigerator. 5–8 pounds. 75 days.

CHAPTER TWELVE

Fruit Encyclopedia

Sweeten your table with fruit crops. From apple to strawberry, the following pages are filled with tips for growing sweet treats in your landscape.

193

199

211

Apple
Malus domestica

Apples are the most widely adapted deciduous fruit trees. This favorite crunchy snack fruit thrives from frigid Zone 3 to nearly tropical Zone 10.

Planting & Growing

Apples are divided into three groups based on when their fruit ripens. Early season varieties are some of the first apples to ripen in mid- to late summer. Midseason apples follow in early fall. Late season apples are the last to ripen, in mid- to late fall. Late season apples often store well; some keep for up to six months.

Standard apple trees grow 20 to 40 feet tall and wide. Scientists have developed dwarfing rootstocks that prevent apple trees from growing to such heights. For easy harvest and pruning, choose a 10-foot-tall dwarf apple cultivar or a 15-foot-tall semidwarf cultivar. Bred to be shorter than standard varieties, dwarf and semidwarf apples produce the same size fruit as standard varieties but often fruit earlier and are easier to care for and harvest. Most common apple varieties are available in these smaller forms.

Generally, apples are considered self-incompatible, meaning they cannot pollinate themselves or any flowers of the same variety. The best fruit is harvested when cross-pollination occurs. Ensure cross-pollination by planting two different apple trees that bloom at the same time and have compatible pollen. Two early season varieties usually pollinate each other well, as do two midseason varieties and so on. There are some exceptions. A few varieties, such as 'Winesap', 'Mutsu', and 'Stayman', produce sterile pollen and will not pollinate themselves or any other apple; other apple trees can pollinate them.

Ample sunlight is essential. Plant an apple tree where it will receive at least eight hours of direct sunlight per day. Take the growth of nearby trees into consideration. Apple trees can live 50 years or more; do not plant them where nearby trees will cast shade in years to come. Apples are hardy in Zones 3 to 10.

Plant bare-root trees in late winter or early spring. Plant container-grown trees anytime during the growing season.

EARLY-SEASON VARIETIES

1. **EIN SHEMER** is a yellow variety with crisp, sweet-tart flesh. Pollinate with 'Dorsett Golden'. Zones 8–10.

2. **ANNA,** a very early green apple with a red blush, is crisp and sweet. Pollinate with 'Ein Shemer'. Zones 8–10.

3. **EMPIRE** has dark red skin and creamy white, tart flesh. Pollinate with 'Freedom' or 'Liberty'. Zones 4–8.

To plant a bare-root tree, dig a hole wide and deep enough that the roots are not crowded or bent. Plant so the graft (bulging area low on the trunk) is at least 2 inches above the soil to prevent the stem from rooting. Space trees as far apart as they will be tall when mature, or as close as 6 feet for hedgerows. Refill the planting hole with the excavated soil, forming a basin around the trunk for water.

Plant a container-grown tree by digging a hole as deep as the container and slightly wider. Remove the tree from the pot and place it in the hole so that the graft (bulging area low on the trunk) is at least 2 inches above the soil to prevent the stem from rooting. Using the excavated soil, backfill the planting hole, tamping the soil as you go to prevent air pockets. Water newly planted trees for at least six weeks after planting, longer if the weather is dry. Aim to moisten soil to the depth of 12 to 18 inches.

In early summer when apples are about the size of a golf ball, thin them by hand to one apple per cluster or about one for every 6 inches of stem. Thinning will produce large, more uniform fruit and prevent branches from breaking from excess fruit production. If necessary, support fruit-laden branches through summer and until harvest with a sturdy post. The post will prop up the branch and prevent it from breaking under the weight of the developing fruit.

Apple trees don't require fertilization for good growth, but fruit yield can be improved with an annual application of compost or a balanced fertilizer. If using compost, spread a 2-inch-thick layer of compost over the soil under the canopy in early spring. Or fertilize using a 10-10-10 fertilizer product applied at the rate of 1 pound for one-year-old trees, 2 pounds for two-year-old trees, and so on until 5 to 6 pounds are applied per year. In late winter or early spring, prune the tree, removing any broken, crossing, or rubbing branches.

Harvesting

Expect to wait three to five years after planting for your first apple harvest. Fruits ripen 70 to 180 days from bloom, depending on the variety. A ripe apple separates easily from the fruiting spur and has firm flesh. Soft, overripe fruit can still be used in cooking. Late varieties are best for long-term storage at cool room temperature. The best place to store apples is the crisper drawer of the refrigerator; they can stay there for many weeks.

MIDSEASON VARIETIES

1. HONEYCRISP is a popular variety that has a distinct flavor and stores well. Pollinate with 'Empire', 'Liberty', or 'Gala'. Susceptible to fire blight. Zones 3–7.

2. GOLDEN DELICIOUS, prized for its excellent flavor, bears young and annually. It is a self-fertile variety that is a good pollinator to others. Susceptible to many diseases. Zones 5–9.

3. LIBERTY is the most disease-free apple. Very productive, it often requires fruit thinning. Pollinate with 'Honeycrisp'. Zones 3–5.

LATE-SEASON VARIETIES

4. WINESAP has an intense sweet-tart aroma. This heirloom is a heavy producer. Pollinate with 'Empire' or 'Honeycrisp'. 'Winesap' has sterile pollen and will not pollinate other varieties. Zones 5–8.

5. GOLDEN RUSSET is an heirloom with very sweet flesh. It produces good cider. Pollinate with 'Golden Delicious'. Zones 4–5.

6. MUTSU produces large apples good for baking and storage. Pollinate with 'Empire' or 'Liberty'. Mutsu has sterile pollen and will not pollinate other varieties. Zones 4–8.

Apricot
Prunus armeniaca

Apricots are fast-growing small trees. One tree reliably produces more than 100 pounds of fruit in moderate climates. New cultivars make it possible to have fruit in cool climates, too.

Planting & Growing

Plant in full sun and well-drained soil. Apricots bloom in early spring, and flowers are often nipped by frost in cold climates. Prevent frost damage by planting in a site that is protected from winds and frost. A north-facing slope, because it is slow to warm up in the spring and revive dormant trees, is best if spring frosts are a factor. Apricots are hardy in Zones 4 to 10. Plant bare-root trees in late winter or early spring. Plant container-grown trees anytime during the growing season. Space standard-size trees about 25 feet apart, semidwarfs 15 feet, and dwarfs 6 feet.

Prevent late-spring frost damage by covering trees with tarps or sheets if a frost is predicted. Apricot trees do not tolerate drought. Keep the soil consistently moist but never waterlogged. Water deeply every week during warm weather.

Apricots grow best when the area under the canopy is free of grass and weeds. Vegetation competes for water and nutrients, slowing the growth of the tree. Skim away the sod as the canopy expands. To control weeds, spread a 3-inch-thick layer of organic mulch, such as wood chips or compost, in a circle under the tree canopy. Be sure to keep the mulch away from the trunk, where it could cause rot. Replace the mulch annually. After normal fruit drop, thin to the healthiest fruit on each spur and leave about 3 inches between fruits.

Harvesting

The apricot harvest season occurs for two or three weeks anytime from late spring through early summer, depending on the apricot variety, weather, and regional climatic conditions. For the richest flavor, let the fruits ripen on the tree, and pick them once they develop full color with the flesh just starting to soften slightly.

VARIETIES

1. **HARCOT** is a very productive variety with good disease resistance. The medium to large fruits have an excellent flavor. Zones 6–7.

2. **MOONGOLD** is exceptionally hardy and bears medium-size sweet, tangy fruits. It requires another variety for pollination. Zones 4–8.

Avocado

Persea americana

When grown in a moderate to tropical climate, full sun, and well-drained soil, an avocado tree will produce an abundant harvest of rich, buttery fruit. Leathery foliage provides year-round shade.

Planting & Growing

The various types of avocado are Mexican, Guatemalan, and West Indian as well as hybrids of these groups. The Mexican, Guatemalan, and hybrids are best adapted to California and the Southeast. West Indian varieties are best adapted to south Florida and Hawaii. Guatemalan avocados are restricted almost exclusively to frost-free Zone 10.

Plant in full sun and well-drained soil. Avocados are hardy in Zones 9 to 11. The best time to plant avocados is in early fall once the air temperature has begun to cool but the soil is still warm. Or plant at any time of the year, except in the high heat of midsummer. Space trees so their canopies will not touch when they reach their mature size.

Fertilize trees with a transplant starter at planting time. Water young trees frequently until well-established, then water only during times of drought. In winter, prune plants to control size. Spread a 3-inch-thick layer of organic mulch under the tree canopy to suppress weeds and prevent soil-moisture loss. Be sure the mulch does not touch the trunk.

Harvesting

Trees usually bear fruit one to five years after planting. Depending on the avocado variety, ripening occurs 6 to 18 months after fruit sets. Because the trees bloom over a long period, fruits will not mature all at once. Use external coloring as a guide to ripeness. Pick the largest, fullest avocados first, using hand pruners to cut the stems. Fruits soften at room temperature in 5 to 10 days.

YOU
— SHOULD KNOW —
It's important to know the mature color of the avocado variety you are growing; it might be medium green, dark green, deep purple, or black when fully ripe.

VARIETIES

1. PINKERTON is a heavy producer that bears small to medium, excellent-quality fruits on a medium, upright tree. Zones 9–11.

2. GWEN is a dwarf tree, growing just 12 to 14 feet tall and bearing small fruits with good flavor. Zones 9–11.

3. HASS is a popular hybrid that produces small to medium fruits with a nutty flavor. Zones 9–11.

Blueberry
Vaccinium species

Flowers in spring, purple berries in summer, and red and yellow color in fall make blueberries an ideal plant for the edible landscape. Use these low-growing or tall woody plants as a hedge or colorful shrubs in a foundation planting or mixed border.

Planting & Growing

The three main kinds are highbush blueberry (*Vaccinium corymbosum*), rabbit-eye blueberry (*V. ashei*), and half-high hybrids of highbush and lowbush (*V. angustifolium*).

Highbush blueberries produce the berries found in most markets. Most varieties grow to 6 feet high or more, though there are varieties that are much lower-growing. These blueberries thrive in the East (particularly around the Great Lakes), the Northeast, and the Northwest. The fruits ripen from late spring to late summer depending on variety.

Lowbush blueberries grow just 1 foot tall and spread by underground stems to form a dense mat.

Half-high hybrids grow 2 to 4 feet high and wide and have greater cold tolerance than highbush berries. They are best adapted to northern climates.

Rabbit-eye blueberries are grown in climates that are too warm for highbush blueberries, mainly in the Southeast. The fruit has thicker skin and less flavor than highbush berries.

Both rabbit-eye and half-high varieties require cross-pollination. Plant at least two varieties of these types of blueberries for best fruit set.

Plant in full sun and moist, well-drained, acidic soil. Blueberries require an acid soil with a pH of 4.0 to 5.5. Test your soil to learn its pH. Note that you would like to grow blueberries on the testing form. A quality soil-testing lab will provide soil test results and recommendations to lower soil pH if necessary. The lab will likely suggest that you incorporate a specific amount of sphagnum peat moss or sulfur to acidify the soil. Blueberries are hardy in Zones 3 to 9.

VARIETIES

1. BLUECROP is a highbush variety and the most popular blueberry. It is more cold-hardy and drought-tolerant than other varieties. Zones 4–8.

2. COVILLE is a vigorous, productive highbush with very large, aromatic, slightly tart berries that hold well on the bush. Canker-resistant. Zones 4–8.

3. ELLIOTT produces medium-size, firm, light blue fruit. This dense highbush is great for the landscape, too. Zones 4–8.

Plant blueberries in early spring where winters are cold and in fall where winters are mild. Plants are available either bare-root or in containers. Space highbush and rabbit-eye varieties 6 feet apart, lowbush 2 feet apart, and half-high 3 to 4 feet apart.

Blueberries are very susceptible to drought. In warm areas without regular summer rainfall, water blueberries weekly, moistening the top 18 inches of soil.

Prune blueberries annually to remove old canes. In the first two years of growth, remove weak, diseased, and damaged canes only. In subsequent years, remove weak, diseased, and damaged canes along with some of the oldest canes. Remove excess young canes to encourage the growth of others, and prune to reduce the density of branches at the top of plants. Canes decline in productivity after five to six years. Rabbit-eye blueberries need little or no pruning.

Fertilize plants every year at flowering time with compost or a low-nitrogen plant food for acid-loving plants, such as one designed for azaleas and rhododendrons.

Harvesting

Blueberries turn from green to pinkish-red to blue, but not all blue ones are fully ripe. Hold a container in one hand and use your other hand to gently loosen ripe berries from the cluster so they drop into the container. Store blueberries unwashed in the refrigerator.

BHG TEST GARDEN TIP
GROW FRUIT IN CONTAINERS

If you don't have the space to grow blueberries in the ground, try them in containers. These small shrubs are low-growing, making them ideal for planting in a large container. Make sure they are sited in full sun. The potting soil you use may need to be amended so the soil pH is appropriate for growing blueberries. In addition to offering fruit in hand on a patio, these small shrubs also provide fall color.

(4)

YOU
— SHOULD KNOW —
Blueberries are easy to freeze. Arrange them in a single layer on a tray. Put the tray in the freezer; as soon as the berries are frozen, place them in containers and put them back in the freezer.

(5)

VARIETIES

4. PATRIOT is a highbush with large clusters of flavorful berries. Its berries are slightly smaller than other varieties. Perfect for eating fresh or making into jams, jellies, and pies. Zones 4–8.

5. JERSEY is an easy-to-grow highbush with medium-size firm fruit that resists cracking and keeps well. Bushes grow 6 to 8 feet tall. Zones 4–8.

6. NORTHCOUNTRY is a half-highbush that produces fruit with sweet, wild blueberry flavor. It is good for northern regions and has sky blue flowers. Zones 3–7.

7. NORTHBLUE is a half-high cultivar that produces large, dark blue fruit that is superior to many highbush varieties. It grows less than 3 feet tall and has attractive, ornamental qualities. It is self-fertile, but yield improves if planted with 'Northcountry'. Zones 3–7.

(6)

(7)

Brambles: blackberry, raspberry

Rubus species

A small patch of brambles—blackberries and raspberries—will easily provide enough berries for a family of four for fresh eating, baking, making jams, and freezing.

Planting & Growing

There are many different types of brambles that you can grow successfully in your backyard.

Red and yellow raspberries are genetically similar plants with 7-foot-long semierect canes. The average plant produces 2 to 3 pounds of tender, juicy fruit in summer or fall, depending on the variety. Red raspberries send out underground shoots and slowly spread from the original planting spot.

Black raspberries, or blackcaps, are borne on trailing thorny canes that reach 8 feet long; these are the least cold-hardy and productive raspberries, and they are more susceptible to diseases. They produce about 2 pounds of fruit per plant.

Purple raspberries are hybrids of red and black raspberries with canes 7 to 8 feet long. Like black raspberries, they do not spread and they produce about 2 pounds of fruit per plant.

Blackberries produce fruit on their two-year-old canes and may be either erect or trailing canes. Blackberries are some of the most productive brambles, producing 5 to 7 pounds of fruit per plant.

Trailing blackberries include marionberry, boysenberry, loganberry, youngberry, and thornless evergreen.

Plant in full sun and moist, well-drained soil. Although brambles tolerate a wide range of soil types, they grow best in soil that drains well. If a well-drained site is not possible, plant brambles in a raised bed that is at least 10 inches tall. Before planting, incorporate a 2-inch-thick layer of compost into the site. Brambles are most productive when they receive 1 to 2 inches of water per week. Consider placing your berry patch near a water source. Brambles are often planted in hills or hedgerows. Plants grown in hills are spaced 4 to 10 feet apart, and weeds are controlled by cultivation

BLACKBERRY VARIETIES

1. **CHESTER** has large, very sweet fruit. The plant is thornless, upright, productive, and resistant to cane blight. It grows well in the South. Zones 5–9.

2. **ROSBOROUGH** bears large, glossy blackberries. This erect, thorny shrub grows well in extreme heat and is drought-tolerant. Zones 5–9.

3. **THORNFREE** has large, tangy, tart blackberries on thornless, semierect stems. It grows best when trellised. It is disease-free. Zones 5–9.

4. **LOGAN** has light-red, tart berries that are prized for their unique flavor. This trailing berry grows best when trellised. Zones 5–9.

5. **MARION** produces large berries with a mild blackberry flavor for weeks on end in midsummer. The trailing canes have many large thorns. It is popular in Washington and Oregon. Zones 7–10.

between and within the row. Plant black and purple raspberries and blackberries in hills. Hedgerows are a good choice for red and yellow raspberries. A hedgerow is a continuous row 12 to 24 inches wide. Brambles are spaced 24 to 26 inches apart within the row. This space-saving planting method is especially good for plants that produce many suckers. Cultivate both sides of the hedgerow to control the brambles' outward spread.

In cold-winter regions, plant brambles 1 inch deeper than they were grown at the nursery. In mild-winter regions, plant them at the same depth they were previously grown. After planting, cut the canes back to 6 inches tall to spur root growth. The plants will not fruit the first season but will produce a small crop the second.

Blackberries and raspberries are biennial. Their canes grow one year, bear fruit, and then die at the end of year two. New canes emerge the following season. Canes of everbearing raspberries begin fruiting the first year in the garden and die the second year.

Annual pruning is essential. The most common downfall of a backyard bramble patch is lack of pruning. In short order, the canes ramble out of control. Each type of bramble has a unique pruning requirement. They are most often pruned in early spring and late summer. Remove weak, diseased, and damaged canes at ground level. Then remove two-year-old canes called floricanes. These canes produced fruit and will die soon if they are not already dead. They will be quickly replaced by new canes called primocanes.

Harvesting

Harvest ripe berries when they taste sweet and are easy to pull from the plant, preferably in the early morning when fruits and plants are dry and cool. Ripe blackberries are easy to identify: They're glossy, soft, and deeply colored. A blackberry's small, soft green core separates from the plant when the fruit is ready to pick. Ripe raspberries will have full color (red, yellow, purple, or black) characteristic of the variety.

Carry berries in shallow trays because they are easily crushed. They also are perishable; keep picked berries in the shade and move them to a cool location as soon as possible.

EVERBEARING VARIETIES

1. HERITAGE is widely adapted with firm, mild-flavor berries. Exceptionally productive, it has strong, upright stems and produces suckers. Zones 4–9.

2. AUTUMN BLISS bears large, firm berries with a mild flavor. It is earlier-fruiting than many other raspberries. It is considered superior to 'Heritage' by some. Zones 3–8.

3. FALL GOLD has large, sweet, soft fruit on upright stems. It is an excellent all-purpose choice best in the Upper South and nearby mountains. Zones 4–8.

SUMMER-BEARING VARIETIES

4. KILLARNEY produces large, high-quality fruit with good flavor. It has strong, thick, upright canes. It is a good all-purpose raspberry. Zones 3–7.

5. ALLEN produces a large crop of glossy, sweet black raspberries. This easy-to-grow cultivar is widely adapted. It is good for jam and jelly. Zones 4–8.

6. ROYALTY has very large, sweet, tangy fruit that ripens late in the season. A vigorous plant, it is immune to the raspberry aphid and resistant to the raspberry fruit worm. It is a good all-purpose raspberry. Zones 4–8.

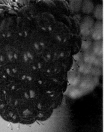

Cherry
Prunus species

Whether you like them sweet or sour, cherries are beautiful fruit trees for the home landscape, and their flowers are a harbinger of spring. One or two trees provide a large-enough crop for plenty of fresh eating as well as preserves.

Planting & Growing

Plant a variety of sweet and sour cherry trees in your yard, and you will have an ongoing supply of fruit for pies, jams, and jellies. Cherries are big producers.

Sweet cherries are more challenging to grow than sour ones. The trees can be big, up to 30 feet tall and wide or more, making maintenance and harvest difficult.

Sweet cherries grow best in mild climates. Spring frosts sometimes damage flower buds, and summer heat over 100°F stops fruit growth. Many sweet cherry varieties require cross-pollination. Be sure to plant two different varieties if necessary.

Standard sour cherry trees are smaller than sweet cherries, topping out at 15 to 20 feet tall and wide. They regularly survive temperatures as low as -35°F and, because they bloom later than sweet cherries, are less likely to be damaged by spring frosts. Sour cherries are self-fruitful and, unlike sweet cherries, do not require a second cultivar planted nearby for fruit production. Both sour and sweet cherry trees are available grafted onto dwarfing rootstocks.

Plant in full sun and fertile, moist, well-drained soil. If late-spring frosts are common in your area, choose a cool, north-facing location if possible to help keep the trees dormant until frost danger is past. Cherries are hardy in Zones 3 to 9.

Cherry trees are available as bare-root trees or container plants. Plant bare-root trees in early spring and container-grown plants anytime during the growing season.

When shopping for a cherry tree, look for a tree that has ample roots for the amount of branches. Opt for a small tree with a large root system rather than a large tree with a small root system. The tree should have a pleasing symmetrical form.

VARIETIES

1. BING is a favorite sweet cherry in the West. Light bearing, it has large, purple, firm, meaty fruit with excellent flavor. Pollinate with 'Montmorency', 'Rainier', or 'Stella'. Susceptible to cracking. Zones 5–9.

2. STELLA is a self-fertile sweet cherry with dark red, juicy fruit. It is vigorous and productive. Moderate crack resistance. Zones 5–9.

3. SWEETHEART has large, sweet, bright red fruit with outstanding flavor. It is self-fertile and very crack resistant. Zones 5–9.

Space standard varieties 25 to 40 feet apart, semidwarfs 15 to 25 feet apart, and dwarfs 8 to 12 feet apart.

Water newly planted trees until they are well-established. Conserve soil moisture and keep the area under the tree canopy weed-free by blanketing the area with a 3-inch-thick layer of organic mulch, being careful not to allow the mulch to touch the trunk.

Prune cherries annually in late winter to remove dead branches or branches that are crossing or rubbing. Cherries can be trained to a central leader or an open center, but it is not essential to good fruit production.

Harvesting

Sweet cherries begin best production in their fifth year and bear fruit in July. Sweet cherries are enjoyed fresh and as a favorite addition to baked goods and preserves.

Sour cherries begin to bear fruit three to four years after planting. Fruits ripen about 60 days after bloom, from late May to early July. Sour cherries are normally used only for cooking and are too tart to eat fresh from the tree. But a few varieties will become sweet if left on the tree until completely ripe.

Store ripe cherries for up to a week in the refrigerator.

(4)

BHG TEST GARDEN TIP

CHERRY TREE HEALTH

Humidity and heat encourage some diseases such as fusarium wilt, rots, and molds. Clean cultural practices are essential to the health of cherry trees. Remove and destroy diseased fruits, leaves, twigs, and branches. Don't compost this debris. To be a successful cherry grower, chose varieties bred for your weather and soil conditions and that exhibit resistance to the pests and diseases that are common in your area.

(5)

(6)

(7)

VARIETIES

4. ULSTER produces sweet, juicy, high-quality fruit. Pollinate with 'Hedelfingen'. Moderate crack resistance. Zones 5–9.

5. DANUBE is a vigorous sour cultivar producing large crops of juicy, dark red fruit with red juice. It is self-fertile. Zones 4–9.

6. MONTMORENCY is a sour cherry with medium to large, bright red, firm, tangy fruit. The tree is self-fertile. Zones 4–9.

7. NORTHSTAR produces small, sour cherries on a naturally dwarf tree. Zones 4–9.

YOU
— SHOULD KNOW —
Oranges are the most popular citrus. Choose a unique cultivar and enjoy tangy sweetness from your own backyard.

Citrus

Citrus species

Long-lasting plants produce juicy, sweet or tart fruit. In addition, citrus trees have glossy evergreen foliage and fragrant flowers.

Planting & Growing

Try these succulent citrus varieties.

Sweet oranges are the most popular citrus. Select early-, mid-, and late-season varieties and enjoy fruit continuously from early November to July. Two or three orange trees produce ample fruit for one family to eat and share. Sweet oranges include common orange, navel orange, and blood orange.

Grapefruit trees are exceptionally productive, and the fruit they produce stores well. One grapefruit tree is usually so prolific that it's all that is needed in a home landscape.

Mandarins, including tangerines and numerous hybrids of tangerines, grapefruit, and oranges, are a good choice if space is limited. Many varieties grow into 10-foot-tall mature trees.

Lemons are easy to grow in the home landscape or even as indoor plants. The vigorous trees respond well to pruning to keep their size manageable. They grow best in dry climates where disease problems are less severe.

Limes are more sensitive to cold than most other citrus. Small-fruit Mexican, West Indian, and Key limes are easy to grow in the home landscape. Large-fruit Persian, or Tahiti, limes are the types most often grown commercially.

Plant in full sun and well-drained soil. Citrus trees are adaptable to many soil types but grow best in light, well-drained soil. In desert climates, plant citrus where it receives some light shade during the hottest part of the day. The shade will prevent the fruit from getting sunburned. In cool climates, plant in the warmest possible microclimate, such as against a light-color south-facing wall. Avoid low spots where cold air can accumulate.

Where winters are mild and summers are hot, plant citrus in fall. Elsewhere, the optimum planting time is early spring after the last frost. Citrus trees are usually sold as container plants.

ORANGE VARIETIES

1. PARSON is a juice orange that ripens very early. It is best in Florida.

2. CARA CARA is a navel orange with large, seedless, pink-flesh fruit with excellent flavor. It grows well in all citrus regions.

3. MORO is a blood orange with violet or burgundy flesh and a distinctive aroma. It is almost seedless and ripens very early. It tends to bear in alternate years and grows well in California and the Gulf Coast.

When shopping for a citrus tree, look for a tree that has ample roots for the amount of branches. Opt for a small tree with a large root system rather than a large tree with a small root system. The small tree will establish quickly and most likely fruit before a large tree with few roots. The trunk and branches should be free of scrapes, and the tree should have a pleasing symmetrical form.

Plant a container-grown tree by digging a hole as deep as the container and slightly wider. Remove the tree from the pot and place it in the hole so that the graft (bulging area low on the trunk) is at least 2 inches above the soil to prevent the stem from rooting. Using the excavated soil, backfill the planting hole, tamping the soil as you go to prevent air pockets. Using soil, form a 3- to 4-foot-diameter basin around the tree. The basin will help hold water, keeping the tree moist longer after watering, and is especially helpful during the weeks right after planting as the tree is establishing roots.

Most citrus trees are easy to care for, requiring minimal pruning and infrequent pest control. Regular watering and fertilizing is usually all they require for years of good fruit production.

The plants need adequate soil moisture for healthy growth. Drought during bloom causes flowers to drop, resulting in poor, if any, fruit set. Lack of moisture during the growing season causes fruit drop and low yields. Prolonged drought will defoliate and eventually kill a tree. At the other extreme, standing water and poorly drained soil are almost always lethal to citrus. Plant citrus in well-drained soil and water regularly during dry periods, supplementing natural rainfall so trees receive about 1 inch of water per week.

Citrus trees grow best when they are fertilized two or three times from February through September. Use 1 pound of 10-10-10 fertilizer per application per tree the first two years, gradually increasing the amount each year to between 5 and 7 pounds after about eight years. Spread the fertilizer evenly over the tree's root zone. Water well after fertilizing to leach nutrients into the root zone.

Soils in some areas are deficient in micronutrients. In these cases, the tree will need foliar sprays of micronutrients such as copper,

MANDARIN VARIETIES

1. CLEMENTINE has red-orange, sweet, juicy fruit that peels easily. A small tree with an attractive weeping habit, it needs a pollinator such as 'Dancy'.

2. SATSUMA produces mild, seedless, sweet fruit on a slow-growing, spreading tree. Very cold-hardy.

3. PAGE has rich, sweet fruit with few to many seeds. The attractive tree is almost thornless. It grows well in all citrus-producing areas.

zinc, manganese, and boron. Look for these products at your local garden center. Don't overfertilize.

Citrus trees naturally self-regulate the amount of fruit they set and regularly drop small fruit in June, hence the term "June drop." Well-watered and fertilized trees usually drop some fruit, but excessive fruit drop might be an indicator of a problem. Keep trees in good health and well-irrigated to minimize fruit drop.

Most citrus trees require little pruning, though you might want to prune lemons and other vigorous trees to control their size. Pruning to remove dense growth and open the center of a citrus tree is also a good way to keep the tree bearing throughout the canopy and prevent the buildup of insect pests. Most citrus types tolerate shearing into a hedge or being trained flat as an espalier.

Citrus trees vary in their sensitivity to cold, but many are vulnerable when temperatures fall to 29°F for 30 minutes or longer. Protect young frost-sensitive trees by wrapping them with an insulating material, such as cardboard, palm fronds, or cornstalks. Cover the trunks from ground level up to the main branches. Frost will rarely kill a mature citrus tree. If the leaves or twigs show signs of frost damage, be patient and wait until the spring flush of growth to determine the damage.

In cold climates, grow citrus trees in pots and enjoy perfectly ripe oranges, juicy lemons, and many other citrus fruits from your own trees. Because citrus reacts well to pruning, you can maintain a small, productive tree in a container for many years. Small types of citrus, such as calamondin, lime, kumquat, lemon, and limequat, are best suited to container culture.

Begin by selecting a pot. Citrus trees grow well in containers when their roots are somewhat constricted, so choose a smaller pot rather than a larger one. A pot about 15 inches wide and 15 inches deep is a good size for a young citrus tree. As the tree grows, you'll need to either transplant it into a larger pot or prune the roots and foliage and replant it in the same pot. If you choose to transplant the tree to a larger pot, increase the pot size by no more than 25 percent.

Fill the pot with a well-drained potting mix, and plant the citrus tree as you would when growing it outside. The final soil surface

GRAPEFRUIT VARIETIES

1. DUNCAN produces large, seedy, very juicy fruit with white flesh. One of the most cold-tolerant grapefruits, it is best in Florida and the Gulf Coast.

2. OROBLANCO is a pummelo-grapefruit hybrid. It is best in California and the desert Southwest.

3. STAR RUBY is a popular, medium-size, seedless, juicy grapefruit with deep-red flesh. It grows well in all citrus regions.

should be 2 to 4 inches below the container rim. You can add a thin layer of mulch on top of the soil to help conserve soil moisture.

The most challenging aspect of growing citrus trees in cold climates is providing them with enough light indoors. In fall, acclimate trees to indoor lighting by progressively moving them to shadier and shadier spots for about three weeks prior to taking them indoors. Reverse the process in spring as you acclimate the trees to more intense outdoor lighting.

Container-grown citrus trees have exacting water requirements. Most watering mistakes involve overwatering. Wait until the top inch or two of soil is dry to the touch, and then water by thoroughly moistening the soil.

Citrus trees rely on bees for pollination. When your tree is in bloom, be sure it is outside where bees can pollinate it. If that's not possible, pollinate the flowers by whisking a small artist's brush over the yellow pollen-covered stamens until the brush is coated with pollen. Touch the brush to the flower's central pistil.

Harvesting

Citrus fruits mature at various times of the year. Early varieties of oranges ripen in October or November of the year in which they bloom. Late varieties of oranges mature from February to May of the following year. The only sure way to determine maturity is to taste the fruit.

Color is a poor indication of ripeness because many fruits have fully colored rinds months before they can be eaten. Lemons, limes, and other acidic types of citrus are an exception. They can be picked whenever they reach acceptable size and juice content. Once mature, most citrus fruits can be stored on the tree for several weeks and picked as needed.

Most citrus fruits can be stored in the refrigerator for at least two to three weeks. Under dry conditions at room temperature, fruits develop an off-flavor, wither, and become unattractive within 10 days.

LEMON VARIETIES

1. IMPROVED MEYER is a favorite hybrid because of its excellent flowery flavor. It is orange-yellow when mature and holds well on the tree. The small to medium tree, which is nearly thornless, moderately vigorous, and spreading, is good for hedges and containers. It grows well in all citrus-producing regions.

2. LISBON produces highly acidic, juicy fruit with few seeds. It is best picked ripe as it loses acidity if left on the tree. The most productive and cold-hardy of lemons, it grows best in California and the desert Southwest.

3. VARIEGATED PINK EUREKA has very acidic, juicy fruit with few seeds. The tree is eye-catching with dark-green leaves variegated white. It grows best in the desert Southwest and the Gulf Coast.

LIME VARIETIES

4. BEARSS has small to medium, acidic, very juicy limes that are yellow at maturity. It grows well in all citrus-producing regions.

5. MEXICAN produces very small, juicy, acidic limes with a distinctive aroma. Known as the bartender's lime, it is yellow when mature but is picked green.

6. RANGPUR has small to medium, very acidic, juicy fruit that holds well on the tree. Very cold-tolerant, it is not a true lime but a good lime substitute.

Currant, gooseberry, jostaberry
Ribes species

Currants, gooseberries, and jostaberries are all hardy fruiting shrubs that grow well in cool, humid regions of North America. They grow well in partial shade and produce large crops of tart fruit.

Planting & Growing

All types of currants and gooseberries are self-fruitful, but yields improve when two varieties are planted for cross-pollination.

Currants grow 3 to 5 feet tall and wide and have attractive 3-inch-wide leaves on thornless stems. In early fall, the foliage turns brilliant orange or red. Clusters of creamy white flowers in early spring are followed by midsummer fruits in red, white, or black.

Gooseberries are similar to currants in every regard but their large, tart fruits and thorny stems. The fruits are often harvested while still green. Mature fruits are purple.

'Jostaberry', a hybrid of black currant and gooseberry, has more in common with currant.

Plant in full sun or part shade and moist, well-drained soil. All are hardy in Zones 2 to 9. Plant in late winter or early spring as soon as the soil is workable. Plants produce well when watered regularly; provide about 1 inch per week. Spread a 2-inch-thick layer of mulch around plants to conserve soil moisture and stifle weeds. Apply a nitrogen fertilizer in fall or early spring.

During the dormant season after the first year's growth, select six to eight of the strongest and best-positioned stems and remove the others to the ground. A year later, choose three or four good one-year-old shoots and remove the rest; choose four or five of the best two-year-old shoots and remove the rest. After the third year, select shoots so that the bush has three or four shoots that are one, two, or three years old.

Harvesting

When all the berries in a cluster attain full color, they're considered ripe. They gradually become sweeter with ripening.

VARIETIES

1. ROVADA is a productive red currant that is good for preserves. Zones 3–7.

2. POORMAN is a long-time favorite gooseberry that produces large amounts of fruit. Zones 4–6.

3. JOSTABERRY is a fast-growing cross of black currant and gooseberry with reddish-black fruits. The thornless plant is more vigorous and earlier-bearing than either parent, and it is resistant to both mildew and white pine blister rust. Zones 4–7.

Elderberry, sweet elder
Sambucus nigra canadensis

Easy to grow and productive, elderberry's only downside is its enthusiasm—it spreads fast. In early summer, the plant is covered with clusters of purple-black berries.

Planting & Growing

Plant in full sun and moist soil. Elderberry thrives in moist soil but will not grow in soil that is poorly drained or boggy. The plant grows best in fertile soil. Mix a 2-inch-thick layer of compost into the soil before planting. Be sure to plant where elderberry has plenty of space to spread. Each plant should have at least 6 square feet of growing space. Elderberry is hardy in Zones 3 to 9.

Plant container-grown plants in early spring. Space them 6 to 10 feet apart. Elderberries are self-unfruitful, requiring two cultivars planted within 60 feet of each other for fruit set. Water shrubs well after planting. Elderberry is easy to grow. It responds well to fertilization. Spread a 2-inch-thick layer of compost over the root zone in early spring, or fertilize with a balanced fertilizer product, such as 10-10-10, according to package directions.

Weeding is one of the most challenging aspects of growing elderberry. Because it has a very shallow root system, cultivating around plants with a hoe or tiller is not a good idea. Instead, hand-pull weeds and mulch plants with a 2-inch-thick layer of organic mulch.

Prune annually to prevent elderberry from spreading vigorously. Cut out dead branches as they appear. Keep plants dense by pruning hard in late winter, removing oldest stems completely and shortening others. Rejuvenate overgrown elderberry plants by cutting off all stems just above ground level.

Harvesting

Pick berries once they're ripe by raking through the clusters with your open fingers. Use the berries at once for juice, jelly, syrup, or pie, or freeze them for later use.

YOU
_ SHOULD KNOW _
Purple-black elderberries have a flavor similar to that of blueberries. Both the flowers and fruit are famous for making wine. The berries are also used for juice and pies.

①

VARIETIES

1. ADAMS NO. 1 and its close relative, 'Adams No. 2', are strong, vigorous, productive, and hardy varieties that bear large fruit clusters. They ripen late and have been the standard since 1926. Zones 4–9.

YORK is often more productive than the Adams series, and the berries tend to be larger. Zones 4–9.

Fig
Ficus carica

Figs are remarkably adaptable. They are productive with little care. Even if the plant freezes to the ground in winter, it often recovers, bearing fruit the following summer. The silvery branches add drama to the landscape, and the fruit is a delicious addition to meals.

Planting & Growing

Plant in full sun and well-drained soil. Figs grow in sandy soil if watered regularly. Ample sunlight is key to good fig production. Site the tree where it will receive at least eight hours of direct sunlight per day. Figs grow 10 to 30 feet tall and wide; plant them where they have plenty of space to expand. Fig trees are hardy in Zones 8 to 10.

Plant container-grown fig trees in fall. Set the trees 2 inches deeper than they grew in the nursery container. Space them 10 to 25 feet apart, depending on the fig variety. In climates where temperatures fall below 18°F, grow a fig in a 10- to 15-gallon half barrel or other large container so you can move it to a protected location for winter. Fill the container with a potting mix enriched with compost.

Fig roots are close to the surface, and the trees dry out quickly. Water plants during hot, dry weather to prevent premature fruit drop, but avoid allowing the trees to stand in water. Spread a 3-inch-thick layer of mulch over the tree's root zone to conserve moisture.

Because they fruit on new wood, fig trees normally fruit the first year after planting. Shade young trees from the hot midday sun. Apply low-nitrogen plant food twice a year to in-ground trees, or use fruit tree fertilizer spikes for trees in containers. When the trees are dormant in fall or winter, prune heavily to remove buds of the spring crop to increase the main crop. Figs are fruitful for up to 15 years.

Harvesting

Unripe fruits are gummy with latex, which can irritate the skin, so wear gloves when working with your trees. Most varieties bear two crops each year; the breba, or spring, crop is generally inferior in quality to the main crop. Ripe fruits become soft. Protect ripening figs from birds.

VARIETIES

1. **BROWN TURKEY** produces a spring crop of brownish-purple fruits. Zones 8–10.

2. **LSU GOLD** fruits have yellow skin and pink-red flesh. The figs are very large and sweet. This variety produces best in the South. Zones 8–10.

3. **CELESTE** bears small figs with purplish-brown skin and reddish amber flesh. It has good cold hardiness and pest resistance. Zones 8–10.

Grape
Vitis species

There are grape varieties for all regions. These easy-to-grow vining plants do well on simple trellises or rambling over pergolas in the home landscape.

Planting & Growing

The best time to plant grapes is late winter or early spring. Dig a planting hole 1 foot in diameter, leaving adequate room to place a stake, post, or trellis before the roots are positioned. Position the lowest bud on the trunk even with the soil line. Tamp the soil lightly over the roots and flood the hole with water, repeating until the soil settles at ground level.

Avoid fertilizing grapes. Highly fertile soil often detracts from the flavor of grapes, especially wine grapes. An annual 2-inch-thick layer of well-rotted compost or manure spread around the root zone will provide sufficient nutrients. Train grapevines to a trellis, sturdy fence, or arbor. An arbor is a particularly good choice for a small garden to use vertical space.

Annual pruning is essential in growing good grapes. Home gardeners commonly don't prune severely enough. About 90 percent of the twigs must be removed each year to spur the formation of large, healthy fruit clusters.

Thinning fruit bunches helps the remaining grapes to grow large and sweet. In cold-winter areas, spread mulch around the base of the vines for winter protection. In extremely cold regions, untie the vines and bend them to the ground, then cover them with soil or straw. Uncover and retie the plants to their supports in spring.

Harvesting

Clip grape clusters from the vines with sharp scissors, and handle them as little as possible to avoid damage. Picking bunches with grapes of varying degrees of ripeness is desirable for making jelly and jam. Pick grapes for fresh eating and juice two or three times over a period of several weeks as the grapes ripen. Store them in the refrigerator for up to two weeks.

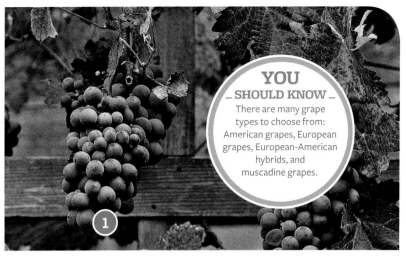

YOU
— SHOULD KNOW —
There are many grape types to choose from: American grapes, European grapes, European-American hybrids, and muscadine grapes.

VARIETIES

1. CONCORD is an American grape that is popular for making juice. It is dark blue, seedy, and fruits in large bunches. Zones 4–8.

2. NIAGARA produces yellow-green, seedless, large, thick-skin grapes. This American grape has a sweet, strong "foxy" flavor. Zones 4–8.

3. SCUPPERNONG is a muscadine with large, speckled, bronze, thick-skin fruit. Use it fresh and for wine. It requires a pollinator. Zones 7–9.

4. HIMROD bears gold-yellow, seedless, large grapes in long clusters. Deliciously spicy-sweet, this very early-ripening grape is good fresh or dried and stores well. Moderate disease resistance. Zones 5–8.

5. RELIANCE produces pale red, seedless fruit in large clusters. Good disease resistance. Zones 4–8.

6. THOMPSON SEEDLESS is a popular pale green-gold, seedless, sweet grape. Thin clusters for larger fruit. Zones 7–9.

Kiwifruit, hardy kiwifruit
Actinidia species

These egg-shape fruits with shimmering, emerald green flesh and delicious berry flavor are making inroads in home gardens. The vigorous, heavy vines need sturdy support and heavy annual pruning. Train the vines over a pergola to shade a patio.

Planting & Growing

The familiar kiwifruit has 5- to 8-inch dark green leaves that are round with a fuzzy white underside. Both male and female plants must be present for pollination.

Hardy kiwi plants look similar, but the fruit is smaller and its skin is edible. Some hardy varieties may not require a male, but fruiting is better if a male and female plant are present.

Plant in full sun and well-drained soil. Kiwis thrive in deep, fertile loam. Enrich the planting site with a 2-inch-thick layer of compost. Plants are susceptible to damage from frost and wind, so locate them in a protected area near your house or an outbuilding. Kiwi is hardy in Zones 8 to 11, and hardy kiwi in Zones 5 to 9. Plant kiwi in fall once summer temperatures begin to moderate. Plant hardy kiwi in early spring as soon as soil is workable. Space plants 15 to 20 feet apart, and be sure to leave space to erect a trellis.

The vines require plenty of water. Irrigate deeply and often when the vines are blooming or fruiting. Mature vines need 10 pounds of 10-10-10 fertilizer every year. Because young vines are sensitive to excess fertilizer, apply about 4 ounces the first two years and increase the amount as the vine grows. Spread fertilizer evenly under the entire canopy. Feed plants in spring through midsummer.

Kiwi vines need regular pruning to prevent them from becoming a tangled mess. Let young plants grow with minimal pruning for a year or two after planting.

Harvesting

Fruits mature in late fall or early winter. Pick them while they're still hard and let them ripen off the vine like pears. A change of color from greenish-brown to brown is a sign the fruit is almost ripe.

VARIETIES

1. HAYWARD is the most common kiwi in North America. Zones 7–9.

2. VINCENT is a kiwi that is ideal for mild climates as it requires little cold weather to produce fruit. Zones 8–9.

3. ISSAI is a hardy kiwi that is self-fruitful but produces better with a pollinator. Zones 5–9.

Mango

Mangifera indica

Mangoes have a bold presence in the landscape. Their thick, leathery, pointed leaves are 1 foot or more long and 3 inches wide. Their fruits dangle at the ends of 6- to 8-inch-long stalks.

Planting & Growing

Plant in full sun and moist, well-drained soil. Enrich the soil before planting by incorporating a 3- to 4-inch-thick layer of compost into the planting site. In the desert, plant trees in part shade to protect fruit from sunburn. Mangoes are hardy in Zones 10 to 11.

Plant container-grown mango trees in the fall when daytime high temperatures become more moderate. When shopping for a tree, look for a small tree in a large container, as opposed to a large tree in a small container; a large tree in a small container usually has constricted roots that will inhibit future growth. Wear gloves while working around mango trees because sap in the leaves and fruit skins can irritate skin.

Keep the soil around mangoes consistently moist until the fruit is harvested. Weekly irrigation is required during warm weather, though in the desert, trees may need daily watering until harvest. Fertilize a mango tree regularly from February through July; spread a 2-inch-thick layer of composted manure over the tree's root zone once a month until July. A commercial fertilizer product can also be used. Don't overfertilize; too much nitrogen increases the likelihood of disease. Prune in winter or early spring to control a tree's size and shape. Thin flower clusters and fruits to encourage annual bearing.

Harvesting

The fruits mature 100 to 180 days after the flowers bloom. The fruits ripen from May to September in most locations. Mangoes are ripe when they develop a consistent round shape and are slightly soft. Tree-ripened fruits have the best flavor, but pick all fruits from late-bearing trees if temperatures fall to 40°F. Ripe fruits will keep in the refrigerator for up to three weeks.

YOU — SHOULD KNOW —
To peel a mango, slice the flesh away from the hard core so you have chunks of flesh with peel attached. Slide a knife between the flesh and peel to separate the two.

VARIETIES

1. AH PING has large, yellow-and-orange, fiberless fruits with small seeds. It ripens in July and grows best in Hawaii.

2. KENT bears large green, red, and yellow fiberless fruit with small seeds. It ripens in July and August and grows best in Florida.

3. MANILA has small to medium yellow fruit that is nearly fiberless. It ripens in late fall and grows best in California.

Peach, nectarine
Prunus persica

Few fruits say summer like a perfectly ripe homegrown peach or nectarine. These are among the smallest deciduous fruit trees. Properly pruned standard-size trees are easily maintained at 12 to 16 feet tall.

Planting & Growing

Plant in full sun and rich, moist, well-drained soil. In the South and parts of the West, peaches and nectarines are simple to grow. They thrive in sunny, hot weather. Growing peaches elsewhere takes some skill and a little bit of luck, but these adaptable plants can be grown in many regions.

In cool climates, choose a protected site—a south-facing slope is best, although a spot on the north side of your property is good if late spring frosts are a problem in your area. Plant trees in a protected location that is sheltered from wind. Peaches and nectarines are hardy in Zones 5 to 10.

Plant dormant, bare-root trees in late winter or early spring as soon as the soil is workable. Container-grown trees should go into the ground in fall in hot-summer areas, but they can be planted anytime where summers are cooler.

If your soil drains slowly or is high in clay—the trees do poorly in either situation—plant on a mound of soil or in a raised bed. Plant trees so the graft union (swelling on the main trunk above the roots) is several inches above the soil surface. Allow 18 to 24 feet between standard-size trees and 5 to 8 feet between dwarfs.

Of all the deciduous fruit trees, peaches and nectarines benefit most from regular applications of nitrogen fertilizer. A yearly application of 1 to 1½ pounds of actual nitrogen ensures vigorous growth and annual renewal of fruiting wood. Avoid unnecessary feeding because it causes excess succulent growth, which is susceptible to frost damage and pests.

Peaches and nectarines need heavy pruning every year to stimulate the new growth that will bear fruit the following season. Early each spring as the new growth is just starting, take time to remove up to two-thirds of the shoots that fruited the previous year

VARIETIES

1. BRIGHTON is a semifreestone, round, juicy peach. Vigorous, productive, and an early ripener, it is prized for its high-quality fruit. Zones 6–8.

2. ELBERTA is a good all-purpose, freestone peach. It is widely grown, available, and adaptable. Zones 5–9.

3. VETERAN produces large, freestone, round peaches that peel easily. It produces reliably in cool, wet weather and is a good all-purpose peach. Zones 5–9.

and leave the thicker of the new growth, cutting the longer shoots back about halfway. Prune more in the upper, outermost parts of the tree to force fruiting on stouter wood. Because lower shoots on peach trees are easily killed by shade, thin the branches so that ample sunlight reaches the interior of the canopy.

Thin fruits to 6 inches apart once they reach 1 to 1¼ inches in diameter and after normal fruit drop. Thin early varieties and heavy producers to 10 inches apart. Use stakes to prop up any sagging fruit-laden limbs to keep them from breaking under the heavy fruit load.

Prune out diseased and damaged wood immediately, and keep the ground around the trees cleared of dropped fruit and prunings, which potentially harbor pests and diseases. Avoid most diseases by choosing resistant varieties, and practice clean cultural habits to prevent pest infestations.

Harvesting

Peach and nectarine trees begin bearing two to three years after planting. Fruits ripen from midsummer to midautumn, depending on the peach or nectarine variety and your Zone. Pick them when all green coloration is gone.

Ripe fruits easily come off the tree with a slight upward twist, but handle them gently because they bruise easily.

Peaches and nectarines can be stored in the refrigerator for a few days.

BHG TEST GARDEN TIP

PRUNE OUT PROBLEMS

Prune out diseased and damaged wood immediately, and keep the ground around the trees cleared of dropped fruit and prunings, which potentially harbor pests and diseases. Avoid most diseases by choosing resistant varieties, and practice clean cultural habits to prevent pest infestations.

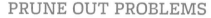

VARIETIES

4. RARITAN ROSE is a striking reddish freestone peach. The medium to large, tender, juicy fruit ripens early in the season. Zones 6–8.

5. MERICREST bears dark red freestone nectarines. The medium-size fruit with yellow flesh is juicy. It is the hardiest nectarine. Zones 5–8.

6. DURBIN produces large, semifreestone nectarines with sweet, yellow flesh. The tree has very good disease resistance. The fruit quality is excellent. Zones 5–9.

7. NECTACREST bears medium-size freestone nectarines with sweet white flesh. The very dwarf trees grow only 10 feet tall and are exceptionally productive. Zones 6–8.

Pear

Pyrus species

A soft, ripe pear is hard to pass up. So planting a pear tree in your yard that produces bushels of juicy ripe fruit is a dream come true. Pears are easy to grow where spring is warm and dry. Pear trees are beautiful in all seasons, making them ideal landscape additions.

Planting & Growing

Pear trees are attractive in both an orchard and a garden; they are as ornamental as they are useful. They feature brilliant white flowers in spring, followed by bright green, leathery leaves that look lovely all summer. And in the autumn, they produce bushels of luscious fruits.

Asian pears are less susceptible to fire blight than their European pear counterparts. Asian and European pears differ in shape and skin texture, too, but perhaps their greatest difference is flesh texture.

European pears are variously described as soft, creamy, and smooth, while the flesh of Asian pears is crisp.

Hybrids between European and Asian varieties, called Asian hybrids or hybrid pears, are also available. They are similar in appearance to pears of European heritage but are generally more fire blight-resistant.

Plant pear trees in full sun and well-drained soil. Choose a north-facing location to delay blooming in areas where late spring frosts are possible. Pears are hardy in Zones 3 to 9.

Plant dormant bare-root trees in late winter or early spring. Plant container-grown trees anytime during the growing season. Space standard-size varieties 16 to 20 feet apart and dwarf varieties 10 to 12 feet apart.

In areas where spring is warm and wet, primarily east of the Rocky Mountains, pears are challenging to grow because they are susceptible to fire blight, a disease that thrives in warm, wet weather.

Keep the soil consistently moist; lack of moisture causes fruit to drop. Fertilize only if a soil test indicates the need, because excess nitrogen encourages succulent growth that is susceptible to fire blight. Train young pear trees to either a central leader or an open

VARIETIES

1. **BARTLETT** is a productive and popular European pear. It is partially self-fruitful and can be pollinated with several other varieties. Zones 5–8.

2. **BOSC** produces medium to large, brown-tinged European pears. The tender and juicy fruits develop on slow-growing trees. It requires a pollinator such as 'Bartlett'. Zones 5–8.

3. **KIEFFER** is a hybrid pear that is good for canning and cooking. Zones 4–9.

center form. An open center is easier and may reduce the extent of damage in the event fire blight strikes.

Like apple trees, pears produce fruit on stubby branches called spurs that remain productive for five to seven years. Prune mature trees to control their height, and thin out the branches so light can reach the fruiting spurs. Remove crossing limbs, dead wood, and watersprouts. Prune hardest in the upper, outermost parts of the tree so that most fruit is borne on the lower, stronger limbs. After normal fruit drop, thin the remaining fruits to one fruit every 6 to 8 inches for best size.

Pear trees usually mature about 25 feet high and wide so they are ideal for even small landscapes. A tree on a dwarfing rootstock is one-half to one-quarter as large.

Pears do better in pairs. All pear trees are more productive if a compatible variety is planted nearby to allow for cross-pollination. European pears are productive in the South and mild-winter West, and others are hardy in cold climates.

Harvesting

The harvesting time and technique of pears is based on the variety type. Standard pear trees begin to bear fruit five or six years after planting. Dwarf trees bear fruit quicker, in just three or four years. The fruits ripen in August through September. Pick pears by hand before they are completely ripe, except for Asian pears, which are best picked when fully ripe and their stems separate easily from the tree. Just grasp a fruit and twist to break the stem.

Pick European pears and hybrids when they reach full size but are still hard and green. They are easy to ripen off the tree at room temperature. If they are left on the tree too long, they become soft and mushy around the core before the outside is ready to eat.

Eat pears fresh or bake them into tarts and other desserts. You can also make pear sauces and jellies to freeze and eat later, enjoying the sweet tastes of summer in the middle of winter.

VARIETIES

4. 20TH CENTURY is a very productive Asian pear that is excellent fresh and stores well. It requires fruit-thinning and is disease- prone. Partially self-fruitful. Pollinate with 'Bartlett'. Zones 6–9.

5. SHINKO is an Asian pear with a distinct flavor. It is resistant to fire blight and codling moth. Pollinate with '20th Century' or 'Bartlett'. Zones 5–8.

Plum, prune, plum hybrids
Prunus species

Of all the stone fruits, none is more varied in origin, size, color, and flavor than a plum. Plum trees can be kept relatively small, growing 12 to 15 feet tall if the tree is pruned annually.

Planting & Growing

European plums are good for canning, drying, or freezing and occasionally eating fresh. They thrive in cold-weather areas and produce small, oval fruits with various colors of skin and flesh.

Japanese plums are the favorite plum for fresh eating and typically produce large, sweet, juicy fruits with red skin. Because Japanese plums flower early, they do not grow well where late frosts occur. They are commonly grown in California and other moderate climates.

Damson-type plums are small, tart fruits that are most often used for cooking and preserves. Compact and cold-hardy, they're easy to grow in many climates.

Plum hybrids result from crossing plums with other stone fruits such as apricots and peaches. The results are completely new fruits with different varieties reflecting various degrees of one parent or the other.

Plant plums in full sun and rich, well-drained soil. If late spring frosts are a problem in your area, plant on the north side of your property; otherwise a south-facing slope is the best site. Plums are hardy in Zones 2 to 9.

Plant bare-root trees in late winter or early spring. Plant container-grown plants anytime during the growing season. Space standard-size trees 20 feet apart, semidwarf trees 15 feet apart, and dwarf trees and shrubs 8 to 10 feet apart.

After planting, spread a 2-inch-thick layer of compost or well-rotted manure under the canopy of the plum tree, and cover it with a 2-inch-thick layer of organic mulch such as wood or bark chips. Repeat this compost and mulch layering every spring.

VARIETIES

1. DAMSON is a small, dark blue plum with tart, juicy, yellow flesh. It is self-fruitful. Zones 5–7.

2. METHLEY is favored for its vigorous production of large, juicy, sweet Japanese plums. The early-blooming tree grows well in many soils and bears excellent all-purpose fruit and is self-fruitful. Zones 5–9.

Be sure trees receive at least 1 inch of water per week for the first two months after planting, supplementing rainfall with hand-watering as needed. Prune trees after flowering to remove dead or diseased wood. The fruits develop on long-lived spurs. Thin interior branches to promote ripening and to make harvest easier.

Thin fruits by hand after normal fruit drop, leaving only the best plum on each spur and 4 to 6 inches between fruits. Red-fruit varieties need more thinning than blue ones, and heavily fruiting branches may need to be propped up.

Plums are susceptible to black knot, a fungus that produces hard black bumps on twigs and branches. Prune out infected areas in winter by cutting the wood well below the knots and destroying the cuttings; sterilize your pruning tools between cuts. Use a labeled disease-control product to prevent brown rot. Prune away diseased and damaged wood immediately, and keep the ground around trees clear of dropped fruit and other plant debris, which can harbor pests and encourage diseases.

Harvesting

Plums are ready to harvest when they come off in your hand with a gentle twist. Sample a few from different parts of the tree before harvesting a significant amount.

European plums must ripen on the tree but should be picked before they are mushy; ripe plums left on the tree will rot. Pick Japanese plums before they are completely ripe; they will continue to ripen off the tree. Damson plums are ready to harvest when they are soft.

All types of ripe plums can be stored for up to two weeks in the refrigerator. Plums can be frozen to use later in desserts or made into jams. They will keep in the freezer for about a year.

YOU
_ SHOULD KNOW _
Japanese plums are favorite plums for eating fresh. The flesh and skin color vary by cultivar, but the flavor is sweet and intense.

VARIETIES

3. GREEN GAGE is a European plum with sweet, juicy flesh. The low-branching, productive tree is self-fruitful but produces best with a pollinator. Zones 5–9.

4. STANLEY produces medium to large, dark blue European plums with richly flavored flesh. Zones 4–8.

5. FLAVOR DELIGHT is a plum-apricot hybrid. It has yellow flesh and a unique flavor. Self-fruitful, it is better pollinated by any apricot. Zones 6–9.

Strawberry

Fragaria × ananassa

Growing about 6 inches high, strawberry plants have pretty semievergreen leaves and white flowers in spring. Red berries follow the flowers in early summer or throughout the summer, making them a good plant for edible landscaping.

Planting & Growing

Strawberries are either June-bearing (also called spring-bearing) or day-neutral (also called everbearing). June-bearing types respond to the lengthening days and shorter nights of spring by flowering and setting a crop that matures in late spring or early summer. In some climates, June-bearers may also set another small crop during the short days of fall. This type of strawberry is best for jams, jellies, and preserves because a large crop of berries ripens at once. Day-neutral strawberries flower and produce fruit anytime the temperatures are between 35°F and 85°F. Instead of one main crop in early summer, the harvest is spread through the summer into fall.

Plant in full sun and loose, well-drained soil. Loam or sandy loam is preferred. Good drainage is important because ripening berries rot in standing water. If your soil is predominately clay, plant berries in raised beds at least 6 inches deep. Mix a 2-inch-thick layer of compost into the soil prior to planting.

Grow strawberries from bare-root or container-grown plants. Bare-root plants are easy to establish and economical. Plant in early spring where winters are cold and in either late winter or fall where winters are relatively mild. Before planting, apply a 10-10-10 fertilizer, digging it into the soil 6 to 8 inches deep.

Dig a hole large enough so the roots can extend, then cover plants with soil to just below the crown (the place on the main stem where the leaf shoots emerge). Do not bury the crown. Plant container-grown plants at the same depth they were growing in the container. Plant June-bearing strawberries in rows 3 to 4 feet apart. Space plants 12 to 24 inches apart within the rows. Mulch plants with a 2-inch-thick layer of straw right after planting. Remove the flowers the first season to encourage the growth of runners.

JUNE-BEARING VARIETIES

1. HONEOYE produces large, bright red, slightly tart berries on vigorous plants. Fruit ripens early and over a long season. Susceptible to soilborne diseases. Zones 3–8.

2. ALLSTAR has large, light orange-red berries with sweet red flesh late in the season. Good disease resistance. Zones 4–8.

3. EARLIGLOW is prized for the outstanding flavor of its large, shiny, dark-red berries. Disease-resistant. Zones 4–8.

4. JEWEL has large delicious, rich red berries. It is widely grown. Susceptible to verticillium wilt and red stele. Zones 4–8.

5. LATEGLOW produces very large, good-quality berries late in the season. Susceptible to leaf blight and anthracnose. Zones 6–8.

Because day-neutral strawberries do not send out as many runners as June-bearers, manage them differently. Plant them in either single rows or staggered double rows. For single rows, space plants 5 to 9 inches apart in rows about 42 inches apart. For double rows, stagger plants 10 to 18 inches apart in two 8-inch-wide rows that are 42 inches apart. Mulch plants with a 2-inch-thick layer of straw after planting. To maximize the yield of berries, remove all runners the first season. Remove flowers until the end of June, and then allow the flowers to remain to set fruit for a small crop of summer berries.

Strawberry plants need about 1 inch of water each week. Water at times other than late evening to avoid keeping the plants wet for long periods, which encourages disease. Soaker hoses are useful for watering strawberries. Hoses woven through a strawberry bed will slowly deliver water to the roots without getting the foliage wet.

Keep the strawberry patch weed-free, especially in the first few months after planting. Renovate June-bearers immediately after harvesting to reduce diseases, stimulate vigorous new growth, and prolong the life of your planting. Renovation is as simple as mowing or clipping the plants to a height of 3 inches.

Fertilize with 1 pound of 10-10-10 fertilizer per 100 square feet after renovation. Fertilize day-neutral berries with a 10-10-10 fertilizer each month from June through September the first year, and May through September in subsequent years. Overwinter the plants by covering them with straw.

Harvesting

Begin harvesting June-bearing strawberries the year after planting—about 14 months from planting in northern climates and 9 months in warmer regions. Day-neutral plants will be ready to harvest about 90 days after planting. The highest yields come from the youngest plants. The berries ripen about a month after the plants bloom.

Regardless of size, strawberries are ripe when they attain full color for their variety. Ripe berries left on the plants will quickly become overripe and start to decay and attract pests, so collect all the ripe berries each time you pick. Harvest as frequently as every other day at the peak of the season. Fruit harvested in the morning usually has a longer shelf life. Store harvested berries in the refrigerator.

DAY-NEUTRAL VARIETIES

1. TRIBUTE produces medium-size, bright-red berries with a pleasing acid flavor. Good disease resistance. Zones 3–10.

2. TRISTAR is similar to 'Tribute' but has smaller and sweeter berries. It is widely available and adapted. Good disease resistance. Zones 3–10.

3. RUGEN alpine has large, flavorful berries. The plant is vigorous and low-growing. It grows in partial sun and does well in containers. Zones 3–9.

CHAPTER THIRTEEN

Food Processing

After you've grown the garden of your dreams, gather up the produce and make something wonderful with it.

224

226

229

Know your produce

Not all tomatoes are created equal. Or cucumbers. Even grapes. Understand key differences among fruits and vegetables to make sure canning projects turn out perfectly.

Undamaged and unblemished

When you put top-quality produce in a jar, you get top-quality food from it. Use produce within a day or two of harvesting or purchasing. Store in the refrigerator if necessary (except for tomatoes). Discard produce that is diseased, moldy, or insect-damaged, though you can cut out small bruises and spots.

Sweetness and ripeness

Choose produce that is moderately ripe. Avoid fruit that is overripe or underripe (with the exception of recipes that specify, say, green tomatoes). Fully ripe yet firm fruit has the best, fullest flavor and processes the best. In some cases, recipes specify the ripeness of the fruit—it's that critical.

Acidity

Some fruits and vegetables have higher acid levels than others. Acidic produce is naturally easier to preserve because acid inhibits the growth of some microorganisms. This is the reason that many home canning recipes rely on vinegar. Other recipes call for a small amount of lemon juice to boost acidity.

Pectin

This natural substance occurs in a variety of fruits and is the substance that causes jams and jellies to gel. Most recipes call for the addition of pectin, but some fruits, such as gooseberries, naturally have so much pectin that adding more isn't necessary. Underripe fruit is high in pectin; overly ripe fruit is low in pectin. Making preserves with overripe fruit might result in a runny product. Because the sugar in each recipe interacts with the pectin, do not alter the amount of sugar. If you want low- or no-sugar jams and jellies, follow low- or no-sugar recipes.

The right type of produce

Some varieties or cultivars of produce process better than others. Paste-type tomatoes, sometimes called roma or plum tomatoes, are firmer and meatier with fewer seeds and juice than beefsteak or slicing tomatoes. Pickling cucumbers, sometimes called Kirby cucumbers, are firmer and stand up to the brining process better, remaining crisp.

top Fresh green beans should be processed as soon as possible after picking to keep peak flavor. ***above and opposite*** Berries, such as blueberries and raspberries, and other fruits at the peak of their flavor will mash to the correct consistency and produce the most delicious jams and jellies. Underripe or inferior berries have less flavor and less-than-ideal texture.

How to prep produce

Before making pickles, preserves, or any other type of canned or frozen produce, simple produce preparation is necessary. Here's how to professionally prep even large amounts of fruits and vegetables.

Picking

For freezing or canning, use only produce that is at its peak of ripeness and flavor. Farmer's market produce and homegrown fruits and veggies should be processed within a few days. For example, pickling cucumbers and raspberries have short shelf lives and can wither or mildew in just a day or two.

Washing

Use only water, rinsing thoroughly in a large colander. Washing removes dirt, insects, and bacteria. Use a scrub brush to get dirt off rough root vegetables such as carrots.

Blanching

Some recipes specify blanching—simply putting produce into rapidly boiling water for a short time, usually a minute or two. Blanching, most often called for in freezer recipes, further cleans produce and kills some organisms on the surface. It also slows or stops the action of enzymes, which causes loss of flavor, color, and texture. Blanching also helps preserve color and vitamin content.

Peeling

For tomatoes, peaches, and other soft-flesh produce, blanching makes peeling easy. Hot water heats and softens the flesh right beneath the skin. Plunging the produce in cold water causes steam, which cools and leaves tiny air pockets that allow the skin to slip off easily. But only peel when the recipe specifies it. Some peels are left on because they contain valuable pectin, which helps thicken the product. In other cases, the peel helps to keep the produce intact.

PREP GUIDE 101

TOMATOES
Make an X at the blossom end of a tomato, then blanch. The X encourages the tomato skin to split so you can slip off the skin easily with your fingers.

STRAWBERRIES
Cut out the stem end of strawberries. This process is called hulling.

APPLES
Make processing apples a breeze by investing a few dollars in an apple corer. Simply push it firmly into the apple, twist, and pull.

HOW TO PEEL PEACHES AND TOMATOES

Blanching produce loosens the skin, making peeling a snap.

1 BOIL
Bring a large pan of water to boiling. Add the produce and leave in for 30 to 60 seconds or until skins start to split.

2 PLUNGE
Remove and plunge produce into a large bowl of ice water. Remove from the cold water after a few minutes. Use a knife to easily pull off the skin.

Food preservation methods

Once you have your hands on all that delicious produce, you'll find several ways to preserve its goodness. Choose the right method to achieve the best results.

The method used to process produce depends on the desired result. Should raspberries be made into a sweet jam, frozen, or elegantly brandied? Should tomatoes be made into a rich sauce, frozen whole, or dried? Here's an overview of basic processing methods.

Boiling-water canning

A boiling-water canner, opposite, is simply a very large pot with a rack in the bottom and a lid on the top. Jars are submerged in boiling water for a specified time. They are heated to a temperature of 212°F. This method is used mainly for fruits, pickles, salsa, and other high-acid foods. It's also used for some tomato recipes.

Pressure canning

A pressure canner, top left, has a lid that locks on and a dial that allows you to regulate the steam pressure building up inside by turning the burner heat up or down. Pressurized steam is much hotter than boiling water—pressure canning heats jars to 240°F. This higher heat kills tougher microorganisms that can thrive in low-acid foods such as green beans, soups, and sauces with meat.

Freezing

An easy way to preserve garden produce, freezing maintains texture in a way that canning doesn't. Freezing is also easy—just put food into airtight containers or bags, top right, remove excess air, and stash in the freezer!

Brining

Merely by marinating some foods in a vinegar-base brine, you can preserve them for weeks longer than they would otherwise stay fresh. Simply make the brine, pack into scrupulously clean containers, middle left, and store in the refrigerator up to the maximum recommended time.

Drying

Food dries most reliably in a dehydrator, bottom, a small electric countertop appliance. You can also dry foods in the oven with some success, as with dried tomatoes and apples, which intensifies flavor and alters texture.

Freezing vegetables

ASPARAGUS

PREPARATION: Allow 2½ to 4½ pounds per quart. Wash; scrape off scales. Break off woody bases where spears snap easily. Wash again. Sort by thickness. Leave whole or cut into 1-inch lengths.

HOW TO FREEZE: Blanch small spears for 2 minutes and large spears for 4 minutes; cool quickly in cold water. Fill containers; shake down, leaving no headspace.

BEANS: BUTTER, LIMA, OR PINTO

PREPARATION: Allow 3 to 5 pounds unshelled beans per quart. Wash, shell, rinse, drain, and sort beans by size.

HOW TO FREEZE: Blanch small beans for 2 minutes, medium beans for 3 minutes, and large beans for 4 minutes; cool quickly in cold water. Fill containers loosely, leaving a ½-inch headspace.

BEANS: GREEN, WAX, SNAP, OR ITALIAN

PREPARATION: Allow 1½ to 2½ pounds per quart. Wash; remove ends and strings. Leave whole or cut into 1-inch pieces.

HOW TO FREEZE: Blanch for 3 minutes; cool quickly in cold water. Fill containers; shake down, leaving a ½-inch headspace.

BEETS

PREPARATION: Allow 3 pounds (without tops) per quart. Trim off beet tops, leaving an inch of stem and roots to reduce bleeding of color. Scrub well. Cover with boiling water. Boil about 15 minutes or until skins slip off easily; cool. Peel; remove stem and root ends. Leave baby beets whole. Cut medium or large beets into ½-inch cubes or slices. Halve or quarter large slices.

HOW TO FREEZE: Cook unpeeled beets in boiling water until tender. (Allow 25 to 30 minutes for small beets; 45 to 50 minutes for medium beets.) Cool quickly in cold water. Peel; remove stem and root ends. Cut in slices or cubes. Fill containers, leaving a ½-inch headspace.

CARROTS

PREPARATION: Use 1- to 1¼-inch-diameter carrots (large carrots may be too fibrous). Allow 2 to 3 pounds per quart. Wash, trim, peel, and rinse again. Leave tiny carrots whole; slice or dice the rest.

HOW TO FREEZE: Blanch tiny whole carrots for 5 minutes and cut-up carrots for 2 minutes; cool quickly in cold water. Pack tightly into containers, leaving a ½-inch headspace.

CORN, CREAM-STYLE

PREPARATION: Allow 2 to 3 pounds per pint. Remove husks. Scrub with a vegetable brush to remove silks. Wash and drain.

HOW TO FREEZE: Cover ears with boiling water; return to boiling and boil 4 minutes. Cool quickly in cold water; drain. Use a sharp knife to cut off just the kernel tips, then scrape cobs with a dull knife. Fill containers, leaving a ½-inch headspace.

CORN, WHOLE KERNEL

PREPARATION: Allow 4 to 5 pounds per quart. Remove husks. Scrub with a vegetable brush to remove silks. Wash and drain.

HOW TO FREEZE: Cover ears with boiling water; return to boiling and boil 4 minutes. Cool quickly in cold water; drain. Cut corn from cobs at two-thirds depth of kernels; do not scrape cobs. Fill containers, leaving a ½-inch headspace.

PEAS, EDIBLE PODS

PREPARATION: Wash Chinese, snow, sugar, or sugar snap peas. Remove stems, blossom ends, and any strings.

HOW TO FREEZE: Blanch small flat pods 1½ minutes or large flat pods 2 minutes. (If peas have started to develop, blanch 3 minutes. If peas are already developed, shell and follow directions for green peas.) Cool in cold water, drain, and fill containers, leaving a ½-inch headspace.

PEAS: ENGLISH OR GREEN

PREPARATION: Allow 2 to 2½ pounds per pint. Wash, shell, rinse, and drain.

HOW TO FREEZE: Blanch 1½ minutes; cool quickly in cold water. Fill containers, shaking down and leaving a ½-inch headspace.

FREEZING HERBS

Some herbs keep their flavor when frozen. Simply clean the leaves, dry them, and put them in sealed plastic bags (remove all the air before sealing) or freeze them in an ice cube tray. These herbs freeze well: basil, borage, chives, dill, lemongrass, mint, oregano, sage, tarragon, and thyme.

PEPPERS, HOT

PREPARATION: Select firm jalapeño or other chile peppers; wash. Halve large peppers. Remove stems, seeds, and membranes. Place, cut sides down, on a foil-lined baking sheet. Bake in a 425°F oven for 20 to 25 minutes or until skins are bubbly and browned. Cover peppers or wrap in foil and let stand 15 minutes or until cool. Pull the skins off gently and slowly using a paring knife.

HOW TO FREEZE: Package in freezer containers with as little air as possible.

PEPPERS, SWEET

PREPARATION: Select firm green, bright red, or yellow peppers; wash. Remove stems, seeds, and membranes. Place, cut sides down, on a foil-lined baking sheet. Bake in a 425°F oven for 20 to 25 minutes or until skins are bubbly and browned. Cover peppers or wrap in foil and let stand 15 minutes or until cool. Pull off the skins gently and slowly using a paring knife.

HOW TO FREEZE: Quarter large pepper pieces or cut in strips. Fill containers, leaving a ½-inch headspace. Or spread peppers in a single layer on a baking sheet; freeze until firm. Fill container, shaking to pack tightly and removing as much air as possible.

APPLES

PREPARATION: Allow 2½ pounds per quart. Select varieties that are crisp, not mealy, in texture. Peel and core; halve, quarter, or slice. Dip into ascorbic acid color-keeper solution; drain.

HOW TO FREEZE: Use syrup, sugar, or dry pack, leaving the recommended headspace.

APRICOTS

PREPARATION: Allow 2 to 2½ pounds per quart. If desired, peel as for peaches, page 225. Prepare as for peaches.

HOW TO FREEZE: Peel as for peaches, page 225. Use syrup, sugar, or water pack, leaving the recommended headspace.

BERRIES

PREPARATION: Allow ¾ to 1 pound per pint. Can or freeze blackberries, blueberries, currants, elderberries, gooseberries, huckleberries, loganberries, mulberries, and raspberries. Freeze (do not can) boysenberries and strawberries.

HOW TO FREEZE: Slice strawberries, if desired. Use syrup, sugar, or dry pack, leaving the recommended headspace. Or place berries (strawberries, blueberries, raspberries) in a single layer on a baking pan and place them in the freezer. Once they're frozen, put the berries in freezer containers or plastic freezer bags and seal. Stored this way, berries will keep in the freezer up to 1 year.

CHERRIES

PREPARATION: Allow 2 to 3 pounds per quart. If desired, treat with ascorbic acid color-keeper solution; drain. If unpitted, prick skin on opposite sides to prevent splitting.

HOW TO FREEZE: Use syrup, sugar, or dry pack, removing excess air.

MELONS

PREPARATION: Allow about 4 pounds per quart for honeydew, cantaloupe, and watermelon.

HOW TO FREEZE: Use syrup, sugar, or dry pack, removing excess air.

NECTARINES OR PEACHES

PREPARATION: Allow 2 to 3 pounds per quart. To peel peaches, immerse in boiling water for 20 to 30 seconds or until skins start to crack; remove and plunge into cold water. (Peeling nectarines is not necessary.) Halve and pit. If desired, slice. Treat with ascorbic acid color-keeper solution; drain.

HOW TO FREEZE: Use syrup, sugar, or dry pack, leaving the recommended headspace.

PEARS

PREPARATION: Allow 2 pounds per quart. Peel, halve, and core. Treat with ascorbic acid color-keeper solution; drain.

HOW TO FREEZE: Not recommended.

PLUMS

PREPARATION: Allow 2 to 3 pounds per quart. Prick skin on two sides. Freestone varieties may be halved and pitted.

HOW TO FREEZE: Halve and pit. Treat with ascorbic acid color-keeper solution; drain well. Use syrup pack, removing excess air.

RHUBARB

PREPARATION: Allow 1½ pounds per quart. Discard leaves and woody ends. Cut into ½- to 1-inch pieces.

HOW TO FREEZE: Blanch for 1 minute; cool quickly in cold water and drain. Use syrup or dry pack, leaving the recommended headspace. Or use a sugar pack of ½ cup sugar to 3 cups fruit, removing excess air.

USDA plant hardiness

Where you live dictates what you can plant. The Zones of your garden will help you determine which fruits and vegetables will excel where you live.

Each plant has an ability to withstand cold temperatures. This range of temperatures is expressed as a U.S. Department of Agriculture Hardiness Zone—and a Zone map shows where you can grow this plant.

Planting for your Zone

There are 11 Zones from Canada to Mexico, and each Zone represents the lowest expected winter temperature in that area. Each Zone is based on a 10-degree difference in minimum temperatures. Once you know your hardiness Zone, you can choose plants for your garden that will flourish. Look for the hardiness Zone on the plant tags of the perennials, trees, and shrubs you buy.

Microclimates in your yard

Not all areas in your yard are the same. Depending on your geography, trees, and structures, some spots may receive different sunlight and wind and consequently experience temperature differences. Take a look around your yard, and you may notice that the same plant comes up sooner in one place than another. This is the microclimate concept in action. A microclimate is an area in your yard that is slightly different (cooler or hotter) than the other areas of your yard.

Create a microclimate

Once you're aware of your yard's microclimates, use them to your advantage. For example, you may be able to grow plants in a sheltered, south-facing garden bed that you can't grow elsewhere in your yard. You can create a microclimate by planting evergreens on the north side of a property to block prevailing winds. Or plant deciduous trees on the

Zone map

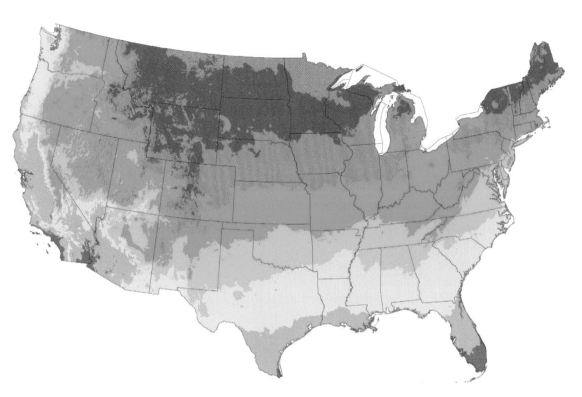

RANGE OF AVERAGE ANNUAL MINIMUM TEMPERATURES FOR EACH ZONE

Zone 3: -40 to -30°F (-40 to -34°C)
Zone 4: -30 to -20°F (-34 to -29°C)
Zone 5: -20 to -10°F (-29 to -23°C)
Zone 6: -10 to -0°F (-23 to -18°C)
Zone 7: 0 to 10°F (-18 to -12°C)

Zone 8: 10 to 20°F (-12 to -7°C)
Zone 9: 20 to 30°F (-7 to -1°C)
Zone 10: 30 to 40°F (-1 to 4°C)
Zone 11: 40 to 50°F (4 to 10°C)

left Every perennial fruit and vegetable, such as this plum, have USDA Hardiness Zone ratings. Select a plant that is hardy in your area, and it will likely overwinter well in your garden.

Frost maps

SPRING The average date of the last spring frost is a valuable guide for determining when to plant many annual crops.

Average Dates of
Last Spring Frost
May 30 or after
April 30 to May 30
March 30 to April 30
Feb. 28 to March 30
Jan. 30 to Feb. 28
Jan. 30 or before

Tomatoes and peppers are usually planted after the last average spring frost. Lettuce and radishes, on the other hand, are often planted three to four weeks before the last average frost date. Many factors combine to determine the actual date in your garden. Weather combined with the contours and orientation of your land are major contributors. More often than not, if you abide by the average date of last spring's frost for your area, your crops will thrive.

FALL The average date of the first autumn frost is helpful for deciding when to plant late season crops.

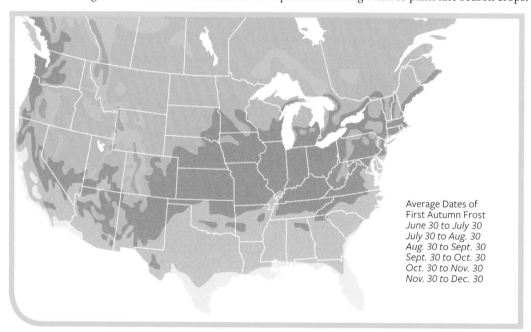

Average Dates of
First Autumn Frost
June 30 to July 30
July 30 to Aug. 30
Aug. 30 to Sept. 30
Sept. 30 to Oct. 30
Oct. 30 to Nov. 30
Nov. 30 to Dec. 30

The average first autumn frost date, in combination with the average last spring frost date, defines the number of frost-free growing days. Frost-free growing days are particularly important to tender plants such as tomatoes, peppers, and squash. Be sure to choose a cultivar that will mature before the first average autumn frost in your area.

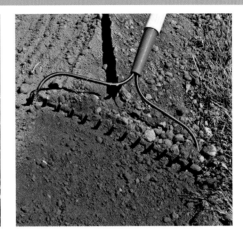

Vegetables

ANNIE'S ANNUALS
annniesannuals.com
888.266.4370
Unique vegetable and herb plants.

BAKER CREEK HEIRLOOM SEEDS
rareseeds.com
417.924.8917
Organic vegetable, herb, and flower seeds. Heirlooms from more than 50 countries.

THE COOK'S GARDEN
cooksgarden.com
800.457.9703
Culinary vegetables, herbs, and flowers. Salad mixes.

GURNEY SEED & NURSERY
gurneys.com
513.354.1491
Vegetable and flower seeds, some fruit trees, and berries.

HENRY FIELD'S SEED & NURSERY CO.
henryfields.com
513.354.1494
Vegetable and flower seeds, some fruit trees, and berries.

JOHNNY'S SELECTED SEEDS
johnnyseeds.com
877.564.6697
Vegetable, herb, and flower seeds; and seeds for cover crops.

J.W. JUNG SEED COMPANY
jungseed.com
800.297.3123
Vegetable and flower seeds.

NICHOLS GARDEN NURSERY
nicholsgardennursery.com
800.422.3985
Vegetable and herb seeds and herb plants.

PARK SEED COMPANY
parkseed.com
800.845.3369
Vegetable, herb, and flower seeds and plants.

RENEE'S GARDEN SEEDS
reneesgarden.com
888.880.7228
Vegetable, herb, and flower seeds. Many heirlooms.

SEED SAVERS EXCHANGE
seedsavers.org
563.382.5990
Heirloom vegetable and herb seeds.

SOUTHERN EXPOSURE SEED EXCHANGE
southernexposure.com
540.894.9480
Heirloom vegetable, flower, and herb varieties adapted to the South.

TERRITORIAL SEED COMPANY
territorial-seed.com
800.626.0866
Vegetable, flower, and herb seeds and plants.

THOMPSON & MORGAN SEEDSMEN, INC.
tmseeds.com
800.274.7333
English vegetable, flower, and herb seeds and plants.

TOMATO GROWERS SUPPLY COMPANY
tomatogrowers.com
888.478.7333
Tomato and pepper seeds.

VERMONT BEAN SEED COMPANY
vermontbean.com
800.349.1071
Vegetable, herb, and flower seeds, and small fruit plants.

W. ATLEE BURPEE & CO.
burpee.com
800.888.1447
Vegetable, herb, and flower seeds and plants.

Fruits

MILLER NURSERIES
millernurseries.com
800.836.9630
Fruit trees, berries, and garden supplies.

STARK BRO'S NURSERIES & ORCHARDS
starkbros.com
800.325.4180
Fruit trees and berries.

Index